ETHNICITY AND WOMEN

VOLUME V

ETHNICITY AND
PUBLIC POLICY
SERIES

ETHNICITY AND PUBLIC POLICY
SERIES

*　　　*　　　*　　　*　　　*

iv

ETHNICITY AND WOMEN

WINSTON A. VAN HORNE
EDITOR

THOMAS V. TONNESEN
MANAGING EDITOR

UNIVERSITY OF WISCONSIN SYSTEM
AMERICAN ETHNIC STUDIES COORDINATING
COMMITTEE/ URBAN CORRIDOR CONSORTIUM

University of Wisconsin System American Ethnic Studies
Coordinating Committee/Urban Corridor Consortium
P. O. Box 413, Milwaukee, WI 53201

International Standard Book Number ISBN 0-942672-08-9 (cloth)
International Standard Book Number ISBN 0-942672-09-7 (paper)
Library of Congress Catalog Card Number: 86-50361

UNIVERSITY OF WISCONSIN SYSTEM AMERICAN ETHNIC STUDIES COORDINATING COMMITTEE

DR. WINSTON A. VAN HORNE
University of Wisconsin–Milwaukee
Chairperson, AESCC

DR. MARVIN P. DAWKINS
University of Wisconsin–Parkside

DR. PETER J. KELLOGG
University of Wisconsin–Green Bay

DR. WILLIAM J. MURIN
Director, Urban Corridor Consortium

MR. THOMAS V. TONNESEN
Program Coordinator, AESCC (ex-officio)

DR. ALAN V. WIEDER
University of Wisconsin–Oshkosh

The University of Wisconsin System American Ethnic Studies Coordinating Committee (AESCC) wishes to acknowledge the contributions of its former members, as well as those of the Urban Corridor Consortium Steering Committee and the University of Wisconsin System American Ethnic Studies Advisory Committee.

PREFACE

It is with no little irony that this volume entitled *Ethnicity and Women* appears at this point in time. As we move into the latter half of the 1980s, the struggle for equality on the part of both ethnic minorities and women is being questioned on more and more fronts. At the level of government and public policy, utterances are being made by public officials to the effect that the time for special attention to racial problems is rapidly drawing to a close. Although the term itself is seldom heard, a drive for a more laissez-faire philosophy of government seems to be rampant. Such means as affirmative action and school desegregation are meeting with increased skepticism and even disdain, not only on the part of government officials and large sections of the white community, but also, perhaps ironically and surprisingly, on the part of disparate groups within ethnic-minority communities. Buttressed by the current trend in public policy, we hear more talk of a move toward a self-help philosophy by these latter individuals. Many of these persons, of course, are ethnic-minority group members who have achieved a degree of middle-class status (no doubt through individual initiative, but also not without government support), although one cannot deny that this self-help strategy has attained at least some measure of currency among lower classes as well. Such talk, albeit from a minority within a minority, is somewhat novel, and thus not only draws the attention of the nation's media, but also allows those in the political arena who desire government retrenchment in this area to use it as justification and vindication. Public opinion, no matter how amorphous, is often formed thusly.

What has been described above is not only true when speaking of racial issues. The feminist or women's liberation movement has always had its vehement critics. In some ways, the struggle to free women from their subordinate position has been more threatening to American society than the quest for equality by ethnic minorities. Those who fear and condemn the movement have not only been male, but to a greater degree than in the cause for racial justice, have also come from within. Ironically, these female opponents have had their status improved by the movement's successes just as ethnic-minority proponents of self-help have been aided by government involvement. The point, though, is that the drive and support which buoyed the women's

ix

movement over the past two decades seem to be eroding. In addition to predictable attacks from pro-lifers, religious fundamentalist groups and the like, some supporters of the movement are increasingly questioning aloud and in print how liberated a career, a marriage, children and a home have left them. This, of course, depends upon one's definition of liberation. If it means increased opportunity, there is no question that the movement has brought women progress. If it means increased freedom from work and responsibility, one has to wonder. Obviously the movement never meant it to mean the latter, and there is no doubt that the former is the more enlightened definition of liberation. But we can understand, though still lament, how the hectic lives of women with a career and a family may lead many to lean toward the latter. All of this, coupled with increased government reticence on women's issues and the failure of the gender factor to effectively materialize as hoped in the 1984 presidential election, seem to portend some rough times for the continued success of the women's movement in the near future.

But perhaps all of the above is much too dismal a description. There is little doubt that both the quest for racial equality and the struggle for women's equality are not currently sailing with the prevailing political winds. This may be useful though. As the goals and objectives of both racial equality and women's equality gained a good degree of acceptance in our societal fabric, an attitude of automatic progression may have set in. There is no disputing that those individuals involved in these movements deserved a period of relaxation, but both current and other history inform us that the lack of constant vigilance leaves the door ajar for more reactionary forces and ideas to enter. To return to the wind metaphor, a wind in one's face will always rouse one more than a wind at one's back. It is our hope that the essays in *Ethnicity and Women,* by addressing issues of both race and gender and how the two intertwine, will call attention to what should be by now an awakening breeze. If not, we will *all* be pushed back.

There is always a great sense of relief after a work such as this one has been completed. There is also a great sense of gratitude. We should begin with mentioning Sharon Gutowski, who is an important cog in organizing the colloquium. Despite the trials of completing law school and embarking upon a career, Joanne Brown has provided us with meticulous copy editing. Heretofore an unsung hero, Ellen Baugher has again deciphered the scribblings of the editors as she played her word processor like a virtuoso. Linda Jallings has again been our guide through the production phase, and Lisa Keys has very competently assumed responsibility for marketing and sales. Support over the years at the University of Wisconsin System level, especially from Vernon Lattin and Dallas Peterson, can also not go unmentioned. As we turn our attention to the next volume in the *Ethnicity and Public Policy* series, we trust we can count on the continued advice and support of all these individuals. If not, our task will be much more difficult.

THOMAS V. TONNESEN

CONTENTS

xiii

INTRODUCTION

Winston A. Van Horne

University of Wisconsin-Milwaukee

Toni-Michelle C. Travis

George Mason University

On June 30, 1982, the congressional deadline for the ratification of the Equal Rights Amendment (hereinafter ERA) to the Constitution of United States passed. The amendment prescribed that "Equality of rights under the law shall not be denied or abridged by the United States, nor by any State, on account of sex," and thus proscribed conduct that either harmed or disadvantaged women solely because of their gender. It sought to write into the organic law of the land the principle of gender-neutral equality of rights. To many this principle was highly evocative and provocative, and it excited the desires and passions of both protagonists and antagonists of the amendment. The writing of women's rights into the Constitution, even though the language of the amendment said nothing about women's rights, seemed to many to trammel the organic law of the body politic, as well as distort and confound its purpose. How joyless an outcome to a struggle in the United States that covered much of the twentieth century, a struggle for the equality of rights of women which more than two thousand years ago Plato took for granted, believing in the natural equality of men and women.

In the *Republic* Plato informs us that

> there is no occupation concerned with the management of social affairs which belongs either to woman or to man, as such. Natural gifts are to be found here and there in both creatures alike; and *every occupation is open to both,* so far as their natures are concerned . . .[1]

It is Plato's conviction that in the organization and management of the commonwealth, "the same natures must be allowed the same pursuits,"[2] thus women and men who "are competent and of a like nature"[3] must share together the duties and responsibilities that fall properly to like natures. Indeed, so completely does Plato believe in the the natural equality of women and men—which does not entail that he believes they are equal arithmetically in each and every attribute and property of mind and body—that he permits them to wrestle one an-

other in the nude as they train their minds and bodies for the guardian-
ship of the commonwealth. Plato knows that such an activity "might
be ridiculed as involving a good many breaches of custom . . . [T]he
notion of women exercising naked along with men in the wrestling
schools . . . would be . . . laughable, according to our present no-
tions."[4] Still, Plato perceives nothing base in the nude wrestling of men
and women who, by education and training, have the rational, spirited
and appetitive parts of their souls in proper balance and harmony. The
appetitive part of the souls of such individuals does not overpower the
rational part and lead to illicit and base sexual activity. Rather, the
appetite obeys the dictates of reason, and calm bodily control results in
the exercise serving its proper purpose. So confident is Plato in the
soundness of his convictions pertaining to the equality of women and
men that he observes that what he proposes pertaining to the proper
relation of men and women is neither impossible nor visionary, "since
it [is] in accordance with nature. Rather, the contrary practice [of
treating women as unequals] which now prevails turns out to be
unnatural."[5]

We find Plato's views to be intriguing, compelling and resonant. He
is one of the first Western political philosophers to recognize clearly
and distinctly the power, force and imperative of education and training in bringing out the best in both women and men. A good education
and proper training harmonize the mind and body of the individual,
and impel one to eschew that which is foul, folly or base as one strives
to be the very best that one can be by one's nature. The critical point
that Plato is making in his advocacy of nude wrestling of men and
women as a part of their physical development and moral growth is
that differences of gender are irrelevant to the exercise of reason's natural authority over the soul; and self-discipline, self-control and responsible behavior are as natural to women as they are to men. Even more
important for our purposes is the fact that Plato believes that those
who "are competent and of a like nature . . . *must* be allowed the same
pursuits."[6] The term must here entails the terms can, ought to and
should. Women who by their training, education and experience possess the same attributes as men to "keep watch over the commonwealth"[7] are empirically capable of ruling political society, and can
rule it. Women who can rule political society ought to be permitted to
rule it in so far as they suffer no natural nor rational disabilities of dis-
qualification. Women who can and ought to rule should be permitted to
rule; indeed, they must be allowed the same pursuits as their male
counterparts. This is Plato's admonition; this is the moral axiom that
forms the touchstone of women's struggle for equality in America's political society.

The architectonic attributes of Plato's ideas in Western political philosophy have long been recognized, yet it is truly striking how little influence his observations pertaining to the equality of men and women have had on the societies of the West—or societies elsewhere in the world for that matter. Men keep watch over the commonwealth; women keep watch over the home. This has been, and for the most part continues to be, the grounding axiom of gender-based inequalities in most societies of the world.

In the United States, "[b]lack women and white women, although not without dissension, have been working together to improve the condition of women since the abolitionist societies of the nineteenth century," according to Toni-Michelle Travis. The struggle over the abolition of slavery had the unintended consequence of unmasking before the eyes of white women their own social inequality, and made them conscious of the rigid gender-grounded stratification of the society. (Stratification by race was unmistakeably obvious to them; stratification by gender was not quite so obvious.) Increased activity in the abolitionist movement had the corresponding effect of enhancing the social consciousness of white women, which, in turn, increased their activities not only in behalf of black slaves but also themselves. One thus observes a significant correspondence between activity and conciousness—consciousness and activity—as women in the United States engaged the struggle for liberation from both race-grounded and gender-grounded inequalities in the society. The struggle has yielded substantial results in the context of both legal justice and social justice. Invidious discrimination grounded in race and/or gender now violates the sensibilities of much of the populace, and is repugnant to the canons of law as well as to the prescriptions and proscriptions of a range of moral and ethical precepts that give form and substance to the social order. Still, much work remains.

Over the past decade, women, especially white women, have altered their role in American society significantly by leaving the private sphere of the home to enter the public arena. It is as if Plato's admonition that those who "are competent and of a like nature . . . must be allowed the same pursuits"[8] finally echoed across the millenia and rang clearly, distinctly and loudly in their ears. Their behaviors demonstrate that they have heeded his voice, though many, perhaps most, do not know him.

After working in the civil rights movement, female activists of the 1960s, as was true of their counterparts in the 1830s, became painfully aware of their subordinate status in American society. They observed that in spite of undeniable gains that had been made, the reproduction of sexism and racism in the culture occasioned the persistence of a

range of undue inequalities in the society. It became increasingly clear
to them that just as invidious racial discrimination and insidious cultural obstacles constrained severely the life chances of blacks, invidious
and insidious gender-grounded dicrimination created wrongful barriers
to the full political participation and occupational mobility of women.
As they scanned their environment, women found blatant discrimination in pursuing an education in scientific and technical fields, in obtaining employment in male-dominated professions, in securing occupational advancement and in climbing the ladder of political success.

As they scrutinized with increasing logical, conceptual and empirical rigor the structure of the social order and their roles in it, women
advanced both theoretic arguments and concrete proposals designed to
make Plato's admonition a reality in American society. Refusing either
to be silent or remain confined to their traditional roles which constrained their participation in discourse and activities that were politically significant and relevant nationally, women engaged the society's
political economy and found once again that they could have an impact
outside the home. As they became more active in the political economy, women sought to articulate and aggregate their interests through
conventional group politics, the electoral process, and pressure group
activities that breeched the customs of the social order. They founded
new organizations through which they called attention to a range of
issues, a key one being the enactment and ratification of the Equal
Rights Amendment to the Constitution of the United States. Increasingly, they found that they had clout in the politial economy. This was
the antithesis of the traditional conception and perception of the
American woman.

Traditionally, the American female was portrayed in the roles of
wife, mother and homemaker. She ran the household, cared for the children, and supported her husband in all of his activities. As portrayed in
popular literature and television, the image of the American female
was that of a white woman who placed the interests and purposes of her
family first, and subordinated her personal and career goals to the family's well-being. In a very real sense, the individual identity and consciousness of the female were dissolved into the collective identity and
consciousness of the family, which was supported materially by the
male. In the 1950s and early 1960s television presented this homogen-
ized perspective of the American family in such series as "Father
Knows Best," "Ozzie and Harriet," and the "Donna Reed Show." The
tranquility of white suburban life was not touched by the rude blows of
unemployment, the brutality of family violence, the callousness of violence in the schools and the savagery of violence in the streets; nor dis-

turbed by the arrival of neighbors who were black, Hispanic, Asian or Native American.

The happy, contented and amiable American family was rocked by the shock waves of the activities emanating from the civil rights movement and the Vietnam conflict, and was awakened to the larger issues of racism, war, poverty and sexism in the society. Television coverage, as well as coverage by other media, depicted graphically "the other" America[9]—one of blight, social marginality, hopelessness, despair and rage. This was an America where black men sought constantly to secure steady employment in order to support their families, where black women were socialized to believe that working outside the house was one of the givens of their lives, and where black children struggled with the realities of racial discrimination which they could not understand. Across the country television screens were filled with images on the nightly news of Americans who were disfranchised, unemployed, being drafted in large numbers for the Vietnam war, and of black women and Hispanic women who were not housewives but domestic servants or agricultural workers for whom a ten- to twelve-hour workday was a commonplace. Both the medium and the message had a profound impact on the national soul of the United States. As the nation-state was hammered by a series of all too familiar blows, the imperative of social change became a commonplace in the land. There were disagreements, indeed sharp cleavages, pertaining to the form, substance, scope, method(s) and rate at which the change(s) should happen. But most of the populace subscribed to the proposition that noteworthy social changes *ought to* occur. Thus did the structure of cultural values that determined in large measure the life chances of women and minority groups in the United States begin to be reconstituted in the 1960s.

This volume scrutinizes rigorously the theoretic structure, the social logic and the empirical dynamic of change in the life chances of American women. It unmasks the relation between race, ethnicity, gender and social state. It lays bare a range of undue inequalities suffered by women, and articulates a vision of women who not only keep watch over the home but over the commonwealth as well. In a very real sense, the authors make use of Plato's vision of the equality of men and women, even though this is not done explicitly, as they paint images of the limits and possibilities of the lives of women in the society.

Sidney Bremer scrutinizes women as they are depicted as leaders in literature that embodies and reflects a range of cultural values. Her study of contemporary literature gives one considerable insight into changes that have taken, and continue to take, place in the society. Through the medium of storytelling, those segments of the society that are not well-represented among policymakers and have either little or no priority on the political agenda are given a voice. Literature thus provides an instrument for expressing critical concerns pertaining to leadership.

Bremer's approach to the subject of women, ethnicity and public policy is novel, and her arguments intriguing. Its novelty lies in its success in using literary inquiry to describe, explain, justify and prescribe behaviors by ethnic-minority women that are germane to the structure of public policy in the society without " 'reducing literature to sociological footnotes.' " Its intrigue lies in its insights pertaining to the historicity of vision in storytelling as "a power essential to democracy."

Bremer observes that storytelling is a means whereby one sings " 'the song of the people.' Whatever the outcome of public policy decisions, the decision-making process must include the voices of all. That's no luxury for us to indulge when we have the time. It's a matter of life and death." Given male dominance in the society and "the heterosexual bias in our culture," as well as the pervasiveness of gender oversights and the "double trouble when ethnic women are invisible minority groups within minority groups," Bremer believes that the ideas of fairness, equity, equality and social justice that are intrinsic to our democratic social order necessitate the resonance of women's voices in order to shatter their "image of the silenced majority." She perceives clearly the empirical fact that "silenced people cannot name their reality for themselves or to others." A silenced people are not a democratic people. Silence is the hemlock of democracy. It is axiomatic in a democracy, and a categorical imperative of a democratic social order, that the people's voices should be heard. One may not like what is heard, and may wish that what is heard was not said, but if a democratic social order is to persist, prosper and flourish, the noise of a cacophony of named realities is inescapable. If silence is the hemlock of democracy, noise and disagreement are its honey.

Women who are silenced by the norms, mores, customs, ethos, traditions and institutions of the society are not good democratic citizens, even though they may be good women. Aristotle, who does not share Plato's views on the equality of men and women, draws a sound distinction between the good man and the good citizen. He observes that "the good man is a man so called in virtue of a single absolute excellence,"[9] that is, one who by contemplation and action conflates his intellectual and moral virtues to produce the greatest possible harmony in his life. A good citizen, on the other hand, is "a man who shares in the administration of justice and in holding office,"[10] that is, he rules and is ruled in turn. It should be noted that when Aristotle uses the term man he means male literally, but this matters not for our concern here. The critical point we wish to make is that Aristotle recognizes the fact that the responsibilities and duties of citizenship require the citizen to participate in keeping watch over the commonwealth. One may participate directly or indirectly in "the management of social affairs,"[11] but one must participate.

If one must participate, logically and empirically one must have the right to participate; for participation implies the right to participate, tautologically. The right to participate in the management of social affairs and keeping watch over the commonwealth are intrinsic to the idea of the good citizen, and the good citizen is one who exercises this right. The expansiveness and robustness of this right vary with the constitution of the commonwealth, as Aristotle aptly observes, and so the form and substance of the right's exercise are contingent upon the kind of polity in which it exists. Bremer knows all of this. Hence, she is impelled to argue that our democratic polity falls far short of its democratic ideal, insofar as values are reproduced which proscribe the full participation of women in the variety of structures and activities that gives form, substance, purpose and meaning to social life in the United States.

It is in this context that Bremer perceives the historicity of vision in storytelling. The stories she discusses present moving images of slices of reality in American society over historical time. The images inform through motion, as the present is linked in dynamic continuity with the past and future. Indeed, the images are but " 'song[s] of the people, transformed by the experiences of each generation, that hold them together, and if any part of [them] is lost the people suffer and are without soul.' " The historicity of vision in storytelling is transgenerational. Bremer finds in this a major impulse for social change. Each generation is made more conscious through the resonant voices of women—as well as of men, of course—of the necessity of activities which occasion the formulation and implementation of public policies that make more likely the convergence of the good individual and the good citizen in a truly democratic social order. In the genre of *The Lord of the Flies*—but applied to the interests and purposes of ethnic-minority women, and by extension of all women—Bremer's discourse makes a noteworthy contribution to the use of literary inquiry in the study of public policy.

If vision and resonant literacy voices animate Bremer's chapter, the ones by Jo Freeman, Toni-Michelle Travis and Elizabeth Almquist are energized by women's activities in the political system. Feminist organizations have led the struggle for greater political participation, more roles for women in the private and public sectors of the society, and the passage of the ERA. Freeman's analysis of the battle for the enactment and ratification of the ERA scrutinizes the internal dissension among female activists, as well as the legal and social implications that the amendment's passage would have for the society as a whole.

First proposed in 1921, the ERA has had ardent supporters who believe that a constitutional amendment is a necessary though not sufficient condition to secure the rights of all women, as well as determined opponents who believe that the strict enforcement of the relevant statute laws and administrative codes, in conjunction with the filing of suits under the Fourteenth and Fifteenth Amendments, are sufficient empirically to guarantee women's rights. Freeman documents meticulously the form and substance of the countervailing forces in the struggle over the ERA. She observes what may be called the irony of competing desirables as the National Women's Party was forced to abandon its position that the ERA would not undo desirable protective labor legislation, and stake out a position that the elimination of such laws was desirable because they "only limited women's opportunities." And she perceives what may be termed the paradox of intergenerational transposition as by 1976 ancient foes of the ERA on the political left became the bedrock of its support, while long-term supporters on the political right became its implacable antagonists.

The irony of competing desirables and the paradox of intergenerational transposition provide the conceptual framework within which Freeman discusses the empirical significance of the struggle for the ERA. She is acutely conscious of the fact that the ERA brings into sharp relief fundamental values of the society, and is most sensitive to its significance for the status of women. The conflict over the ERA is grounded in legal, moral/ethical and social principles and concerns. Passage of the ERA would be a singular victory for those who believe women's possibilities should not be delimited by gender; for it is right and proper that those who are competent and of a like nature should be allowed the same pursuits. It would affirm through the body of the organic law of the land the right of women to be good citizens. It would signal the propriety of women to be wage earners and single parents heading households, as well as leaders in the public and private sectors of the society. Freeman believes that many neither desire these outcomes nor deem them to be desirable.

It is Freeman's conviction that the ratification of the ERA would be adverse to the interests of those who subscribe to patriarchal principles of social organization. She observes that

> any racial or ethnic group for whom patriarchal family structure and a sexual division of labor are desired norms and part of its basic identity will find the ERA inimical to its interests. If achievement of the ERA is perceived as resulting in a loss of prestige to patriarchy, then ethnic groups who value patriarchy or the

patriarchal family will also lose prestige. Conversely, those groups which have been derogated for being matriarchal will gain in prestige.

Freeman believes that "[a]lthough most of the opponents as well as the proponents of the ERA are white, and not identified with any particular ethnic group," black Americans should be one of the primary beneficiaries if the amendment were incorporated into the organic law of the land. This is so because black Americans have had to bear the stigma of matriarchy in a society that enthrones patriarchy—even though anthropological research and demographic findings have established that approximately 80 percent of Western Africa from which black slaves were transported to the United States was marked by patriarchal family organization. The patriarchal family structure of West African slaves was corroded by the barbarism of New World slavery. Their culture was assaulted unrelentingly, and there was a ceaseless attack upon the masculinity and manhood of black males. Little wonder, then, that black females, though brutalized by the savagery of slavery, should have been beaten down less than black males, and thus able to harness within themselves a reservoir of energy that gave them the strength to succor and nurture progeny through whom the race survived. African matriarchy in the United States was a European construction of the slaves' lives. Insofar as it exists today, it most assuredly epiphenomenal of the reality of black people's lives prior to the trauma and tragedy of the bondage of their forebears.

Freeman notes that "[b]lack society is hardly matriarchal in any abstract sense of the word, but it has been labeled as such because black women are more likely to be the sole supporters of their families than are white women. Compared to black men, black women have also exercised more power and responsibility within their own communities than white women have compared to white men." Freeman believes that given the empirical fact that the institutions and values of white middle-class society are biased toward the patriarchal family, "[a] governmental action which confers status on women, and enhances the prestige of those values associated with the women's movement, should undermine [the] degradation of the black family structure." The ERA is thus conceived of as an instrument for the transvaluation of values, as phenomenal reality displaces epiphenomenal images.

The theme of the empowerment of women is continued in Travis' chapter. She notes that along with the high hopes that women would achieve equality through the ERA has been the dream that policy changes could be accomplished through the electoral process. The 1984 presidential election offered an opportunity for women to coalesce across racial-ethnic lines to vote against the policies of President Ronald Reagan and his administration. Such was not the case.

As noted earlier, white women and black women have had a long history of working together. This can be traced back to the nineteenth century abolitionist movement. Joint efforts continued, although there was friction over priorities in the suffrage movement and over black representation during the club movement era. What is the current status and potential of racial cooperation at a time when most of the newer women's organizations, both black and white, are concentrating on political objectives?

American women have matured politically. The increased sophistication of their political approach is observable in the formation of such organizations as the National Organization for Women (hearinafter NOW), the National Women's Political Caucus, and the Coalition of 100 Black Women, along with the increased role women now play in the Democratic and Republican parties. Women are now mobilizing their resources to get women elected to office and to criticize those of Reagan's policies which affect them adversely.

The 1984 election was seen as a great opportunity for women, who constitute a majority of the voting population, to make their political clout felt. Clearly this did not happen, as black women remained with the Democratic Party and a considerable number of white women supported Reagan and the Republican ticket. What happened to the potential power bloc and the possibility of future interracial coalitions?

Politically active women were thought to be united on the issue of defeating Reagan and voting for the Democratic ticket. However, the fragile coalition suffered a severe blow at the Democratic national convention when the question of priorities arose again. White women opted for a female vice-presidential candidate, while black women still saw race as a priority and supported Jesse Jackson's candidacy for the nomination.

Black women left the Democratic convention, as they had left so many others since the days of the abolitionists, determined to build and head their own organizations where race would remain a priority issue. Many black women supported Jackson at the convention, nonetheless they gave their complete support to the Mondale-Ferraro ticket in the election. The question remains: Will white women activists seek to build another coalition with black women in 1988 when they did not achieve success with their first priority, a female candidate, in 1984?

The question above is not asked rhetorically. It calls attention to a problem most fundamental in women's struggle for social justice and equity, namely, the intergenerational reproduction of racism in the culture. Cultures reproduce themselves; individuals are the instruments through which they are reproduced. True, the instruments of reproduction can and do change that which is reproduced. Still, the process and product of cultural reproduction are only nominally the work of individuals *qua* individuals. Attributes of a culture that are reproduced in individuals are not erased from the culture by the behavior of this or that individual. They are erased only transgenerationally by the progressive blotting out of the collective memory of the social efficacy of particular forms of behavior. Racism has been and continues to be socially efficacious in the society. It is one of the key attributes of the culture that gives form and substance to our society. Accordingly, it is reproduced in the culture which sustains structural arrangements and patterns of behavior for which racism is socially efficacious. Travis is conscious of this when she writes: "Politically active black women have declared that they will no longer be subordinates to white female leaders, nor brokers for the black community. Those women who faithfully supported the 1984 Democratic ticket feel that they have paid their dues, but that *white women will not accept them as equals* with legitimate political priorities." The force of race as a hard line of demarcation between black women and white women is all too obvious here, and it calls out a problem in the relations between blacks and whites that is older than the republic itself—racism. Will common interests of gender transverse the racial divide as women engage the 1988 presidential election? The history of the interactions between black women and white women that Travis presents cannot but make one less than sanguine about the prospects of shared activities to advance common interests.

Racism and oppression have accompanied one another in the society. This does not entail that there has been a one-to-one corresondence between racism and oppression in the United States over historical time. It does entail that racism has been a key occasioning factor, if not the efficient cause, of oppressive social wrongs that non-white peoples have experienced in the society. One of the truly damnable effects of racism and oppression has been the mistranslation of common interests by the oppressed, mainly due to the skewing and distortion of their perception of reality by their social state. As one scans the tablets of recorded history, one cannot but marvel at the ease with which the few have ruled the many, and the host of frictions that have tended to divide the oppressed. Almquist is troubled by this as she observes that the goals of feminist organizations have been hampered because of limited support from black women. Suffering under the double jeopardy of racism and sexism, black women have had limited resources they could contribute to feminists causes. Although occupational mobility has been minimal because of the policies imposed by a dominant white culture, black women have continued to play a strong role in the family and in the civil rights movement. As a dual minority, black women have felt that the well-being of their family and political rights were primary objectives, while issues of feminism were only of secondary importance.

Almquist uses the internal colonialism model—which gained quite a bit of currency in the late 1960s and early 1970s, and has been the subject of well-known critical scrutiny in the literature of the social sciences—to describe and explain the limits of ethnic-minority women's participation in both social movements and social movement organizations. Believing that "[a]mong several possible social science perspectives, the internal colonialism model provides the most useful interpretation of the unique situation of racial and ethnic groups in this country," Almquist seeks to demonstrate "that the United States has practiced a number of policies which placed racial-ethnic minorities in roughly the same situation that European powers placed the people in the territories they conquered." This is the axiomatic assumption that grounds the internal colonialism model.

Almquist continues Travis' observations on the divisiveness of race among women by conjoining racism and internal colonialism, and showing their common effect on interracial/interethnic, gender-grounded group solidarity. She observes that "Black women, Asian women, Native-American women, Mexican-American women—all have little sense of sharing a common design for living with each other or with Anglos. Internal colonialism and racism practically guaranteed that these groups would have no sense of solidarity with each other." Since group solidarity is one of the necessary conditions that constitute the *sine qua non* of the long-term persistence of social movements, as well as social movement organizations, one observable empirical effect of racism and internal colonialism is the failure of women to sustain interracial/interethnic activities designed to have transracial/transethnic gender benefits. This is so in spite of the fact that a range of structural and cultural barriers that heretofore constrained participation in shared activities has been eroded. What, then, is the future of transracial/transethnic gender-grounded alliances? This question impels one to consider the mobilization of resources, which Almquist does with great care.

Ethnic-minority women are still constrained in their life chances by racial barriers and low incomes. Yet, there are indications that they might participate in social movements that emanate from conditions in the workplace. Though the double jeopardy of racism and sexism continues to be a stubborn reality of their everyday lives, it is nonetheless the case that "[w]orkplace organizing holds high potential for increasing structural ties and for highlighting common interests, identities and issues that transcend racial lines," says Almquist. Informed and sensitive public policy should encourage this, for as all women become increasingly good citizens, the society benefits as a whole.

The necessity of informed and sensitive public policy, with effective enforcement mechanisms where appropriate, is made all too obvious in the chapters by Mary Romero as well as by Jeanne Gordus and Marian Oshiro. Both chapters discuss the occupational status of ethnic-minority women in the private sector in the context of a common question: How much progress has been made, and at what cost to whom?

Gordus and Oshiro examine the salience of race and ethnicity as constraints which prevent ethnic-minority women from achieving sufficient occupational mobility to become officials and managers in private corporations. This is a most interesting chapter, for it calls out a range of difficulties that women in general, and ethnic-minority women in particular, have in penetrating the opportunity structure of the corporate world—especially its upper echelons. It also focuses attention on the possibilities and limits of public policy in fostering the penetration of the corporate opportunity structure by ethnic-minority women who desire to become officials and managers. Additionally, it corroborates important observations that we have made thus far.

Gordus and Oshiro call attention to the significance of "sameness" and "belonging" in achieving occupational mobility in the corporate world. They write: "It has been said again and again that, in management, much of the reason for career advancement is a perception, not merely of a person's competence, but of her/his 'belonging'—of sharing the same goals and values, employing the same methods and means to agreed-upon ends—and more. The outcome of this attribution of 'sameness' in the hiring and promotion process is to reduce perceived risk." They proceed to observe that "[t]hose who are the 'same' as the decision-makers are perceived—rightly or wrongly—as less risky choices since their future work performance and style are assumed to be similar to those of the people currently making personnel decisions." The points that Gordus and Oshiro make here are well-known, but nonetheless important. (It has been said that truisms become truisms because they make important truths about the world obvious.)

Sameness and belonging are perceived to reduce risk. The reduction of risk is believed to limit cost. The limitation of cost increases profit. There is thus a strong indirect link in the causal chain between the social-psychology of sameness and belonging and the political economy of profit that obtains in the corporate world. The political economy of the impetus for profit and the reduction of risk reinforce the social-psychology of sameness and belonging, which, in turn, reinforces behaviors that limit risk in the equation of profit making. Here one observes a conceptual, if not an empirical, circularity between sameness and belonging, risk reduction and profit making. What is the significance of this for ethnic-minority women?

There is a strong propensity in the corporate world, particularly at the level of officials and managers, to hire and promote "our kind of person." Who is "our kind of person?" One who possesses the attributes mentioned by Gordus and Oshiro. Competence, sameness and belonging form the triad of first choice at the level of officials and managers. The triad is not, however, universal and invariable in its empirical application. There are times when sameness and belonging together have been taken to be empirically sufficient for the award of first choice. There have been occasions when considerations of competence have been empirically sufficient in the award of first choice—superseding ones pertaining to sameness and belonging. However, when there is a pool of approximately equally competent individuals, given the tradition of the triad of first choice in corporations, it is the case that the award of first choice will most likely go to one(s) who possess(es) all three attributes, and is/are not simply judged to be competent. Given the overwhelming dominance of white males as corporate officials and managers, one can readily perceive the problems posed by gender in general—ones which are compounded by the addition of ethnic-minority status. The social-psychology and political economy of corporate traditions, conjoined with the reproduction of racism and sexism in the cultural substratum of the society, severely disadvantage ethnic-minority women in the penetration of the opportunity structure of the corporate world.

Ethnic-minority women "have few role models from whom to learn or after whom to pattern their own behavior." They generally lack "inside contacts," which are difficult to make "without membership in the 'right' country club" where their absence is most conspicuous. Moreover, the "[l]ack of common experiences leaves a gap where one would like to show, 'I am like you, and therefore can be trusted like you.' Rare is the father with accumulated acumen, associations, and wealth to pass on to daughters, the husband to leave to a widow, or other relatives to help the minority women as white women have sometimes been helped," observe Gordus and Oshiro. These obstacles, together with others that Gordus and Oshiro articulate, serve to limit the information that ethnic-minority women have about, and their access to, corporate life.

If competence, sameness and belonging form the triad of first choice in the corporate world, access and information form the dyad of influence. Access fosters information which, used judiciously, occasions greater access. Lacking in both access and information, ethnic-minority women exert precious little influence in the corporate world. Those who do/have succeed(ed) in becoming managers and officials are invariably confronted with a terrible dilemma. In order to maximize access and information, one is often impelled to show that " 'I am like you, and therefore can be trusted like you.' " This confronts ethnic-minority women foursquare with tough questions pertaining to their identity, by gender as well as by race and ethnicity. Moreover, "[t]he problems multiply (at the very least) geometrically as ethnic standards of femininity compete with those of the majority society as well as with expected and acceptable standards of feminine behavior within the corporate environment, in relation to subordinates and superordinates (male or female)," Gordus and Oshiro point out. Given the commonplace stresses that accompany the management function, and the social-psychological as well as the corporate environmental pressures that confront ethnic-minority women *qua* ethnic-minority women, it is not terribly difficult for a company that "wishes to fulfill its prophecy that women and/or minorities cannot do the job" to do so, observe Gordus and Oshiro.

Still, all is not doom and gloom. "Except during the 1975 recession period, women of all racial and ethnic groups have been improving their representation in most job categories, both in numbers and in share of jobs," note Gordus and Oshiro. They are sensitive to the fact that "the amount of improvement has varied by job category for the four different minorities, and by industry," but they are nonetheless sanguine about the prospects of the upward continuation of the trend line. Women are now making "smarter" career choices, and making more effective use of educational opportunities. Corporations have taken a range of concrete measures to hire, retain and promote women in general, and ethnic-minority women in particular. Public policy which can do little or nothing to change patterns of informal access to official and managerial roles, has done much to alter the patterns of formal access. Still, Gordus and Oshiro believe that more needs to be done if the gains that have been made are not to be eroded as "scarcer-than-normal promotional opportunities . . . [t]hrough the 1980s and 1990s [limit the] career progression" of white males of the baby boom generation.

It is obvious from Gordus' and Oshiro's chapter that there has been no zero sum game in the gains that ethnic-minority women have made as corporate officials and managers. This theme is echoed in Romero's chapter which discusses the relation between affirmative action regulations and the occupational distribution and participation of Mexican-

American women in private industry in California, Texas and Illinois—three of the four states with the largest Mexican-American population. Examining occupational trends from 1971 through 1980, Romero strives to discern answers to the three fundamental questions that organize her presentation: "Has affirmative action been successful in removing white male dominance in prestigious and high-paying occupations? Has affirmative action resulted in upward mobility for women and minorities by eliminating their concentrations within unskilled, low-paying white- and blue-collar occupations? Have white males had to suffer economically for advances made by minorities and women?" These questions emanate from Romero's conviction that "[t]he ten-year period since affirmative action legislation was enacted has provided employers with time to implement affirmative action programs based on anticipated employee turnover rate and new vacancies, as well as time to promote and upgrade qualified Chicanas." Hence, "[o]ne would expect that guidelines providing equal opportunity for advancement within the work force would result in an increase in the number of Chicanas in managerial and professional positions." Romero's findings do not make her optimistic about the payoff of affirmative action for Chicanas, but she wishes neither the weakening nor the abolition of affirmative action legislation and guidelines. This appears somewhat paradoxical at first blush, but there is no paradox here, as one shall see momentarily.

Looking at Mexican Americans, Romero describes the hardship of striving for occupational mobility under the burden of being twice a minority. She is particularly sensitive to the lot of Chicanas, who suffer the cumulative disadvantages of gender, race/ethnicity and language. These disadvantages have had an exclusionary effect over historical time as Chicanas have tried to penetrate the opportunity structure of the work force. Affirmative action was/is a public policy instituted for the purpose of broadening "participation in the political community in general, and the work force in particular, by providing mechanicisms whereby those who have been excluded from a range of societal benefits may have the opportunity to partake of them legally."[12] Chicanas, as well as others who have suffered the effects of undue exclusionary disadvantages, perceive affirmative action as an instrument for their inclusion in the ordinary processes of the distribution of the society's benefits and burdens. The promise of affirmative action has been incommensurate with its performance for Chicanas.

Romero observes from the data she presents that occupational mobility for Chicanas over the decade of the 1970s was minimal. Their entry into official and managerial positions was nominal at best, and "[e]ven less progress was made in professional occupations." Also, their occupational participation in private industry showed only a fractional increase. These observations hardly attest to the erosion of exclusionary barriers by affirmative action.

To what extent has the implementation of affirmative action hurt the occupational status of white males and resulted in reverse discrimination? Romero's data "do not indicate that white males have experienced a downward occupational distribution as a result of the entry of Chicanas or other minorities into managerial and professional positions; on the contrary, white males appear to have made continued progress." Moreover, she observes that "white males have been able to maintain a disproportionate share of the higher-paying and skilled jobs in private industry despite affirmative action," noting that "[t]he slight increases Chicanas have made into professional occupations have not been at the expense of the status quo."

We should now understand why what at first appeared to be paradoxical is no paradox after all. The data indicate no significant payoff for Chicanas from affirmative action. They show that there is no zero sum game involving Chicanas' occupational gains and white males' occupational losses in private industry. They show that affirmative action has had very marginal results at best, and inconsequential ones at worst, in relation to the occupational gains of Chicanas in private industry. Still, the preservation and strengthening of affirmative action are of the utmost importance in the absence of a better public policy to take its place.

Romero is sensitive to the social reality and the historical significance of vigorous implementation and strict enforcement of written and unwritten rules that have disadvantaged racial and ethnic minorities over historical time. She is mindful of the unending struggle to have public policies that advantage racial and ethnic minorities implemented copiously and enforced strictly. It is in this context that she is acutely conscious of the empirical costs that would invariably attend the weakening or abolition of affirmative action in the absence of a sound and effective alternative public policy. Indeed, it may well be that affirmative action as symbol has overshadowed affirmative action as substance, and an inverse relation obtains between the symbol and substance of affirmative action. But symbols are of the utmost importance historically, and when they persist through several cross sections of historical time, they tend to acquire substance that increases exponentially.

Symbol and substance converge in the black family, one of the two most enduring institutions in black America—the other being the church. Elmer Martin and Joanne Martin scrutinize the black family in order to ascertain the differential and changing roles of black women in it over historical time. Beginning with the axiomatic assumption of black women as survivors, achievers and agents of social change, the Martins argue that a strong matriarchy as well as a strong patriarchy have had deleterious effects on the black community. It is their conviction that black women in their roles as survivors, achievers and agents of social change are natural products of black culture, and constitute a powerful counterpoint to "a white racist, sexist society and to male chauvinist deviations in the black community." They suggest "that public policy which seeks to actually stabilize the black family and community would be more effective if it sought, instead, to strengthen black women in these roles, rather than to destroy an alleged matriarchy and establish a black patriarchy."

In their discussion of the black family, the Martins observe that its organization reveals neither matriarchy nor patriarchy but a form of social intercourse that fosters substantive equality between males and females. Substantive equality between black females and black males issues from the structure of the black family over historical time. This is a crucial finding and a profound insight, given its obvious social significance and critical revision of dogma about the black family that obtains in the literature of the social sciences.

Observing a tradition of equality in the black family, the Martins posit that "[i]t is a cruel hoax to demand that black men live up to the patriarchal model and then do practically everything conceivable to make sure that the great majority of them will never be able do so. It is even a more cruel hoax to hold that the black man is ruled by a matriarchy, the very opposite of the patriarchal ideal. In essence, this is saying that the black man is not a man." Here one feels the anger of the Martins at one of the insidious effects of the reproduction of racism in the culture, to wit, the primacy of white constructions of the black family. These constructions ignore the tradition of substantive equality between black males and black females, and downgrade—as well as derogate—black females in their roles as survivors, achievers and agents of social change. It is, then, no wonder that "[v]ery little is done on the public policy level to take advantage of the black woman's tradition as an achiever." The result of this has been that "thousands [one might say millions] of black women have had their promise and potential stifled generation after generation, regardless of those in political office," observe the Martins.

For too long deficit models of the black family have held sway in the society. The Martins desire to undo these, and place in their stead constitutive models grounded in the strengths of the black family. To this end they write: "[T]he stereotypic, racist image of black women as mammies, matriarchs, permissive sex objects, welfare bums and emas-

culators . . . must be totally destroyed so that a more realistic assessment of black women as hard-working, striving, achieving people seeking to improve the quality of their lives can emerge." The Martins'
chapter makes an invaluble contribution to this end.

The family evokes passion and pathos. One glories in its triumphs
and anguishes in its defeats. One takes pride in its accomplishments
and pities its shortcomings. One rejoices in its strengths and sorrows in
its weaknesses. And one is gladened to remember that it is the well-
spring of generations but saddened to recollect that it is the source of
the first murder—Abel's death at Cain's hands.

Violence in the family, always present but more often than not invisible, has become increasingly visible over the course of the past generation, and is the subject of Suzanne Steinmetz's and Joy Pellicciaro's
chapter. Violence entails the intentional and/or deliberate use of force
to occasion injury, harm or damage in order to diminish the value of a
person or property. The purpose of the use of violence is the diminution
of value; this is axiomatic. There is not, however, a one-to-one correspondence between its purpose and its function, and so there are instances in which its function is incommensurate with its purpose. But
in the family, there is a remarkable correspondence between the purpose and the function of violence. Steinmetz's and Pellicciaro's arguments and data demonstrate this.

One cannot but be struck by the fact that in the United States, "a
curvilinear pattern [obtains] between rates of violence and women's
status. The highest levels of violence are in those states where women's
overall status is lowest. The rate drops as status improves," observe
Steinmetz and Pellicciaro. Low status entails undervaluation and devaluation; thus women of low status are undervalued and devalued.
This undervaluation and devaluation of their dignity, worth and person make them ready objects of violence in the same manner that the
weak are prey to the strong. Women of low status are easy prey, and
the violence they suffer only exacerbates their social marginality. The
obvious inference from this is that women of low status should strive to
increase their status in order to decrease the probability of being the
objects of violence. But Steinmetz and Pellicciaro report that "[s]tatus
inconsistency, especially the husband's underachievement in occupation, and status incompatibility, i.e., the wife's occupation is high relative to her husband's, are likely to result in life-threatening abuse—
beating or use of a weapon. Couples with an overachieving husband
experience considerably lower levels of spousal violence." How does
this square with the notion of women increasing their status in order to
decrease the likelihood of suffering violence?

Violence by husbands against wives whose status is greater than their own is designed to cut them down to size, if we may so speak. Its purpose is to diminish them; to reduce them, at least psychologically and emotionally, to a standing that is coterminous, or perhaps a notch below, that of their husbands. This interpretation is surely consistent with the finding that in families where husbands are overachievers, there tends to be less spousal violence. Women thus face a cruel dilemma. If their status is low, they are prime objects of violence; if their status is high, higher than their spouses, they are also prime objects of violence. The implicit message to women thus appears to be: Achieve, but do not achieve too much, and surely not more than your spouses. Steinmetz and Pellicciaro recognize this when they write: "As women continue to strive for equality, a readjustment in the male/female power structure can be expected to produce a short-term increase in violence. Only when egalitarian rather than male-superiority norms prevail can we expect to see a reduction in spousal violence." Put differently, only when those who are competent and of a like nature are allowed the same pursuits can we expect to see a reduction in spousal violence, if Plato as well as Steinmetz and Pellicciaro are correct. How does this square with the Martins' observations pertaining to substantive equality in the black family?

The data presented by Steimetz and Pellicciaro intersect racial and ethnic boundaries. Their key empirical generalizations also intersect racial and ethnic boundaries. It is thus the case that Steinmetz and Pellicciaro do not perceive the black family to be nearly as egalitarian as the Martins believe it to be.

Steinmetz and Pellicciaro believe that there is a cycle of violence that continues from generation to generation, and is "fueled by a lack of education, inadequate financial means, unstable or overstressed kinship networks, insufficient and inappropriate social services, and a value system that rewards male machismo and aggression/violence in general." If this noxious cycle is to be broken, Steinmetz and Pellicciaro are convinced that "[i]nasmuch as economic reforms are more efficacious to legislate than cultural norms . . . public policy must concentrate on extensive structural improvements" in the society.

Conclusion

Over the past generation women have made conspicuous progress. Some have soared in both the public and private sectors of the society, but, taken as a whole, they still have many promises to keep and miles to go before they sleep. Before them is the vision of what they ought to be and can be, behind them is the memory of what they have been, within them is the image of what they were, are, and should be.

Today, women are no longer content with having men determine the contours of their lives. The routine deference of females to males is fast fading from the social landscape. In ever increasing numbers, women are leading organizations, their own and others, that are assaulting the continuing problems of inequality in the society. They are asserting and affirming their rights through interest groups, pressure groups and electoral politics, and taking advantage of employment opportunities in both the public and private sectors of the society. These changes are clearly reflected in the images portrayed by one of the most, if not the most, powerful media in the United States—television. Images of the female homemaker of the 1950s have been replaced by ones of the career woman of the 1980s. As a conduit, reinforcer and transformer of cultural values, television cues the society to the processes of social change. Its images of females over the past three decades have certainly cued one to profound and fundamental changes in the status of women. These changes have been tossed by the ceaseless flux of becoming, which the Greeks understood well, and they will continue until women become all that they ought to be and can be. The process of becoming is not, however, a rectilinear one, and so women will continue to be jolted by the upsweeps and downsweeps of their struggle for equality.

In spite of the progress that has been made, there are still policy-makers who cling to cultural values which would keep women in the home and out of the work force. And they are by no means sociocultural dinosaurs, yet. One has no doubt heard them complain that too many women have entered the work force too fast, noting that this has contributed substantially to the persistent high rate of unemployment. The crucial point here is that much work remains undone if women are to enjoy the fruits of citizenship in a truly participatory democracy.

Despite the common interests and purposes that women *qua* women share, this volume demonstrates clearly and vividly major obstacles that have hindered and continued to impede their struggle for equality. It is obvious folly for one to believe in the likelihood of *all* women coalescing around any *one* concern, problem or issue. Differences grounded in race, ethnicity, generation, status, moral/ethical principles and norms of socialization have often proved to be intractable as women activists strived to forge a united front in relation to a shared interest grounded in gender. All women do not have identical agenda, neither in social intercourse nor political economy. This is human and natural. What is troublesome is the overall effect of radically different agenda on the struggle for equality, and the extent to which these agenda are conditioned by criteria that divide rather than unite women. Here, the cultural reproduction of racism is particularly pernicious. Its devisive effects are known all too well.

In the 1930s a young Richard Wright joined the Communist Party in the belief that, as a part of the class struggle, it would wage war against racism in general and Jim Crow in particular. He was to exit the party disillusioned. He came to the stark and painful realization that though the struggle for racial equality was subsumed by the class struggle logically and conceptually, empirically this was not so. Race and racism were of secondary importance to the party; they were of primary importance to Richard Wright. A half century later one observes a replay of similar images, only this time the gender struggle has replaced the class struggle, and the National Organization of Women has replaced the Communist Party. NOW perceives the gender struggle to subsume the struggle for racial equality logically, conceptually and empirically. Black women might concede to NOW the logical and conceptual soundness of its position; they do not concede its empirical soundness. To black women race and racism are constants of their lives, and thus of the utmost importance. Racism is not a constant of the lives of the white women who form the bulk of NOW's membership, and thus is not nearly as compelling a priority for them as it is for black women. Differences in priorities are accompanied by differences of response. The response of black women, as well as other women who are racial minorities, and the response of white women to the problems of racism, thus vary as its priority on their agenda differs.

American society is steeped in the Hebraic-Christian tradition. Christians believe that one day the New Jerusalem will descend upon the Earth, but in the meantime one cannot escape the realities of the here and now. Although underlying racial-ethnic tensions and frictions persist, much progress has been made to date, and the signs of future progress are encouraging as women forge ahead in their struggle for equality. As members of a political community grounded in the principles of participatory democracy, everyone has a stake in their success. If Aristotle is correct that full participation in the life of the political community is the *sine qua non* of good citizenship in a democracy, activities that are designed to make all women good citizens should be encouraged. If Plato is correct that those who "are competent and of a like nature . . . must be allowed the same pursuits,"[13] women should be encouraged in their struggle; for in securing for themselves what is rightfully theirs they contribute to making the society as a whole what it ought to be and can be. Standing on the shoulders of Aristotle and Plato, we thus say that our democracy and society are strengthened and enriched by the struggle of women for equality.

NOTES

[1]Plato, *The Republic of Plato*, trans., Francis McDonald Cornford (New York & London: Oxford University Press, 1964), V, 455. Hereinafter this work will be cited as *Republic*, and all translations are from this edition. Authors' italics.

[2]Ibid.

[3]Ibid.

[4]Ibid., V, 452.

[5]Ibid., V, 456.

[6]Ibid., V, 455.

[7]Ibid.

[8]See Michael Harrington, *The Other America* (Penguin Books: Baltimore, Maryland, 1963).

[9]Aristotle, *The Politics of Aristotle*, trans. Ernest Barker (New York: Oxford University Press, 1962), III, 4: 3.

[10]Ibid., III, 1: 2.

[11]*Republic*, V, 455.

[12]Winston A. Van Horne, ed., *Ethnicity and the Work Force* (Milwaukee: University of Wisconsin System AESCC/UCC, 1985), Vol. IV, pp. 12-13.

[13]*Republic*, V, 455.

LITERARY PERSPECTIVES ON ETHNIC-MINORITY WOMEN'S LEADERSHIP STYLES

Sidney H. Bremer

University of Wisconsin—Green Bay

A Prologue on Language and Literature

Literary critics do not usually come to mind as public policy experts. It takes a great degree of open-mindedness—or, some might say, fool-hardiness—to solicit such individuals to comment on the public policy issue of leadership styles for ethnic-minority women. Before proceeding with a few particular literary perspectives on this issue, therefore, the implications of the rarity of this enterprise in general should be noted. The usual methodological disjunction between literature and public policy deserves attention, not least of all because it bears a family resemblance to some conceptual problems underlying the focus of this volume on ethnic-minority women.

Crudely put, literature is usually considered too "soft" to hold its own in the public policy arena. Public policy practitioners are expected to be hard-nosed and rational in developing policy, and literary insights seem mushy, certainly crosscut with paradoxes and charged with emotions, at worst sentimental or inflammatory, at best enriching only in indirect ways. Practitioners value literature primarily as a private, auxiliary pursuit. The social science experts, to whom they most commonly turn for "hard" data and recommendations, are professionally a bit more welcoming to their colleagues in literature, at least within the walls. Academic social scientists value literature for fostering the broad perspectives and sensitivities, general cultural awareness, communication skills and conceptual flexibility that are critical to the educational enterprise. My social science colleagues also appreciate literary illustrations for their own theoretical constructs; they have used *1984* to show how people experience totalitarianism, *The Jungle* to exemplify the abuses of monopolistic capitalism, *The Lord of the Flies* to dramatize social contract theory. But they question whether literature can generate any useful theories of its own. And literary critics, in return, are leery of "reducing literature to sociological footnotes," in the words of an humanities colleague. Few literary critics have bent their energies toward bringing imaginative literature to bear on the institutional arrangements, hard data, and other bottom lines of social issues. In fact, literary critics expend a lot of energy to save Great Books and Great Ideas for "purely" aesthetic or contemplative purposes. So literature remains a largely private pleasure, something that is nice to come home to after a hard day in the trenches.

This image keys one of the connections to be made in this extended prologue. Women, like literature, have been regarded as "soft," mistresses of feeling and nurturers of private relationships, someone nice to come home to after a hard day in the trenches. And even though we have all come a long way, we are still very new at the large job of bringing women's perspectives and resources fully to bear on our thinking about public concerns.

Within that framework, this whole volume is an extremely ambitious act of imagination: It dares to stretch and to test our fundamental understandings about ethnicity and public policy by focusing on women. Willy-nilly, it challenges its own terms in the process. Even if *ethnicity* is rooted in familial experience, our "social generalizations" about the Japanese American, the Jew, the Chicano, et al., remain all too often cast in terms of male experience—"in fact based on the masculine population" even when "stated sweepingly to cover the entire society," to use historian David Potter's formulation for the gender bias in social studies generally.[1] There is point as well as sardonic wit in the title of a recent work on black women's studies: *All the Women Are White, and All the Blacks Are Men, but Some of Us Are Brave.*[2]

Now obviously—and make sure that the obvious is understood—gender oversights are not peculiar to ethnic studies. But it is a double trouble when ethnic-minority women are invisible minority groups within minority groups. And this is an issue that centrally involves language and literature—what our words mean, whose voices resonate. So it is not surprising that ethnic-minority writers of imaginative literature have taken the lead in developing our primary metaphor for the minority status of women generally: the image of the silenced majority. Two of our most gifted contemporary writers, both Jewish-American women, have authored theme-setting essays about muffling women's voices: Tillie Olsen in *Silences*,[3] and Adrienne Rich in *Lies, Secrets, and Silences*.[4] Moreover and more generally, because silenced people cannot name their reality for themselves or to others, humanity's symbol-making capacities are handicapped and human knowledge is grossly incomplete. Ethnic-minority women have also contributed to literature's realization of that awful consequence for all of us. It is epitomized in the title of a recent collection of writings by Jewish-American women, *The Woman Who Lost Her Names*,[5] and in the opening chapter of one of the literary works to be highlighted in this chapter, "No Name Woman" in *The Woman Warrior* by Chinese-American autobiographer, Maxine Hong Kingston.[6] In particular, women's voices and the naming of women's experiences from within can challenge our understandings of what public policy might concern.

Our stereotypes have, in effect, set women outside the terms of debate, outside the public sphere of purposive, rational, long-range policy, and inside the private sphere where intuitive insight, emotional relationships and unchanging cycles (like daily cooking, weekly washing, and "monthlies") properly belong. The problem is not only a matter of stereotypes, either. We are now regularly impeaching stereotyped statements that all women are "just" wives and mothers, and slowly we are setting aside the knee-jerk assumptions that such statements bring into the open. But the stereotypes have some analogues in reality. In fact, women's common experiences have been focused on the so-called private sphere in American culture generally and in our ethnic cultures variously. Women have been encouraged to develop intuitive and emotional skills and a strong sense of continuity. This is not to say that women have not also exercised leadership, and lots of muscle, in public affairs and rational policymaking. Shirley Chisholm, Dianne Feinstein and Sandra Day O'Connor come quickly to mind. But it is meant to say that our conventional understanding of public policy does not comprehend the full range of women's leadership perspectives and skills. We need to question those terms, *public* and *policy*, to expand their meanings in order to take full advantage of what women can offer to our public life and policy formation. Questions about the relationship of private to public affairs need to be raised. Feminist scholars have established solid grounds for recognizing that such private matters as domestic violence and sexual harassment are public concerns, and that such public matters as spheres of influence, constitutional amendments and the GNP depend largely on private preferences and domestic arrangements. Questions also need to be addressed about the kind of thinking and the range of considerations that ought to inform public policy.

This brings us back to literature, ready now to make the claim: Literature can give us access to dimensions of human experience that lie beyond our established concepts and institutional *modi operandi*. Because literature is an experiential and synthesizing language act, rather than conceptual and analytic, it can give us access to knowledge that our conventional concepts cannot comprehend and our analyses often misconstrue. Literature speaks in what philosopher Susanne

Langer calls "presentational" language, by arranging metaphors and incidents and characters in interactive structures—rather like a kaleidoscope. Literary language presents dimensions of human life that resist the linear logic of problem analysis, data, and, to use Langer's terminology again, "discursive" argument.[7] In particular, literature can name insights and experiences of ethnic-minority women that fall outside the conventional spheres of public policy debate.

One purpose of this chapter, then, is to explore a few literary examples of ethnic-minority women's leadership styles. It is intended to focus on four images of women leaders: the leader as medium; the leader as story and storyteller; the leader as warrior/slave; and the leader as mother and sister. These complex images center some of the most outstanding literature of the past ten years: the novels *Meridian* by Alice Walker[8] and *Ceremony* by Leslie Marmon Silko,[9] Maxine Hong Kingston's award-winning autobiography *The Woman Warrior*,[10] and the "novel in seven stories" that earned the American Book Award for 1983, Gloria Naylor's *The Women of Brewster Place*.[11] They have been singled out as exceptionally rich works that present women as leaders whose power extends beyond their own domestic relationships. These particular literary works have been chosen to explore ethnic-minority women's leadership styles because they are rooted in several distinctive cultural contexts—those of Native Americans, of once enslaved Afro-Americans, and of immigrant Chinese Americans. It must be insisted though that their four leadership images are being offered as *metaphors*. They present rather than analyze ethnic-minority women's leadership styles. It is not claimed that they represent typical or average experiences; it is not even claimed that they represent the central myths from their respective cultures. What is claimed is sufficient: that these are profound images firmly rooted in their cultures, deeply moving and radically challenging.

Now the second purpose of this chapter can be admitted. Rather than pursue the question of how "representative" *each* image is of women in its particular ethnic group, we desire to use the *set* of images as a heuristic device to help us think about ethnic-minority women and leadership styles generally. Focusing on ways in which the four images overlap and echo other literary works by ethnic-minority women, we aim to explore the questions about leadership that they raise: How do these images of women as leaders relate to women's sexual vulnerability and private affairs? How do they relate to the primary goddess figure of the mother, to biological mothers and motherhood, to other women and to men? Why do mystical and organic power sources figure so prominently in these works? Why are there so few examples of individual "public" leadership in ethnic-minority women's literature? And

finally, how might we give voice to such profoundly, richly, powerfully
and dangerously "soft" concerns in public policy affairs?

The Images

Because it takes shape in a context that we easily recognize as central
to ethnicity and public policy, we start with the image of the leader as
medium in Alice Walker's novel, *Meridian*. The work is set in the decade following "Freedom Summer" 1964, as the civil rights movement
shifted into its black power phase. The name of the title character even
memorializes the hometown of one of that summer's martyrs, James
Chaney of Meridian, Mississippi. But women remain the least familiar
of the leaders who gave their lives during the civil rights movement,
listed as a collective epitaph for the novel's second chapter, thus:

MEDGAR EVERS/JOHN F. KENNEDY/MALCOLM X/
MARTIN LUTHER KING/ROBERT KENNEDY/CHE
GUEVARA/PATRICE LAMUMBA/GEORGE JACKSON/
CYNTHIA WESLEY/ADDIE MAE COLLINS/DENISE MC-
NAIR/CAROLE ROBERTSON/VIOLA LIUZZO.[12]

Walker's fictional character, Meridian Hill, performs the least visible
"woman's work" of the movement, the typing and sexual servicing expected by male organizers of female volunteers, even though she has
never typed before. She does much more, of course, but also without
full credit. Her bravery as a freedom teacher and protest marcher is
trivialized. Although a supposedly protected women, she is nonetheless
physically attacked and jailed by whites, and sexually harassed by
black men as well as white men. So, "You women sure are lucky not to
have to be up against'em all the time," quips Truman Held, the male
organizer she sees as an Ethopian "prince," as he proceeds to take full
advantage of her sexual vulnerability.[13]

Above all, Meridian's most distinctive leadership style goes un-
celebrated. She seems "weird," even to many of the black townspeople
for whom she faces off against a tank in the opening chapter set in the
mid-70s. In this epitomizing "performance," Meridian asserts the
rights of the black community's children to view a freak-show
mummy. The specific occasion is trivial, and the height of the civil
rights movement is long past, but the incident nonetheless exemplifies
her devoted and costly leadership style: As a medium between the living and the dead, Meridian enacts the black community's most ambiguous desires, " 'volunteers to suffer' " for them, collapses into an un-
conscious paralysis when the job is done, and is carried like a
" 'corpse' " back to her "cell" in the house they have provided for

her.[14] Meridian has kept faith by living among " 'the people . . . like Civil Rights workers used to do.' " She has done so instead of going with the "revolutionary . . . intellectuals"[15] who have transplanted themselves to New York and pledged to kill as a matter of abstract principle — principle of the sort Albert Camus developed in the last chapter of *The Rebel* (1951), entitled "Thought at the Meridian."[16] In Walker's *Meridian*, the better road to such a commitment is communal and mystical, not abstract. Finally, Meridian Hill is able to move on— to recover from her paralytic fits and "to walk behind the real revolutionaries—those who know they must spill blood in order to help the poor and the black"— only by listening to the will of the people and affirming the leadership role of the medium.[17] As a leader, she also passes that role on to others. In particular, Truman Held, transformed from civil rights prince to revolutionary artist with a Che Guevara beard, but still drawn to Meridian by something now beyond sexual energy, makes some voter registration visits with her. He learns to appreciate as effective leadership the matter-of-fact way in which she accepts the oldest of human beings on their own terms. It is he who takes a "dizzy" fall into "vision" at the end of the novel, putting on the cap and ancient role she has left behind, and accepting, too, "the sentence of bearing the conflict" of humanity's life and death "in [his] own soul."[18] Walker's novel shows how Meridian herself comes to and through this costly leadership experience, which Truman then emulates.

Powerfully and centrally, Meridian's leadership is rooted in a communal mysticism; it is organic rather than abstract in its origins. Jewish-American poet and novelist Marge Piercy was first to recognize "the progress of a saint" in Meridian's ecstatic seizures and haloed weakness.[19] Piercy's early *New York Times* review did not, however, recognize that Meridian is a peculiar saint, a medium inspired not by heaven's god but by earth's humanity—first, specifically, in an Indian burial ground. (Piercy's oversight is odd because she herself wrote a 1973 cycle of poems on mystic power, a Tarot reading called "Laying Down the Tower," which uses an Indian "communal longhouse" to epitomize its vision of an alternative to hierarchy.[20]) Meridian's paternal great-grandmother had "stepped into another world" in the center of a burial mound called the Sacred Serpent, where the earth "began to spin" and she fell down "as from some strange spiritual intoxication." Meridian is drawn to the Sacred Serpent by this family story of "ecstasy" and by her own father's "compassion" for the Indian ancestors of the land he holds. "And it had happened to her." Entranced, her spirit "expand[ed] the consciousness of being alive" beyond her body, "there where the ground . . . was filled with the dead."[21]

The living power of that organic connection to past generations embodies itself a second time for her, during her civil rights college days, in a campus landmark called the Sojourner tree. Just as the Sacred Serpent gathers up lost Indians, so the Sojourner gathers together college girls afraid of being lost in pregnancies. The tree, too, is "magic," grounded in an old story of a slave woman whose tongue was cut out for telling tribal stories.[22] Both Sacred Serpent and Sojourner are landmarks, rooted in the earth, linked to death and tribal stories and a female spirituality from earlier generations, bringing oppressed people together. They are talismans of Meridian's leadership as a medium. But both are vandalized, so "there is no center any longer, and the sacred tree is dead," in the words of Oglala Sioux seer Black Elk, quoted in the novel's preface. Thus they can provide only crippled power sources for Meridian's self-paralyzing leadership as a medium. They are finally superseded by a more lively source of communal power, a "militant" black church that also sustains stories of the dead by bringing people together. Its preacher's mimicry of Martin Luther King is "keeping that voice alive," Meridian realizes, and its congregation pledges to carry on a local martyr's life beyond death by " 'gathering ourselves to fight.' "[23] This humanly sacred home, grounded like the earlier talismans in generational continuities between life and death, allows Meridian to recover her physical health and move on to other communities.

What is troubling about the resolution of Meridian's story is the loss of a female context for her new stage of leadership. (That may be why she does not, cannot, act it out within the pages of the novel, as Marge Piercy complains.) The church's preacher and martyrs are men, and the inheritor of Meridian's cap is a man also. There are spiritual fathers and brothers here, but no mothers or sisters. Indeed, an underlying theme throughout *Meridian* is the failure of contemporary motherhood and sisterhood for the woman who leads. Even the power of the Sacred Serpent and the Sojourner come to Meridian from ancient generations of women long dead. In contrast, Meridian's own mother disdains the Indian burial mound and rejects her daugher for failing to get religion in the conventional way, then for being "monster" enough to give up her own biological child.[24] The conflict between Meridian and her mother is stark: Meridian put an unwanted, and yet beloved son up for adoption in order to go to college and join the civil rights movement, while Mrs. Hill bowed to the old notion "that her personal life was over" when she became a mother.[25] Meridian suffers both from her mother's consequent frustrations and from her own rebellion against the traditional bind on women's autonomy. She "felt deeply" the rightness of the path she chose, but "on some deeper level," her lost mother and son haunt her.[26]

In the end it is an unrelated man, finally-faithful Truman Held, who offers Meridian the "maternal" care she so badly needs.[27] Biological mother and motherhood still remain lost to her, "magnificent giants" whose touch she is denied.[28] That is a very hard loss to be borne by a leader who expresses such a maternal concern for her people and all their children. It is an especially great loss in an ethnic culture where mothers supposedly have so much social as well as mythic power. What is more, the female intimacy of "sisters" that Meridian shares with Truman's Jewish former wife is limited, not strong enough to bear the hard truth of the white woman's rape by a black man.[29] So procreation and sex limit the possibilities of women's solidarity here, even as Meridian bases her leadership on the continuity of human death and life, the power of the medium.

Like *Meridian*'s mothers, the female leaders in Leslie Silko's *Ceremony* have more mythic than literal presence. The protagonist of Silko's novel is a man—like Silko herself, a half-blood Laguna Pueblo. Tayo returns from World War II sickened by his sense of responsibility for others' deaths. By joining his half brother Rocky in the white Americans' war against the Japanese, Tayo has betrayed his brotherhood with other nonwhite people, failed to prevent Rocky's death in battle, and left his uncle without the help he needed to raise a new breed of cattle resistant to drought. In purging his own illness, Tayo learns that it is part of a greater world sickness, a "witchery" of destruction that makes whites into thieves and nonwhite people into irresponsible victims, with neither side willing to break the circle of hate. Presumably women as well as men are caught in that circle. But it is specifically against Anglo *men* that Tayo must struggle to reclaim the cattle for which his uncle died. And it is specifically against Indian *men* that he must struggle to keep himself out of the circle of hate, even though he cannot prevent the murderous destruction that his old drinking buddies wreak upon themselves. Finally, it is to the old *men* of the kiva that Tayo reports his story so that the entire community might possess its healing power. Only two women, Tayo's grandmother and a beautiful, mysterious stranger, participate directly in his quest.

Nonetheless, women figure importantly as the source of life and the story that Tayo must join to win his struggles with and against other men. Interwoven with Tayo's story is a series of tribal myths, legends and chants that center on female forms of leadership. Indeed, Tayo's story and the very novel that contains it are both part of a larger "story that was still being told." It is a story told by Thought-Woman of creation and human witchery and worldwide drought and a hoped-

for reconciliation through ceremony with the abundance of Corn Woman.[30] Thus the boundaries between Silko's historical world and
Tayo's fictive world, between both these worlds and the worlds of myth
and legend, break down. As at the center of the Sacred Serpent in *Meridian*, so in *Ceremony* the whole of life embraces many worlds, the living and the dead. In *Ceremony* that whole is bound together by the
power of storytelling, and the leadership of the storyteller and the
story is profoundly female.

Before Silko begins telling her story, which ends with Tayo telling
his, she invokes the archetypal storyteller Thought-Woman. In effect,
the novel begins before itself, in the mind of the goddess, thus:

> Ts'its'tsi'nako, Thought-Woman,
> is sitting in her room
> and whatever she thinks about
> appears.
> . . .
> I'm telling you the story
> she is thinking.[31]

Thought-Woman's story is of her own naming of the universe created
by her sisters, Nau'ts'ity'i and I'tcts'ity'i (who are themselves namers
of the universe in other tribal versions of this myth of origin). Moreover, Thought-Woman is also "the spider" weaving a web from her
own body here. She is both "the storyteller and the story," as the Mo-
hawk editor of a recent collection of North American Indian women's
writing also claimed herself to be.[32] And so, of course, are both Silko
and Tayo. But the primary stories that Thought-Woman tells are fe-
male-centered: the creation and naming of the universe by herself and
her sisters; then within that frame, the primary myth of Corn Woman
on which Tayo's story is threaded—an earth-mother story of the
drought and barrenness willed by Corn Woman when human beings
fail in their proper homage to her, of their lengthy quest to purify
themselves, and of Corn Woman's just bounty in the end; and intertwined with this, mythic stories of Spider-Woman's grandson and of a
legendary guide named Elk-Woman.

In a further blurring of the boundaries between worlds, Elk-Woman
breaks into Tayo's story twice. Most obviously, she is embodied in the
mysterious stranger who joins his quest. A Mexican/Indian/goddess
woman of several names, she helps Tayo find his uncle's cattle, loves
him, and prepares him for his final showdown with his Indian antagonists. But Elk-Woman is also indirectly invoked earlier in the novel by
Tayo's grandmother. It is Grandma who takes him to the medicine
man Betonie, whose story leads in turn to the mysterious stranger,
Montaño/Ts'eh/Elk-Woman. Grandma begins Tayo's ceremonial

healing when "she reached out for him. She held his head in her lap and she cried with him, saying 'A'moo'oh, a'moo'ohh' over and over again."[33] Her comfort word *a'moo'ooh* readies Tayo for the medicine man, and it is cognate to the kiva's salutation in the end, when the old men recognize Elk-Woman in Tayo's story:

> "A'moo'ooh! A'moo'ooh!"
> You have seen her
> We will be blessed
>   again.[34]

A'moo'ooh is also, importantly, "the Laguna expression of endearment for a young child" that Silko's own grandmother used to speak to her, until she thought her grandmother's "name really was 'A'mooh,' " as she writes in her more recent book *Storyteller*.[35] So the line of human storytellers for both Tayo and Silko begins with a grandmother and links up, through the invocation *a'moo'ooh*, with the mythic women of the stories themselves.

This is the female leadership of "the storyteller and the story," grounded as much in thought as in earth, as much in verbal guidance as in generativity. It is a female power even when it is embodied in a male storyteller. An entire people's survival depends on it. The prefatory pages of *Ceremony* make this clear. Right after it all begins with Thought-Woman, "the story she is thinking" begins by explaining the power of story itself. A microcosmic "Ceremony," a prefatory poem in the voice of a medicine man, asserts that "stories . . . are all we have . . . to fight off illness and death," that stories are the "life" of the people. The verbal guidance of stories *is* generativity. It is also profoundly female, even equated with carrying babies:

> He rubbed his belly.
> I keep them here
>   . . .
> There is life here
> for the people.[36]

So all of Silko's storytellers embody the power of a pregnant woman who gives life to a whole people. That is the story beneath Tayo's story, too: *Ceremony*'s mythic image of the woman leader as guide and life-force, as "the storyteller and the story." If it is disappointing that Silko dramatizes her image of female leadership through a male protagonist, perhaps it was a necessary first step. *Ceremony* was the only novel listed in Beth Brant's 1983 bibliography of writings by Native American women.[37] So it broke ground, and sowed Silko's image of female storytelling in a male protagonist's story. (In fact, the Tayo plot of *Ceremony* closely conforms to the battle-fatigued quest of M. Scott

Momaday's Kiowa hero in *House Made of Dawn*.[38]) And already a Laguna Sioux woman has come forth with a novel in which a female protagonist embodies that power. In *The Woman Who Owned the Shadows*, Paula Gunn Allen presents a half-blooded sister to Tayo. This Native American woman marries one of the war's Japanese-American victims, challenges white women's stereotypes of Indians as passive victims, draws strength from the stories she tells of her mythic ancestors, and even becomes one of them, the Sky Woman whose fall began the human race.[39] Such is the leadership potential of the story-teller and the story.

Storytelling and stories also figure centrally in *The Woman Warrior*. Maxine Hong Kingston does not concern herself with the chronology of external circumstances that conventionally frames autobiography. Her self *is* stories, the legends and histories, memories and fantasies she carries around in her head. They are not all life-giving stories, however. Many are American " 'chink' words and 'gook' words" that she, as a Chinese American, needs to exorcise.[40] Many are misogynous Chinese sayings that she, as a Chinese-American woman, needs to exorcise: "Feeding girls is feeding cowbirds." "There's no profit in raising girls. Better to raise geese than girls." "When you raise girls, you're raising children for strangers."[41] And all the stories threaten to confuse her: "How do you separate what is peculiar . . . from what is Chinese? What is Chinese tradition and what is the movies?" she wonders.[42] And worse, what is real and what is made up? Her life is a struggle with that issue and especially with her mother's fabulous ability to "talk-story." Her mother's stories were supposed "to warn us about life." But they also painfully "test[ed] our strength to establish realities."[43] So adolescent Maxine finally cries out in anger, "You lie with stories. You won't tell me a story and then say, 'This is a true story,' or 'This is just a story.' I can't tell the difference . . . I can't tell what's real and what you make up."[44] Yet storytelling is also Maxine's own way of developing autonomy, so her tirade to her parents continues, "Ha! You can't stop me from talking." The resolution of her autobiography comes when she marks her maturity by telling her mother, "I also talk-story"; then she and her mother tell a final story together.[45]

This profoundly personal struggle with storytelling is intertwined with the Chinese stories of Fa Mu Lan and Ts'ai Yen to create an image of the leader as warrior/slave. Ostensibly, "the woman warrior" of Hong Kingston's title is the legendary Fa Mu Lan. The story is that Fa Mu Lan developed extraordinary powers of body and mind under the tutelage of mountain divinities and animals in her childhood, then offered to take her father's place in battle, headed her own army, secretly consummated her marriage and bore a son while disguised as a huge soldier, and avenged her village against its powerful enemies. Hong Kingston tells Fa Mu Lan's story here as her own, in the first person. The legend is intimately familiar to her, as well as culturally renowned. She embraces it as an antidote to the assumption that Chinese girls grow up "to be but wives or slaves." As a child, she learned to sing the story of Fa Mu Lan with her mother, who "said I would grow up a wife and slave, but . . . taught me the song of the warrior woman."[46] It is both a contradiction and a challenge to women's extreme, cruel subordination by a foot-binding culture.

Paradoxically, the woman warrior is also bound. She carries into battle her parents' revenge carved on her own back. She is the bearer of their anger in two senses, as its avenger and as its victim, as its warrior and slave. And when Fa Mu Lan frees a group of foot-bound, "cowering, whimpering women" who have been enslaved—her supposed opposites—they turn into "swordswomen." Unlike Fa Mu Lan's army of men, theirs is a "mercenary army" of "witch amazons" who wear women's clothes and kill men.[47] Nonetheless, they are also women warriors and onetime slaves. The fusion of warrior and slave is made even more pointed in the last chapter of Hong Kingston's autobiography. "A Song for a Barbarian Reed Pipe" creates several fusions and represents a tremendous achievement. Begun by her mother and completed by Maxine Hong Kingston herself, its storytelling involves the reconciliation between mother and daugher that eludes *Meridian*. And it tells the story of Ts'ai Yen, like *Ceremony*'s Thought-Woman, an image of the woman leader as storyteller and story, fused now with the warrior/slave.

Having claimed her own voice and acknowledged that "I also talk-story," Maxine Hong Kingston assumes a creative place in her family's female line for this finale. Her mother begins now with a story of her own mother's love for the Chinese theater and its stories, and a humorous "proof . . . that our family was immune to harm as long as they went to plays." This is similar to *Ceremony*'s claim that stories protect the life of a people. But Hong Kingston takes that power even further—toward the possibility of reconciliation between peoples, even enemies—when she supposes that "at some of those performances [her mother's family] heard the songs of Ts'ai Yen, a poetess born in A.D. 175."[48] As *The Woman Warrior* tells the story, Ts'ai Yen's poetry comes out of her experiences as a warrior who is at the same time a slave. A Chinese woman captured, raped and kept by a barbarian chieftain, she fights as one of the "captive soldiers" in his army and bears two children. But her great achievement comes the night she realizes the full humanity of her captors and responds across the cultural chasm between them. She learns that the barbarians' reeds can make the "yearning" music of flutes as well as the "death sounds" of arrows. Her enslavers' humanity makes her "ache"—and then sing to them in return. "Her words seemed to be Chinese, but the barbarians understood their sadness and anger." And when she returns to her own people, her song "translated well" for them, too.[49] Awful as it may be that this warrior/slave fights for her enslaver, her own power to hear and sing across a great cultural divide—to mediate and give voice, to lead beyond enmity to greatness—comes from that awfulness.

Awful, too, is the hope that Afro-American Gloria Naylor wrests from pain in The Women of Brewster Place. This "Novel in Seven Stories" does not blind itself to any of the violence of women's supposedly private lives: one mother's baby bitten in bed by a rat, another's little girl electrocuted by a kitchen wall outlet; an abortion to keep a man who does not want more children, and his desertion anyhow; the rape of a lesbian by an alley gang, and her demented murder of a wino who has been a surrogate father to her. Such violence eviscerates what Hong Kingston calls the "American-feminine" dream of being protected by a man and fulfilled by children. It also directs attention to the larger social conditions that breed rats, parental neglect, violence between the sexes and despair.

Those larger social conditions are epitomized by Brewster Place itself. Naylor presents the housing project as a "bastard child." "Conceived" to cover up governmental and economic corruption, crammed into an already "badly crowded district," and later walled off from the city's mainstream of commerce, Brewster Place becomes "a dead-end street," the epitome of a ghetto.[50] Its brick wall cuts off the sunlight of growth and creates an alley for death. But some people must live there anyhow, including the seven "colored daughters of Brewster" who each start elsewhere and all end up there.[51] The first five stories treat individual lives that become progressively intertwined, the sixth a pair of lesbian women together but isolated from the others, and the seventh a block party that involves them all in the anger and hope of community action. Their merging stories create a collective image of women leaders as mothers and sisters to each other.

In their midst is an abstracted counterpart to Meridian Hill, a recognizable type of young social activist named Kiswana Browne. With a fake Afro and a new name, she has left her own middle-class family ostensibly to join " 'my people' " and revolution on Brewster Place.[52] But her rebellion reeks of self-indulgence. She spends her time looking out "over the wall" from her upstairs apartment, reminiscing of past nights with her lover and fantasizing unbound freedom, until a visit from her mother forces her "to see her new neighborhood" in all its "broken," grimy, noisy reality.[53] To ground her commitments, Kiswana needs to acknowledge "that her mother had trod through the same universe," to allow herself again to be called Melanie after her biological grandmother, and to claim her upbringing " 'to meet this world on its own terms.' "[54] Only as a daughter can she approach the other women of Brewster Place as sisters with care and without judgment. Even then her lone attempts to organize a tenants' association flounder. Petty gossip about the two lesbian women who are "*that* way*" divides the women of Brewster Place.[55] They need an inclusive, collective sense of sisterhood. Otherwise the block party that they plan to have underwrite a rent strike will be only an empty gesture against the brick wall.

What makes the difference is a new kind of mothering and sisterly vision rooted in every woman's pain and anger. Out of a death and a rape, Naylor shows what that might entail. In the first instance, a child's electrocution plunges her mother, Ciel Turner, into suicidal despair. But an older woman, one of the maternal "magnificent giantesses" yearned for in *Meridian*, refuses to let Ciel go. Bellowing "No!" with the "huge" force of "a black Brahman cow, desperate to protect her young," a "mammoth" Mattie Michael forces Ciel to open her wound so it can heal. Having "rocked . . . rocked . . . rocked . . . rocked . . . rocked . . . rocked" Ciel back through the bloody history of infant deaths and "back into the womb" to the source of her pain, thus exorcising it, Mattie "slowly, reverently" bathes Ciel like "a newborn," until Ciel can cry and sleep and begin to heal.[56] Ciel gets the maternal care that women traditionally give to infants. It makes her strong enough to accept her own pain, the pain of biological motherhood.

It also makes her strong enough to accept another's pain as her own. Only thus, along with Ciel, can all the women of Brewster Place finally achieve an inclusive sisterhood. At least that is the dream that sees them beyond despair in the end. Specifically, it is Mattie's dream of the block party after one of the lesbian women has been gang raped. Lorraine is presented without a surname or family, with only a wino as a surrogate father, and she is denied the friendship of the other women of Brewster Place. Thus isolated, she acts out their common vulnerability as women unprotected by biological families or men. During the week following her rape and leading to the block party, "every woman of Brewster Place had dreamed . . . of the tall yellow woman in the bloody green and black dress."[57] Naylor makes these dreams, and Mattie's dream which contains them, a reality of the novel, the dawning of a new day that might be. Even Ciel, who has moved away and not met Lorraine nor heard about the rape, dreams of Lorraine and returns to tell of "a woman who was supposed to be me, I guess. She didn't look exactly like me, but inside I felt it was me."[58] The "weird dreams" of the other women build into a collective anger strong enough to tear down walls.[59] When the women of Brewster Place now find Lorraine's blood still on the alley wall, they know it is their blood. And together they dismantle the wall of the ghetto, brick by brick, relaying each brick from hand to hand out of the cul-de-sac. They include Lorraine's lesbian lover, in this revolution more powerful than even Kiswana had "fantasized."[60] Theirs is the visionary, collective leadership, beyond abstract fantasy to bloody dream, of women who are mothers and sisters to each other.

The Issues

"The personal is the political" has been a central insight of the current feminist movement. It challenges the compartmentalization of human life by which women's voices have been diminished, even silenced, in some areas. It points to the continuities through which we must be heard. Certainly that is borne out by the literary works discussed here. Most of the issues they raise about ethnic-minority women's leadership styles turn on the intersection between personal and political dimensions of life. The collective unison and individual profundity of these literary works signal us to listen well. The integrity of their literary structures and the richness of their articulation tell us that they have tapped deep truths. Let us try now to cast some of those issues in discursive language for clarity's sake, knowing full well that this is testing the limits of translation at least as much as did Ts'ai Yen.

First it should be recognized that these works offer no easy integration of leadership with the genital and reproductive aspects of women's lives. The possibility of rape is a serious hindrance to women as leaders. It must not be regarded as a minor public policy issue nor as a danger that can be avoided by staying home. It is neither, as *The Women of Brewster Place* and *Meridian* show. At best it is a profound and painful ground for sisterhood, as worst a rupture in even the most supportive relationships. Lorraine's raped horror of any human movement leads her to murder the father figure whose care has built her self-confidence, and the political dynamite of interracial rape undermines the friendship between Meridian and a Jewish "sister." Even the best possibility of building sisterhood on the ruins of rape is tragic, and does not comfortably include men. The men of Brewster Place are only bystanders as the women together tear down the ghetto wall.

Moreover, the full power of sisterhood deeply challenges the heterosexual bias in our culture, and sexuality generally strains against effective leadership in these women's lives. Mattie Michael is strong enough to confront the possibility that lesbian loving is "not so different" from other loving among women: "Maybe that's why some women get so riled up about it, cause they know deep down it's not so different after all."[61] But Mattie's ability to accept as natural and inevitable that sexual energy in any profound touching, including her bathing of Ciel, is exceptional. It comes at a high price: sexuality is diffused in her life, but never concentrated into a full love relationship. Mattie has only one youthful experience of intercourse, and even that stops short of commitment's "sweetest" intimacy.[62] Indeed, of all the women leaders in these literary works, only Kiswana Browne, the legendary Fa Mu Lan, and the ambiguously human incarnation of Elk-Woman are sexually active. Apparently, for a mature but simply human woman it is extraordinarily difficult to integrate leadership with sex. Neither the "American-feminine" expectations of women's sexual passivity nor the interracial, masculine battles over who can "possess" "our women" encourages initiative on women's part in sexual affairs. Bound sex enslaves women warriors, or at the very least skews their orientation toward activism. At the end of Walker's novel, Meridian Hill manages to move beyond passivity and possession into a love relationship with Truman Held, which may include physical intercourse, "but it was not sexual . . . It was forgiveness."[63] While forgiveness may be a necessary component of love between imperfect humans, it seems barren alone.

Mattie and Meridian are alike in another vital way also: each exercises maternal powers of leadership only after she is separated from her biological son and her biological mother. All four literary works suggest that motherhood is a source of both conflict and power for women. Kiswana Browne and Maxine Hong Kingston are able to reconcile with their biological mothers, and that reconciliation empowers Kiswana to be a sister to other women and Maxine to find her own voice, to talk-story. But these two are not also biological mothers themselves, like Mattie and Meridian. For mothers, the procreative issues of vulnerability and responsibility, desire and guilt lie deep, a kind of body knowledge that cannot be reasoned away. Such unresolved issues are self-alienating and divisive. Thus it is in the context of their own mothering—Mattie having an illegitimate son and Meridian giving up her legitimized son—that each loses touch with her own mother. Particularly in ethnic cultures that put tremendous multiple burdens of child care, economic provision and domestic anchoring on women, this is a powerful detriment to women's leadership potential. Both the leadership loss of women who concentrate on domestic relations, and the inhibiting costs to women who extend themselves beyond family ties, should be issues for public concern. They suggest the need to provide more male and social support for parenting responsibilities, and the

necessity of giving women the kind of nurture they are expected to provide to others.

Conversely, *Meridian* and *The Women of Brewster Place* in particular suggest that figurative mothering can play a powerful role in public
affairs. In order to accept mothering in public places and beyond family
bounds, however, we need to recognize human care and comforting as
adult needs. These are not childish means to avoid challenges, but wise
ways to confront pain and growth, as Mattie and Ciel show us. We
need to free up our image of those "magnificent giants" from our fears
of smothering mothering. In this endeavor, some Native American cultures may be an especial help, grounding images of female leadership in
mythic life forces of both body and mind. Such images expand the
meaning of motherhood and show its equality with wisdom in women's
lives. Both Corn Woman and Thought-Woman have public status in
the Laguna Pueblo world of *Ceremony*, representing fruitfulness and
thoughtfulness as equally female powers and equally sacred.

That illustration brings us to another kind of issue related to minority women's leadership styles, the methodological issue of how we *think*
about public policy matters. Corn Woman and Thought-Woman are,
after all, mythic beings. A strong visionary strain runs through all four
of the literary works: the earthy ecstasy of the Sacred Serpent that
Meridian's great-grandmother discovered, the ceremonial union with
Elk-Woman toward which Tayo's grandmother propels him, the for-
est-trained vision of the woman warrior Fa Mu Lan and the reed flute
songs of Ts'ai Yen, and the sisterhood of wall wreckers dreamed by
"mammoth" Mattie. These moments of vision have several features in
common. All break through the supposed boundaries between reality
and dream. A sense of organic relatedness to non-human life—earth,
plants and animals—is involved in each. This envisioning often belongs
to an intergenerational quest in which older wise women play central
roles. Consistently these features emphasize continuity. That emphasis challenges both the analytic rationality and the objectifying perspective that commonly shape our thinking about public policy.

Specifically, the visionary strain in these literary works challenges
the basic assumption of analytic rationality: that we can arrive at understanding simply by separating out and logically ordering the component parts of reality. Visionary wisdom is synthetic, and it refuses to
privilege logical rationality. If anything it privileges dream, not abstracted fantasy but richly embedded dream, as a way to truth. Certainly it implies that logical rationality abstracts, and thus miscon-
strues, the embeddedness of truth in an interconnected reality of
emotion and thought and body and spirit. This view is particularly
important to women, whose social status focuses so much attention on

the body, whose social responsibilities concentrate on matters of emotion and spirit as well, and whose capacity for thought is considered consequently limited by "raging hormones," emotionalism and idealism.

Visionary wisdom also denies the possibility of objectivity. The visionary seer is *one* with his or her vision, inextricably involved in it, at best at its center. Moments of vision are possible because we are, everyone and always and everywhere, part of a continuous life-world. Paradoxically that *life*-world embraces generations, the dead as well as the living and the unborn, and all earthly forms, stones as well as elks. From this point of view, universality is embedded in particularity, not lifted to transcendence, not separated and objectified. Such a perspective is particularly important to minority persons, whose views of the world tend to be treated as "special interests." It levels the epistemological hierarchy, insisting that those in power have no less "special" perspectives, that such particularity is even the basis of authority, and that the truly great lie is to claim objectivity. Moreover, minority persons, women especially, who must challenge the established structures that our society does misconstrue as objective givens of reality, may need a sense of visionary authority to do so. It is no coincidence that all the women leaders in these literary works are empowered by visions.

Implicit in their visionary perspective is yet another issue pertinent to leadership—the structural issue of the individual's relationship to the collectivity. The visions of the Sacred Serpent, the witchery and the ceremony, Ts'ai Yen and the wall-wrecking sisterhood all emphasize collective forms of leadership. In fact, one is hard pressed to think of any powerful literary works that ethnic-minority women have written about purely independent leaders. Edith Blicksilver's fine and full anthology, *The Ethnic American Woman,* is similarly lacking.[64] In this regard, minority women's literature is not peculiar. Apart from history plays such as Shakespeare's, epic poetry and historical fiction, literature generally pays little attention to the independent leadership of public affairs. The "Great Man" view has dominated history more than literature, our reconstructions of circumstantial facts more than our constructions of moving truths. This suggests that the "Great Man" view of leadership may be imaginatively impoverished—not only limited in its capacity to represent human affairs, as revisionist historians and women's and ethnic studies scholars have been arguing, but also limited in its power to inspire human action. This is good reason to develop collaborative forms of social action, political agency and reflective dialogue in public policy matters. Power *over* or *against* others, in Rollo May's terms, may not be the way things work best, despite our clichés about charismatic leaders. What May characterizes as power *for* and *with* others may indeed be wiser, more compelling and more realistic.[65]

In any event, more collaborative modes of *doing* public policy, as well as an openness to vision in *thinking about* public policy, are important if we are to hear the voices of ethnic-minority women in our public affairs. Although the four books discussed here offer mostly ambiguous, often troubling images of leadership within their pages, each is itself an unambiguous achievement of leadership. Each gives voice to experiences and insights that have been, for the most part, excluded from our public discourse. That is no little matter. *The Woman Warrior* powerfully dramatizes how hard it can be for a person labeled "chink" and "slave" to dare to speak. Hong Kingston's life *is* the struggle to find her voice. Learning to talk-story is the dramatic center of her autobiography, and the autobiography is its fruit. It is not just a personal matter, either. In the process she gives voice to others; she names the reality of "No Name Woman," an outcast within her own family history, and she decries the crimes against her town, her people, and all women—"the words at our backs" that are avenged by being reported.[66] Storytelling is the leader's primary power for and with others in *The Woman Warrior*, as it is in *Ceremony*. It is also the leadership role that Hong Kingston and Silko and Walker and Naylor themselves play out so powerfully.

Finally we must realize that storytelling is a power essential to democracy. As Meridian Hill explains to the people she registers to vote, voting "can be the beginning of the use of your voice. You have to get used to using your voice, you know. You start on simple things and move on . . ."[67] Clearly the medium's role in all that, like the role of the warrior/slave and storyteller and mother of sisters, is to sing "the song of the people." Whatever the outcomes of public policy decisions, the decision-making processes must include the voices of all. That is no luxury for us to indulge when we have the time. It is a matter of life and death. As *Meridian* puts this vital truth, "it is the song of the people, transformed by the experiences of each generation, that holds them together, and if any part of it is lost the people suffer and are without soul."[68]

NOTES

[1]David M. Potter, "American Women and the American Character," *Stetson University Bulletin*, 62 (January 1962), reprinted in Michael McGiffert, ed., *The Character of Americans* (Homewood, Ill.: Dorsey, 1970), pp. 318-319.

[2]Gloria T. Hull, Patricia Bell Scott and Barbara Smith, eds., *All the Women Are White, All the Blacks Are Men, But Some of Us Are Brave: Black Women's Studies* (Old Westbury, N.Y.: Feminist Press, 1982).

[3]Tillie Olsen, *Silences*, edited by Seymour Lawrence (New York: Dell Publishing, 1979).

[4]Adrienne Rich, *Lies, Secrets, and Silences* (New York: W. W. Norton, 1979).

[5]Julia Wolf Mazow, ed., *The Woman Who Lost Her Names* (San Francisco: Harper and Row, 1980).

[6]Maxine Hong Kingston, "No Name Woman" in *The Woman Warrior* (New York: Random House, Vintage paperback, 1977), pp. 1-19.

[7]Susanne Langer, quoted in Alan Trachtenberg, "The American Scene: Versions of the City," *Massachusetts Review*, 8 (Spring 1967): 284-285.

[8]Alice Walker, *Meridian* (New York: Pocket Books, Kangaroo paperback, 1977).

[9]Leslie Marmon Silko, *Ceremony* (New York: New American Library, Signet paperback, 1978).

[10]Kingston, op. cit.

[11]Gloria Naylor, *The Women of Brewster Place* (Harmondsworth, Eng.: Penguin Books, 1983).

[12]Walker, op. cit., p. 33.

[13]Ibid., pp. 99, 113.

[14]Ibid., pp. 21-27.

[15]Ibid., pp. 28-31.

[16]Greil Marcus, "Limits," *New Yorker*, (June 7, 1976), p. 133.

[17]Walker, op. cit., p. 201.

[18]Ibid., p. 220.

[19]Marge Piercy, "Review of Alice Walker, Meridian," in *New York Times Book Review* (May 23, 1976), p. 5.

[20]Marge Piercy, "Laying Down the Tower," in *To Be of Use* (Garden City, N.Y.: Doubleday, 1973), p. 79.

[21]Walker, op. cit., pp. 57-59.

[22]Ibid., p. 44.

[23]Ibid., pp. 196-199.

[24]Ibid., p. 89.

[25]Ibid., p. 50.

[26]Ibid., p. 91.

[27]Ibid., p. 213.

[28]Ibid., p. 168 (cf. p. 121).

[29]Ibid., p. 173.

[30]Silko, op. cit., p. 258.

[31]Ibid., p. 1.

[32]Beth Brant, "Introduction: A Gathering of Spirit," *Sinister Wisdom*, 22/ 23 (Special edition, 1983): 5. In yet another example of cross-cultural affirmation among minority women, Brant was encouraged to undertake this special issue by Afro-American Michelle Cliff and Jewish-American Adrienne Rich, who have co-edited *Sinister Wisdom* for the past several years.

[33]Silko, *Ceremony*, op. cit., p. 34.

[34]Ibid., p. 270.

[35]Leslie Marmon Silko, *Storyteller* (New York: Seaver Books, 1981), pp. 33-34.

[36]Silko, *Ceremony*, op. cit., p. 2.

[37]Brant, op. cit., "Selected Bibliography," pp. 215-217.

[38]M. Scott Momaday, *House Made of Dawn* (New York: Harper & Row, 1968).

[39]Paula Gunn Allen, *The Woman Who Owned the Shadows* (San Francisco: Spinsters Ink, 1983).

[40]Kingston, op. cit., p. 63.

[41]Ibid., p. 54.

[42]Ibid., p. 6.

[43]Ibid., pp. 11, 5.

[44]Ibid., p. 235.

[45]Ibid., p. 240.

[46]Ibid., pp. 23-24.

[47]Ibid., pp. 52-53.

[48]Ibid., pp. 240-241.

[49]Ibid., pp. 242-243.

[50]Naylor, op. cit., pp. 1-2.

[51]Ibid., p. 192.

[52]Ibid., p. 83.

[53]Ibid., pp. 75-76.

[54]Ibid., pp. 86-87.

[55]Ibid., p. 131.

[56]Ibid., pp. 103-104.

[57]Ibid., p. 175.

[58]Ibid., p. 179.

[59]Ibid., p. 181.

[60]Ibid., p. 75.

[61]Ibid., p. 141.

[62]Ibid., p. 18.

[63]Walker, op. cit., p. 173.

[64]Edith Blicksilver, *The Ethnic American Woman* (Dubuque, Iowa: Kendall/Hunt, 1979).

[65]Rollo May, *Power and Innocence* (New York: W. W. Norton, 1972), pp. 105-113. May describes exploitative and manipulative power *over*, competitive power *against*, nutritive power *for*, and integrative power *with* others—although I think manipulative power works *through* others and may often be an incipient form of power *with* others.

[66]Kingston, op. cit., p. 63.

[67]Walker, op. cit., p. 205.

[68]Ibid., p. 201.

THE QUEST FOR EQUALITY: THE ERA VS. "OTHER MEANS"

Jo Freeman

The Equal Rights Amendment to the Constitution has been a cause of controversy since first proposed in 1921. While its proponents have staunchly held that the ERA was the *only way* to legal equality for women, its opponents have maintained just as staunchly that insofar as women needed legal equality, there were other and better ways. However, the opponents, and the other means that they have proposed, have not remained the same over time. This chapter will review the history of the ERA controversy with particular attention paid to who the primary participants in the struggle have been, and the reasons they have given for their positions on the ERA. It will then look at the alternative strategies that have been proposed for improving the position of women in society, and assess the viability of these approaches with particular attention to whether there would be any differential impact on ethnic-minority women.

The Equal Rights Amendment

"Equality" vs. "Protection": The Original Fight

The women's suffrage movement was not a united one. It had two distinct branches with different strategies and different goals which were not abandoned even after suffrage was attained. The moderate branch was by far the largest and is given most of the credit for the Nineteenth Amendment. Its dominant organization was the National American Women's Suffrage Association which, under the leadership of Carrie Chapman Catt, mobilized the ratification campaign through its state chapters. Even before final ratification, Catt successfully urged her followers to disband the feminist organization and form a non-partisan, non-sectarian League of Women Voters which would encourage women to work within the parties and support a broad range of social reforms.

Under the banner of the National Women's Party (NWP), the militant feminists used civil disobedience, colorful demonstrations and incessant lobbying to get the Nineteenth Amendment out of Congress.

Once it was ratified, they decided to focus their attention on the eradication of legal discrimination against women.[1] Concentrated in Washington and funded more by legacies and wealthy benefactors than by a large membership, the NWP's strategy was suitable to its particular strengths as well as its feminist ideology.

The vehicle through which the NWP sought to attain legal equaltiy was the Equal Rights Amendment, written by its guiding light, Alice Paul. The original version of the ERA stated that "Men and women shall have equal rights throughout the United States and every place subject to its jurisdiction," and was introduced into Congress in 1923 by Rep. Daniel Anthony (Republican of Kansas), nephew of Susan B. Anthony, and by the Senate Republican Whip, Charles Curtis (Republican of Kansas). It was strongly opposed by the League of Women Voters (LWV), the newly-created Women's Bureau of the Department of Labor, the National Women's Trade Union League, the National Consumer's Union, and most other women's organizations. Their opposition was based on the one fact about the ERA on which everyone could agree—that it would abolish protective labor legislation for women.

Protective labor legislation was a generic label for a host of state laws, applicable to women, which restricted the number of hours they could work, the amount of weight they could lift, occasionally required special benefits such as rest periods, and sometimes prohibited their working in certain occupations entirely. Passed at the turn of the century in an attempt to curb sweatshop conditions, proponents of protective labor laws originally intended them to apply to both sexes, but the Supreme Court declared these laws a violation of the right to contract. In 1905, *Lochner* v. *New York* found unconstitutional a New York law that prohibited bakers from working longer than ten hours a day or sixty hours a week because "the limitation necessarily interferes with right of contract between the employer and employes . . . [which] is part of the liberty of the individual protected by the Fourteenth Amendment."[2]

This setback prompted social reformers to turn their attention to laws which applied to women only. The Court was more receptive three years later when it heard *Muller* v. *Oregon*. Strongly influenced by an extensive brief prepared by the National Consumer's League that documented women's physical disabilities, the Court upheld an Oregon law that restricted the employment of women in factories, laundries or other "mechanical establishments" to ten hours a day, on the grounds that women's

> physical structure and a proper discharge of her maternal functions—having in view not merely her own health but the well-

being of the race—justify legislation to protect her. . . The limitations which this statute places upon her contractual powers . . . are not imposed solely for her benefit, but also largely for the benefit of all. . . The reason rests in the inherent difference between the two sexes, and in the different functions in life which they perform.[3]

The NWP did not originally intend the ERA to abolish protective legislation, and initially claimed that it would have no such effect. The ERA was aimed primarily at the plethora of laws which restricted women's property rights, disadvantaged them under state family laws, or barred them from holding office or serving on juries. However, the overwhelming conclusion of legal authorities was that the amendment would nullify or throw open to question all legislation aimed at women. The NWP tried to work with the opposing women's organizations to draft suitable language exempting protective legislation, but agreement could not be reached on the wording. Therefore, the NWP changed direction. It admitted protective laws would be eliminated, but claimed that this would be desirable because such laws only limited women's opportunities.[4]

By 1923 both sides had hardened, and over the next few decades each devoted itself to undermining the position of the other. The Women's Bureau and its allies conducted studies to show that protective labor laws did not handicap women, and testified to this before legislative committees. Its director, Mary Anderson, lobbied against the ERA at every opportunity. The NWP continued to take advantage of any forum to argue for the ERA, even if it had to disrupt the gathering to do so, and to oppose further protective labor legislation. A temporary compromise was reached between these two antagonists in 1926 when they agreed to

> an investigation into the effect of protective labor legislation on the working opportunities of women. The NWP was to have three places on an advisory committee of nine. However, the attempt at reconciliation failed. The National Women's Party insisted upon open hearings, while the rest of the Committee was determined to employ the standard Women's Bureau methods of investigation and analysis of statistical data. Each group believed the other's method would prejudice the outcome; the Committee remained deadlocked until May, 1926, when Anderson dissolved it. The Women's Bureau conducted the study, and predictably concluded that protective laws for women helped rather than hindered them. Each side regarded the other with increasing bitterness.[5]

The result of this stalemate was that each side's efforts to improve the lot of women cancelled the other's. New protective laws continued to be passed, but at a decreasing rate until 1937 when the direction of the Court's 5 to 4 decisions negating laws that protected both sexes was reversed by a single justice.[6] The ERA continued to be bottled up in committee until World War II, when the need to bring women into the labor force brought about a reconsideration. By then, neither side was very strong.

Even when the two antagonists agreed, they were not very successful. Section 213 of the National Economy Act, which prohibited husbands and wives from working for the federal government at the same time, was opposed by all feminists, whether reform-minded or militant, but their combined efforts neither kept it from being passed nor compelled its repeal. Between 1932 and 1937, 1,600 married women were dismissed from the government. However, organized women could not even get the Democratic party to adopt a plank opposing Section 213 in the 1936 platform.[7]

During the late 1930s, the coalition of women's organizations that opposed the ERA slowly disintegrated as the social reform movement which fed them died out. Some of the key organizations of the social feminists completely disappeared. Others, such as the LWV, turned their energies to other problems. At the same time, support for the ERA expanded beyond the NWP to include the National Federation of Business and Professional Women's Clubs (BPW), the General Federation of Women's Clubs, Soroptimists, and organizations of women lawyers, dentists, osteopaths, real estate agents, accountants and physicians.[8]

Over time, the division more and more became one of class, or more specifically, occupation. Women either in or associated with other women working in industry, particularly unionized industries, opposed the ERA because they supported protective legislation. Business and professional women supported the ERA and opposed protective labor legislation, which they saw as a barrier to their effectively competing against men in their professions. Indeed, it was the attempt of protectionists to bring women in business establishments (primarily clerical and retail sales workers) under the protective umbrella that pushed business and professional women's clubs from neutrality to support for the ERA. From the businesswoman's perspective these positions were not industrial ones, and their occupants were potential executives and managers who should not be protected from promotions and the responsibilities that went with them.[9]

To a lesser extent the division was also one of party. The social feminists who supported protective legislation were mostly, though not exclusively, Democrats. Although they overlapped only slightly with Democratic party activists, and could not keep the ERA out of the

Democratic party platform after 1940, they and the unions with which they worked closely did exercise some influence within the Democratic party and virtually none within the Republican party.

With a few notable exceptions, the NWP members were Republicans. While somewhat disdainful of both parties, Alice Paul and her followers had chosen to follow the British example of blaming the party in power for any legislative failures. Woodrow Wilson was a Democrat, and his repeated failure to support suffrage until circumstances forced him to do otherwise forever tainted the Democratic party in Paul's eyes. The Congress which sent the ERA to the states for ratification was a Republican Congress, and twenty-nine of the thirty-six states necessary for ratification had Republican legislatures that year. Furthermore, the NWP's ideology of legal equality and independence, and its opposition to government protection, was much more compatible with the Republican philosophy of laissez-faire.

Equally important, the professional and business women who became the ERA's primary supporters were more likely to be Republicans, the members of Congress who sponsored the ERA were Republicans, and conservative organizations like the National Association of Manufacturers, which opposed any law regulating industry, supported the ERA. In 1928 the NWP even endorsed Herbert Hoover for president, despite the fact that he had not personally expressed support for the ERA. His running mate, Charles Curtis, had been an ERA sponsor, and his Democratic opponent, Alfred E. Smith, was an ardent supporter of protective labor legislation.[10]

There is no evidence that race or ethnicity had any effect on one's position on the ERA, except insofar as it coincided with occupation or party. The National Association of Colored Women supported the ERA and the National Council of Negro Women opposed it. This reflected the positions of their respective founders, Mary Church Terrell and Mary McLeod Bethune, and the years in which these organizations were founded. The former was founded during the suffrage era and the latter during the depression.[11] Black women were certainly more likely to be concentrated in the lower class than white women, and thus might seem more concerned with protection. However, they were also concentrated in occupations which were not covered by protective labor legislation such as domestic service and agricultural labor. Thus, in a very real sense, debate over the ERA was a white women's issue. Even among white women, ethnicity was not crucial. Certain ethnic groups were more likely to be concentrated in industrial jobs at which protection was primarily aimed, but ethnicity was still secondary to class, or occupation, as a prime determinant.

The Transitional Era: 1940-1970

The year 1940 was a transitional one. Younger women who had not been schooled in the suffrage movement began to assume leadership positions in the Democratic party and in many women's organizations. They did not bring with them the deep hostility toward the ERA of the older generation because they had not personally experienced the conflicts on which it was based. It was also a transitional year in that the war in Europe altered national priorities from social and economic concerns to the possibility of war. Democratic ideals and slogans about equality took on a different meaning when the audience was international rather than local.[12]

Declining opposition to the ERA was publicly apparent with the addition to the 1940 Republican party platform of a clause stating, "We favor submission by Congress to the States of an amendment to the Constitution providing for equal rights for men and women." Largely the result of efforts by NWP members in the Republican party, it also reflected a changing balance of power. Once the BPW decided to endorse the ERA in 1937, it made it a legislative priority. BPW members, as well as those of the NWP, were contributors to the Republican party. Since the ERA was not inconsistent with Republican opposition to government regulation, adding support for the amendment to the 1940 platform was easy for the GOP to do. Without offending any existing GOP supporters, it gave them one more way of challenging the Democratic party's claim that the Roosevelt administration represented the true interests of the people.

The Democrats did not follow suit until 1944. In 1940 a committee appointed by the Women's Division of the Democratic National Committee, headed by an ERA opponent, presented an alternative plank to that of the NWP which committed the party to equality "without impairing the social legislation which protects true equality by safeguarding the health, safety and economic welfare of women workers." When Eleanor Roosevelt told the platform committee that the ERA would be "a grave mistake," it accepted the alternative proposal.[13] However, by 1944 the opposition was in disarray. Her attention turned elsewhere, Eleanor Roosevelt failed to speak against the amendment and many other opposition leaders had retired. Emma Guffy Miller, one of the few Democratic party activists who was also an NWP officer, "practically single-handedly" convinced the Democratic Party Platform Committee to follow the example of the Republicans and recognize the contribution of women to the war effort by supporting the ERA.[14]

In 1942 the ERA reached the floor of the Senate for the first time. It was quickly recommitted but reintroduced the following year with new wording approved by Alice Paul. "Equality of rights under the law shall not be denied or abridged by the United States, nor by any State, on account of sex." The House Judiciary Committee voted not to report the amendment at all, but these victories stimulated the NWP to increase its lobbying and organizing activities. While remaining a small, exclusive organization itself, it formed a coalition of all groups supporting the ERA, called the Women's Joint Legislative Committee.[15] In response, opponents formed the National Committee to Defeat the Un-Equal Rights Amendment (NCDURA) late in 1944. Although it succeeded in keeping the ERA from passing Congress, it did not prevent the National Women's Party from garnering increased support. By the end of 1946 the NWP claimed that thirty governors and thirty-three national women's organizations endorsed the ERA.

In order to reverse this flow of support the NCDURA decided to offer a positive "alternative" which would, supposedly, end undesirable discrimination while preserving necessary protection. Called the "Status Bill" and sponsored by two Republicans (Senator Taft of Ohio and Senator Wadsworth of New York), it declared it the policy of the United States that "in law and its administration no distinctions on the basis of sex shall be made except such as are reasonably based on differences in physical structure, biological or social function." Instead of enforcement provisions, it proposed the creation of a Commission on the Legal Status of Women to study sex discrimination. It urged the states to take similar actions. Along with this "more positive" approach the NCDURA decided it needed a more positive name, and changed its to the National Committee on the Status of Women (NCSW), headed by Mary Anderson, former director of the Women's Bureau.[16]

However, this "practical, working program" was not perceived as such by the numerous organizations which now endorsed the ERA. Even many of those opposed to the ERA objected to such vague terms as "reasonably based" and "social functions." Republicans were particularly unhappy.

> The Federation of Women's Republican Clubs of New York State expressed its "unalterable objection" to the "futile" Status bill, and called on Republicans Taft and Wadsworth to honor their party's campaign pledge. E.R.A. sponsor John Robison pronounced the Status bill a "red herring" which would violate the Republican platform.[17]

Thus despite active lobbying by the Women's Bureau, and the belief by some ERA proponents that passage would not preclude later adoption of the ERA, the "Status Bill" failed. The NCSW said that its failure was due primarily to its identification as an anti-ERA measure and the support by both party platforms for the ERA. It turned its attention to removing endorsement of the ERA from the 1948 party platforms, but was unable to do so. Continued support by the Republicans was never in question, and inertia combined with the fact that the Republican convention preceded the Democratic convention that year kept the ERA in the Democratic platform over some opposition.[18]

Alternatives having proved futile, ERA opponents sought to change the wording of the amendment. In January 1950 the ERA was debated on the Senate floor, having been reported favorably by committee. At the end of the debate Sen. Carl Hayden (Democrat from Arizona), at the suggestion of the Women's Bureau, proposed an amendment which read: "The provisions of this article shall not be construed to impair any rights, benefits, or exemptions now or hereafter conferred by law upon persons of the female sex." ERA proponents were caught by surprise, and many senators, whose support for the ERA had been on the record but never very strong, took advantage of the opportunity to vote for both amendments. The Hayden rider passed 51 to 31 and the ERA 63 to 19.[19] This strategy was repeated when the ERA once again came to the Senate floor in July 1953. This time the rider passed by 58 to 25 and the ERA by 73 to 11.[20] Appalled at this turn of events, the NWP allowed the ERA to languish in the House committee.

With the return to power of the Republicans in 1953, ERA proponents thought their time had finally come. The Eisenhower White House supported the ERA, albeit weakly, and the new appointee to head the Women's Bureau, Alice Leopold,[21] withdrew its opposition. The new Republican chair of the House Judiciary Committee also favored the ERA. But this change did not reflect a strong or cohesive policy. Out of deference to organized labor the new secretary of labor continued his department's policy of official opposition, but this too was very muted. In effect the executive branch withdrew from the arena, leaving the battle to Congress where key committees were headed by ERA opponents.

ERA opponents were without their customary leader, the Women's Bureau, and some members of the coalition, such as the National Women's Trade Union League, had disbanded. Others, such as the League of Women Voters, no longer thought it important to actively oppose the ERA. Nevertheless, the opponents found a new deterrent in the Hayden rider. Rep. Katherine St. George (Republican of New York), ERA's sponsor in the House, tried to find substitute language for the Hayden rider which would not undermine the amendment, but since the rider was really just a ploy to kill the ERA, no compromise could be found.[22] The gap left by the defection of the Women's Bureau was filled by the AFL-CIO which, in a campaign orchestrated by Esther Peterson, its legislative representative, lobbied heavily against the ERA. But by this time public interest in the ERA was very low and many NWP stalwarts had died or retired. The organization's journal, *Equal Rights*, ceased publication in 1954. The National Women's Party had been an "exclusive" organization for many years, making no attempt to recruit new members.[23] It could still get promises of support from members of Congress, but it could not get the amendment voted on without the Hayden rider.

Nineteen sixty was both the nadir of the ERA and the beginning of its resurgence. The key person in both these developments was Esther Peterson. As an advisor to presidential candidate John F. Kennedy, she convinced the Democratic party platform to adopt the AFL position and drop its support for the ERA in favor of a vague expression against barriers to employment based on sex and "equality of rights under law, including equal pay." After Kennedy was elected she asked, and received, appointment as director of the Women's Bureau, and was also made an assistant secretary of labor. Few other women received such important appointments, a lack of action for which Kennedy was roundly criticized.[24]

One of Peterson's first recommendations to the new president was the creation of a national commission on women, one of the components of the 1947 Status Bill once proposed by ERA opponents. To avoid the NWP lobbyists, the commission was created by Executive Order 10980 on December 14, 1961. Members were selected to represent mainstream opinion on women to devise suggestions that would be acceptable to the administration. Marguerite Rawalt, a former BPW president, was the sole member who supported the ERA. Eleanor Roosevelt was asked to chair the president's commission, and when she died almost a year later, she was not replaced.

> Peterson . . . and her colleagues used the presidential commission on women to stop the E.R.A. dead in its legislative tracks. Peterson reasoned that Congress would not be likely to act on the E.R.A. while the matter was under consideration by a presidential panel. In addition, she presumed that eventually the Commission would offer substitute recommendations which would continue to stymie the Amendment's progress. But obstructing the E.R.A. was not really her primary motive. Peterson regarded the Commission's most important function to be the creation of an alternative program of "constructive" action to improve women's status, a possibility which before had always been blocked by the E.R.A. dispute.[25]

Despite the fact that opposition to the ERA was foreordained, as were objections from the NWP, the commission did seek a middle ground on the ERA. After much debate and many alternative proposals on wording, the final report declared: "Equality of rights under the law for all persons, male or female, is so basic to democracy . . . that it must be reflected in the fundamental law of the land."[26] The commission acknowledged unreasonable distinctions based on sex in state laws and practices which discriminated against women. It had considered three different ways to achieve "greater recognition of the rights of women": test litigation challenging laws under the Fifth and Fourteenth Amendments to the Constitution, the ERA, and state legislative action. It expressed a preference for the first and third routes, but did not squarely oppose the ERA. Instead, in deference to Marguerite Rawalt, it said the ERA "need not *now* be sought." (My italics.)

> Since the Commission is convinced that the U.S. Constitution now embodies equality of rights for men and women, we conclude that a constitutional amendment need not now be sought in order to establish this principle. But judicial clarification is imperative in order that remaining ambiguities with respect to the constitutional protection of women's rights be eliminated.[27]

Although the president's commission gave Congress an excuse to abstain from further consideration of the ERA, it also was a key element in its resurgence. Its existence prompted governors in all but one state to create their own state commissions on the status of women, which in turn prepared extensive reports documenting discrimination against women in their respective states. The members of these commissions were invited to annual conferences in Washington by the Women's Bureau. It was at the third such conference, in June 1966, that the National Organization for Women was formed. Although NOW almost split over the inclusion of the ERA in the bill of rights it formulated in 1967, it decided to adopt it even when the loss of its union members cost NOW use of the United Auto Workers' Women's Committee's office. However, it was several years before the ERA became a NOW imperative. Initially, NOW was more concerned with changing the guidelines on sex discrimination promulgated by the Equal Employment Opportunities Commission, which was created by Title VII of the 1964 Civil Rights Act.[28]

The addition of "sex" to the section of the act prohibiting discrimination in employment on the basis of race, color, creed and national origin was more opportunistic than planned. It was not brought up in committee and no hearings were held. Instead, it was a floor amendment in the House made by a male ERA supporter from Virginia which received several hours of humorous debate before being passed by a coalition of women representatives and male opponents of the entire act.[29]

Though there was little time for positions to solidify, organizations split along the same lines as they had over the ERA, albeit for different reasons. The NWP basically did not believe in government intervention of this type, but it wanted any such assistance to racial minorities to also be provided to women. It engaged in what lobbying there was on this provision. The Women's Bureau was against it, not only because it feared for protective legislation, but because it felt that the purpose of the Civil Rights Act was to attack discrimination on the basis of race, and that attention should not be diverted from that issue.

The Equal Employment Opportunity Commission (EEOC) chose to follow what it felt was the true intent of Congress rather than the wording of the law; it ignored the sex provision. The first executive director of the EEOC publicly stated that the provision was a "fluke" that was "conceived out of wedlock."[30] Initial guidelines prohibited segregation of want ads by race but permitted listings by sex.[31] The EEOC also decided that

> The Commission will not find an unlawful employment practice where an employer's refusal to hire women for certain work is based on a state law which precludes their employment for such work, provided that the employer is acting in good faith and that the law in question is reasonably adapted to protect women rather than to subject them to discrimination.[32]

The EEOC's attitude and these guidelines had two major consequences of importance to the ERA. First of all, they incensed women, particularly those in the network developed by the president's and state commissions who expected the EEOC to support the law, and led them to form NOW. Second, they compelled women who found the EEOC insensitive to their complaints to go to court. The courts consistently ruled that state protective labor laws were preempted by Title VII and therefore invalid. These rulings in turn paved the way for reconsideration of the Equal Rights Amendment.

Switching Sides: 1970-72

Since the traditional opponents of the ERA had based their opposition on the need to maintain protective labor legislation, its invalidation neutralized them. Many switched sides. Several unions were impressed by the plethora of legal complaints filed by blue-collar women over the restriction of their job opportunities due to protective labor legislation. The United Auto Workers endorsed the ERA in 1970, and it was soon followed by the Communications Workers and the Teamsters. The AFL-CIO did not change its policy until late 1973. The Women's Bureau switched in 1969 when the Nixon administration appointed as its director Elizabeth Duncan Koontz, a black former president of the National Education Association from North Carolina who, like the NEA, was an ERA supporter. She quietly lobbied union women who in turn influenced union men.

Among those groups with a renewed interest in the ERA was the Citizen's Advisory Council on the Status of Women, a small governmental body created to carry out the proposals of the president's commission. Nixon had appointed several strong ERA supporters to it, and its executive secretary had also become convinced that the ERA was of greater benefit to women than protective labor legislation. On February 7, 1970, it officially endorsed the ERA, "sensing that the time had come to advance the cause of justice and equality for men and women."[33] With this endorsement it published a definitive legal analysis of the ERA and transmitted both to Nixon with an appropriate press release. This analysis was written by a lawyer in the Justice Department who had been a founder of NOW and had originally written the paper for NOW. On March 26, it was entered into the *Congressional Record* by Rep. Martha Griffiths.

In May 1970 hearings were held in the Senate Judiciary Subcommittee, now chaired by an ERA supporter. The AFL-CIO still testified against the ERA, but no representatives of women's organizations did so. At the same time the White House released the report of the Task Force on Women's Rights and Responsibilities appointed by President Nixon. It recommended endorsement of the ERA. In June the new secretary of labor added his endorsement.

One of the biggest blockades to consideration of the ERA had been House Judiciary Committee chairman Emmanuel Celler (Democrat of New York). He was challenged by Martha Griffiths (Democrat of Michigan), who obtained signatures from a majority of the House members to discharge his committee from further consideration of the bill. During floor debate in the House even Edith Green (Democrat of Oregon) spoke for the ERA, and it passed 350 to 15. However, the Senate voted to add two amendments; one to exempt women from the military draft and another to permit prayer in the public schools.[34] Thereafter the ERA was dropped for that session.

After reintroduction into a new Congress, the House Judiciary Subcommittee held new hearings. Assistant Attorney General William Rehnquist initially testified against the ERA until ordered by the White House to change his testimony. The "favorable" testimony he finally gave was so full of holes it was quoted by the opposition. Nonetheless, the subcommittee recommended the ERA as written. Unfortunately, Representative Celler still chaired the full committee. He engineered a substitute version which would have reauthorized protective labor legislation. Although it was mostly Republicans who voted for the watered-down version, the final House vote was so overwhelmingly in favor of the amendment and against the substitute that partisanship was not evident. In the Senate eight separate substitutes were proposed, but this time they all met resounding defeat. Here too the final vote was overwhelmingly in favor of the ERA as written.[35]

Defeat: 1972-1982

Even as the ERA was emerging from Congress under the prompting of the new feminist movement, it was stimulating an organized opposition by groups which had not heretofore participated in the forty-nine years of debate. The person most identified with the defeat of the ERA in the states is Phyllis Schlafly, who as late as 1971 did not find it objectionable. However, in February 1972 she devoted an entire issue of her newsletter, *The Phyllis Schlafly Report*, to condemning the ERA for its detrimental impact on the family. Schlafly had long been active in the right wing of the Republican party and, until the ERA came along, her concerns were primarily in the areas of foreign affairs and military policy. These activities, and her publications, gave her a wide base of support among conservative Republicans whom she proceeded to mobilize against the ERA. The response was strong enough to prompt her to form STOP-ERA in October 1972 with herself as chair.

Within a year other right-wing groups such as the John Birch Society, Pro-America Incorporated, the Christian Crusades, and Young Americans for Freedom threw their organizational resources into the fight. Organizations of the religious right were also a major source of ERA opponents. The Mormon Church, the Southern Baptists and other fundamentalist Protestant churches, and portions of the Catholic Church actively fought the ERA in state legislatures. They were joined by newly formed local groups such as Eve Reborn, HOT DOG (Humanitarians Opposed to Degrading Our Girls), AWARE (American Women are Richly Endowed), and POW (Protect Our Women).[36]

There is no consensus on why the ERA ratification campaign failed, but the fact that its emergence from Congress was more spontaneous than strategic must be seen as a major contributor. Twenty-eight states ratified it the first year, but only seven after the opposition became public. None of the feminist organizations which contributed to the effort to get it out of Congress were prepared to replicate in the states the ad hoc lobbying effort that had been created at the national level. States that already had a strong feminist movement (except Illinois) quickly ratified the amendment. Those that delayed acting on the ERA until an opposition had time to coalesce largely did not ratify it at all. Between 1972 and 1977 three separate efforts were made by pro-ERA organizations to put together a centrally directed campaign, but they were marked more by competition than by coordination. State ERA coalitions did form to counter the opponents, but in most states were not capable of achieving more than a stalemate.[37]

In 1977, after years of internal turmoil due to other reasons, NOW assumed leadership of the ratification struggle. With little time left before the ratification deadline, NOW took the unprecedented step of asking Congress to extend the deadline. Although initial reactions were negative, NOW mobilized a professional lobbying campaign backed by hundreds of chapters collecting signatures on petitions and letters. On July 9, 1978, the anniversary of the death of Alice Paul, NOW organized a march of over one hundred thousand on the Capitol, despite so little publicity that many feminists did not know it was being planned. Within four months, the deadline had been extended by a little more than three years.

The length of the extension had been a compromise, and it was a gamble the movement lost. At that point there were not any "undecideds" left among the current state legislators. Success for the ERA required the identification and electoral defeat of enough "antis" to gain the votes necessary when each state legislature met again. For most non-ratifying states, there would be only one election before the new deadline. The nature of the United States political system makes it virtually impossible to change the composition of a legislature in only one election, absent an issue of overwhelming importance. Consequently, while a majority of the American population supported the ERA, the votes of a few kept it from being added to the Constitution by the final deadline of June 30, 1982.

During the ratification struggle the ERA became once again a highly partisan issue. According to Eleanor Smeal, again president of NOW and leader of the ratification struggle during its last five years, 83 percent of Republican legislators in key unratified states voted against the ERA while only 45 percent of the Democrats did so.[38] This time the fight was within the Republican party. Both parties had quietly restored the ERA to their platforms in 1972, after its even quieter disappearance in the sixties. In 1976 most of the women who came to the Republican convention to support Ronald Reagan's candidacy also opposed the ERA. They lost a close vote in the platform committee, but had enough support to file a minority plank. With great reluctance they decided not to demand a floor vote after Reagan stated that he wanted floor fights on only two issues, of which the ERA was not one. By 1980 Reagan came to the convention with the nomination in his pocket, and he supported removal of the ERA from the GOP platform. Opposition to its removal was vocal but nominal. Nonetheless, as a concession to Republican feminists, Reagan mentioned equal rights for women in his acceptance speech. He was for equal rights, but via unnamed alternative means, not the ERA.

In 1980 the Democratic party had its own fight over a minority plank on the ERA, but the issue was not whether to drop it from the platform but whether to "discipline" state legislators who did not support the ERA by denying them party resources. Although the Democratic administration was opposed to the plank, and the party had few resources to discipline its state candidates effectively, it nonetheless was passed at the convention by a floor vote largely because the Democrats did not want to seem to oppose the ERA. Indeed, after the deadline for ratification passed, Democrats quickly reintroduced it into Congress.

Passage of the ERA came at a unique point in its history. It had been debated for years by mutual antagonists who would not compromise an inch. In the meantime, social and legal changes intervened to undermine the basis of the opponents' position. Between 1970 and 1972 opposition was greatly attenuated, and what existed was not partisan in nature. With a few notable exceptions, the ERA became a symbolic issue on which everyone could agree. Yet even as this agreement was reached, a new opposition was developing. Ironically it was from the right, which had mostly supported the ERA during its lengthy stay in Congress. This opposition grew and eventually consumed more moderate forces, even while the ERA gained support from ancient foes on the left. By 1976 party once again had emerged as a major dividing line between opponents and supporters. But by now they had switched sides. The Democrats were virtually all in favor of the ERA, and the Republicans were the major source of opposition.

The Alternatives

The ERA has been held out to be the most direct route to legal equality, but it is not the only one. Two alternative routes have also been proposed: the use of the courts to achieve the same legal status for women that the Fourteenth Amendment grants racial minorities, and legislation to change discriminatory laws while preserving those perceived as beneficial to women. Although one could contend that these alternatives supplement rather than displace the need for an ERA, the preferability of alternatives has been a primary argument by ERA opponents.

The Fourteenth Amendment

During the nineteenth century women tried without success to use the Fourteenth Amendment to strike sex-discriminatory laws. After *Muller* declared that sex was a reasonable basis of classification, further efforts seemed futile.[39] Although the rationale of *Muller* had rested on public concern with maternal health, it was cited as a precedent in support of excluding women from juries, different treatment of the sexes in occupational licensing, and excluding women from state-supported colleges.[40] To understand why *Muller* was so important, one has to understand the structure of legal analysis that has developed around the Fourteenth Amendment. The simple language of Section I imposes restrictions on state action that were previously imposed only on the federal government:

> No state shall make or enforce any law which shall abridge the privileges or immunities of citizens of the United States; nor shall any State deprive any person of life, liberty, or property, without due process of law; nor deny to any person within its jurisdiction the equal protection of the laws.

The Supreme Court ruled in 1872 that the "privileges and immunities" clause did not convey to citizens any rights that they had not previously had, and it thus shut off that avenue of legal development.[41] The "due process" clause was used for many decades to undermine state economic regulations such as protective labor laws applying to both sexes. This left the "equal protection" clause. Initially the Court ruled that race and only race was in the minds of the legislators when the Fourteenth Amendment was passed, but its coverage was soon expanded to include national origin and alienage. However, what is prohibited is not *all* official discrimination, but only *invidious* discrimination. If a *compelling state interest* is served by discrimination—such as the need to integrate school districts—distinct laws or state practices based on race or nationality are permitted. The essence of this approach is that certain classifications made by laws are "suspect" and thus subject to "strict scrutiny" by the courts. Unless there is a "compelling state interest," they will be struck down as unconstitutional. Classifications that are not suspect are not subject to the same searching inquiry by the courts. The state need only show that there is a "rational basis" for their existence, and the court will then defer to the legislature.

In practice, classifications that are subject to strict scrutiny are almost always invalidated as unconstitutional. Classifications that need only a rational basis have almost always survived challenges to their constitutionality. The courts have shown great deference to the state legislature, and have gone out of their way to construct rationalizations for legal distinctions that to the untrained eye seem to have only the flimsiest of reasons.[42] The consequence has been a "two-tier" system in which the type of analysis applied to a classification, rather than the reason for the classification, determines the outcome of its constitutionality. The "strict scrutiny" test is usually fatal, while the "rational basis" test is usually meaningless. Thus, in order to eliminate a legal classification, one has to convince the courts that it should be subject to strict scrutiny.

In 1961, only two years before the president's commission urged courts to examine the validity under the Fifth and Fourteenth Amendments of "laws and official practices discriminating against women, to the end that the principle of equality become firmly established in constitutional doctrine,"[43] the Supreme Court had said that this discrimination was valid. Reviewing the conviction of a Florida women by an all-male jury for murdering her husband, the Court upheld a law exempting women from jury service unless they registered a desire to serve with the clerk of the circuit court. Even though this virtually insured that there would be no women in the jury pool, the Court justified it as due to women's "special responsibilities" as the "center of home and family life."[44]

Despite this decision, at a 1962 meeting of the president's commission, attorney Pauli Murray had distributed a draft memorandum outlining a legal strategy using the Fourteenth Amendment. Her idea was proposed as a feasible alternative to the ERA on which both sides could agree. Murray's strategy was to emphasize functional differences, e.g., pregnancy and motherhood, rather than sex differences. Laws distinguishing people on the basis of the former would be constitutional, while laws based on the latter would not be. Under her proposal the Florida law upheld in *Hoyt* would be unconstitutional, but a law exempting parents responsible for the full-time care of children from jury service would not be. Although many commissioners found Murray's proposal attractive, the final version of its report mentioned it as only one of three alternatives.[45] No existing organizations followed the commission's admonition that "interested groups should give high priority to bringing under court review cases involving laws and practices which discriminate against women."[46]

Nonetheless, only ten years after *Hoyt* and eight years after publication of the commission report, the Supreme Court began to take a different view. The turning point came in 1971 when the Court unanimously held unconstitutional an Idaho statute giving preference to males in the appointment of administrators of estates. In *Reed* v. *Reed*[47] the Court found the "administrative convenience" explanation of the preference for males to have no rational basis. Although unexpected, this development was not unforeseeable. During the previous few years the Court had been adding a bit of bite to the rational basis test by looking more closely at state rationalizations for *some* classifications, even though they did not trigger strict scrutiny. Also, during the previous two years the emerging women's movement had become publicly prominent, and the Equal Rights Amendment had been battling its way through Congress.

One sign of this "sea change" in public attitude was given by the American Civil Liberties Union, a traditional opponent of the ERA. In 1968 its national board had rejected a proposed policy statement concerning women's legal rights based on the Murray-Eastwood analysis. Two years later, after a women's caucus at its 1970 national biennial meeting passed a strong women's right's resolution, the board surrendered to the arguments of its several NOW members and came out in support of the ERA and litigation to foster women's rights. Shortly thereafter a staff member spotted *Reed* in a legal publication while it was still in the Idaho courts. The ACLU became co-counsel and asked Ruth Bader Ginsberg, a professor at Rutgers Law School, to write a major portion of the brief presented to the Supreme Court. This change was not solely due to pressure within. In the preceding few years ACLU affiliates had been bombarded with requests by women to take on sex discrimination cases. Ginsburg's students had likewise brought cases in state courts to her attention. After *Reed* the ACLU obtained a major grant from the Ford Foundation for a Women's Right's Project. Ginsburg argued several key cases before the Supreme Court, and the ACLU wrote amicus briefs in others, but there was never any single strategy to bring cases in a particular order to achieve a particular result.[48]

The next key case was brought before the Court in 1973 after Air Force Lieutenant Sharon Frontiero challenged a statue that provided dependent allowance for males in the uniformed services without proof of actual economic dependence, but permitted such allowances for females only if the women could show that they paid one-half of their husbands' living costs.[49] Eight members of the Court found the statute unconstitutional, but they split on the reason. Four applied strict scrutiny, thus granting sex the long sought status of a "suspect class."

Three applied the traditional rational basis test, but found the statute unconstitutional on the authority of *Reed*. One justice concurred without giving an opinion. Justice Rehnquist was the sole dissenter. If only one more justice had joined the plurality opinion, "legal equality," or at least as much as any other group had, would have been achieved. Ironically, the three justices that deliberately avoided characterizing sex as a suspect classification asserted that

> [t]he Equal Rights Amendment, which if adopted will resolve the substance of this precise question, has been approved by the Congress and submitted for ratification by the States. If this Amendment is duly adopted, it will represent the will of the people accomplished in the manner prescribed by the Constitution. By acting prematurely and unnecessarily, . . . the Court has assumed a decisional responsibility at the very time when state legislatures, functioning within the traditional democratic process, are debating the proposed Amendment. It seems . . . that this reaching out to pre-empt by judicial action a major political decision which is currently in process of resolution does not reflect appropriate respect for duly prescribed legislative processes.[50]

In cases after *Reed* and *Frontiero* the Court applied a "strict rational basis" standard with greater and greater scrutiny, until in 1976 a new standard, subsequently referred to as *intermediate scrutiny*, was articulated. On the surface, *Craig* v. *Boren* did not appear to be a momentous case. It concerned an Oklahoma law that prohibited selling "3.2" beer to men under twenty-one but allowed sales to women over eighteen. The state's rationale for this law was that more than ten times as many males as females between eighteen and twenty-one were arrested for drunk driving. The Court found the law unconstitutional, holding that "classifications by gender must serve important governmental objectives and must be substantially related to achievement of those objectives."[51] The Court was not satisfied that "sex represents a legitimate, accurate proxy for the regulation of drinking and driving."[52]

After *Craig* the Court no longer wrote plurality opinions in which some justices supported use of strict scrutiny in gender cases and other concurred or dissented on a different basis. Instead the heightened intermediate scrutiny standard was applied consistently, though not unanimously, usually to strike down laws that made distinctions by sex.

However, the Court has not ruled against *all* sex distinctions. Both before and after *Craig* the Court has looked favorably on statutes that it felt operated "to compensate women for past economic discrimination." *Califano* v. *Webster* upheld a Social Security provision that, prior to 1972, permitted women to eliminate more of their low-earning years from the calculation of their retirement benefits than men, because it "works directly to remedy some part of the effect of past discrimination."[53] *Kahn* v. *Shevin* upheld a Florida statute giving widows, but not widowers, a $500 property tax exemption. The Court ruled that the state law was "reasonably designed to further state policy of cushioning the financial impact of spousal loss upon the sex for which that loss imposes a disproportionately heavy burden."[54]

The other rationale that the Court has employed to uphold some sex distinctions is that men and women are not "similarly situated." *Schlesinger* v. *Ballard* upheld federal statutes that allowed more time for female than for male naval officers to attain promotion before mandatory discharge on the ground that they served the goal of providing women equitable career advancement opportunities.[55] The Court found that, because women were restricted from combat and most sea duty, it would take longer for them to compile favorable service records than it would for men. Therefore, "the different treatment of men and women naval officers . . . reflects, not archaic and overbroad generalizations, but, instead, the demonstrable fact that [they] are not similarly situated with respect to opportunities for professional service."[56] This explanation was also relied upon to uphold a California statute that made statutory rape a crime that only males could commit against females. The state supreme court had already subjected the classification to "strict scrutiny" and found that the statute served a "compelling state interest" in preventing teenage pregnancies. Applying the lesser standard of "important governmental objectives," the Supreme Court came to the same conclusion, but only by ignoring the dissent's objection that a sex-specific statute was not "substantially related to a stated goal as long as a gender-neutral one could achieve the same result."[57]

These cases led inexorably to *Rostker* v. *Goldberg*, which contested the requirement that males but not females register for a potential draft.[58] Giving great weight to the legislative history, the Court noted that Congress's thorough consideration of the issue had clearly established that its decision to exempt women was not the "accidental by-product of a traditional way of thinking about females."[59] It concluded that the "purpose of registration . . . was to prepare for a draft of combat troops" and that "[w]omen as a group, . . . unlike men as a group, are not eligible for combat."[60] Because men and women were not "similarly situated" with regard to military service, it was not unconstitutional to distinguish between them. "The Constitution requires that Congress treat similarly situated persons similarly, not that it engage in gestures of superficial equality."[61]

Although the Court has not adopted the same standard for sex cases as it has for race, religion and national origin cases, for both categories there are some exceptions to the mandate for equality, usually involving rectification for past inequalities. However, cases permitting different treatment of the sexes on the grounds that they are not "similarly situated" could, under a different Court, light the way to a modern version of *Muller*. On the surface it might seem desirable for the Court to require equality where men and women are similarly situated, and to make exceptions apparently in women's favor where they are not, but there are very few circumstances in which men and women are similarly situated. *Muller* was also perceived to be in women's favor from the perspective of reformers of the time. Yet later courts and legislatures relied on it to restrict women's opportunities.

"Specific Bills for Specific Ills"

Legislation which would focus on removing discriminatory laws and practices that hurt women, while preserving those which aided them, was the original alternative to the ERA proposed by the Women's Bureau and its allies. From their perspective, "true equality" meant acknowledging that women had different needs than men. Their roles in the family and responsibilities as mothers "justified legislation to protect them." The ERA would remove good laws as well as bad, require extensive litigation, and still fail to eliminate discrimination against women deriving from social attitudes and habits rather than law. A piecemeal approach would be, in the long run, more constructive, so the argument goes.

Although most of the laws which discriminated against women were state laws, the coalition opposed to the ERA was organized nationally. Because it had to present alternatives to Congress, they had to be federal in nature. The first such attempt was the "Status Bill" discussed earlier. The second was the Equal Pay Act. However, unlike the case of the Status Bill, not all ERA proponents opposed the Equal Pay Act, and it was eventually enacted into law in 1963.[62] Although the Equal Pay Act was thoroughly debated and is considered to be effectively enforced, no one today views it as an alternative to legal equality, or even as a means to attaining economic equality.

The next serious attempt to propose legislation as an alternative to the ERA was by Ronald Reagan, as part of his campaign for the presidency. Called the "50 States Project," its purpose was "to urge the states to eliminate from their statutory and regulatory codes unfair differentiations on the basis of gender." This project was purely hortatory, having no force of law. Indeed to judge by the information released by the White House, it was and is purely political. The project director is to meet with "both private and public sector representatives" and speak "generally about the Reagan record, emphasizing the President's record on issues of particular interest to women."[63] No current comprehensive report on sex discriminatory laws in the states is available, though many states have conducted reviews of their laws and some have passed omnibus bills. Most of these studies were undertaken in response to efforts to adopt a state ERA or ratify the federal amendment.[64]

The Reagan administration also takes credit for creating the Task Force on Legal Equity for Women in 1981 "to correct discriminatory laws and regulations on the federal level."[65] It has resulted in a bill by Sen. Robert Dole (Republican of Kansas) to remove over 150 discriminatory provisions from the federal code. With a few exceptions, this bill is aimed solely at overt sex distinctions of a non-controversial nature "which are clearly incompatible with settled, well-established public policy."[66] These include extending benefits for wives, widows, or dependent children of males to spouses and children of females, removing some minor barriers to equal opportunity, eliminating preferences for husbands over wives or fathers over mothers, extending definitions of criminal sexual activity to protect males, and adding "sex" to the prohibition against violating a person's civil rights by force or threat of force.

Reports by the Civil Rights Commission in 1977 and by the Civil Rights Division of the Justice Department in 1978 had revealed more than three thousand sections of the United States Code containing sex-based references. The reports noted that many of the discriminatory provisions were obsolete, of relatively minor importance, or involved terminological problems with no substantive effect. Substantive distinctions were found in laws relating to the military, federal retirement policies, and employee benefits. Although neither study resulted in remedial legislation, subsequent efforts to revise portions of the U.S Code incorporated many of their recommendations. Other laws, such as the Social Security Amendments Act of 1983, eliminated additional sex-based distinctions.

What Difference Does It Make?

The governing principle behind this chapter has been that legal equality is a necessary goal for the women's movement. However it is not a sufficient goal. Many countries throughout the world purport to give women legal equality when their real inequality is evident to any observer. Nonetheless, in keeping with this governing principle, the question still remains: What difference does it make? In order to attempt an answer it is necessary to identify the potential costs and consequences of each alternative.

Legal Changes

At this point there are few substantive changes *in the law* left to be made. Most of the laws that existed prior to the start of the current feminist movement that were truly restrictive have been removed, some through legislation, others through executive and administrative action, and still others through court action. Many feminists point out that there are in fact hundreds of discriminatory laws still left on the books, which, at the current rate of legislative activity, would take another century to remove.[67] However, this begs the question. All but a handful of those laws are trivial and legislative activity in one era or state does not predict that in another. Omnibus bills in each state, such as Dole's federal bill, could remove all but the most controversial ones in one sweep. Many of those controversial provisions are not stated in clearly discriminatory language, and thus might well require court interpretation even with an Equal Rights Amendment. Also, most of the current legislative agenda of the women's movement would not be achieved by an ERA because it involves either changes in private behavior or the creation of new governmental programs.

However, the ERA would provide a guide. As Eleanor Smeal observes, "By establishing once and for all the basic national standards for eliminating sex discrimination, the ERA would add constitutional impetus to updating the laws and to preventing women's rights reversals now possible in a hostile environment."[68] To see what kind of a guide the ERA would provide, it is worthwhile to look at court decisions in the seventeen states that have some sort of state ERA. Does the existence of an ERA make much of a difference? Since 1968, fifteen states have added ERAs to their state constitutions or included one in a general constitutional revision: Alaska, Colorado, Connecticut, Hawaii, Illinois, Louisiana, Maryland, Massachusetts, Montana, New Hampshire, New Mexico, Pennsylvania, Texas, Virginia and Washington. Eight use language similar to that of the proposed federal amendment. Most of the others have clauses patterned after the equal protection clause of the Fourteenth Amendment, with sex included as a category. Utah and Wyoming included similar provisions in their original constitutions when they became states in 1896 and 1890 respectively.

Judicial decisions at the state level have been highly varied. Washington and Pennsylvania courts have taken a very strict approach, striking down virtually all gender-based statutes including ones that excluded women from contact sports dominated by men. However, even Washington upheld the denial of a marriage license to two males on the grounds that both sexes were affected equally by the requirements that legal marriages be heterosexual.[69] Several state supreme courts have avoided interpreting their ERAs by deciding cases on other grounds or refusing to review them at all. Utah, Louisiana and Virginia have followed a traditional "rational basis" standard and found virtually all sex-based laws to be reasonable. Several states have applied the "strict scrutiny" standard, but this has not prevented them from upholding school regulations restricting the length of boys' but not girls' hair[70] nor prison regulations that required women visitors to male prisons to wear brassieres.[71] Other states have relied on lesser standards, usually derived from the latest Supreme Court language, or have not articulated a specific standard. Thus laws that have been struck down in some states have been upheld in others. Even in states such as Illinois, where the highest court has held sex to be a suspect class, lower state courts have applied the rule inconsistently, with the result that statutes invalidated in one jurisdiction are upheld in another.[72]

This review should not be seen as an absolute prediction of what the Supreme Court would do. State courts are influenced by the Supreme Court in ways that are not reciprocal. Nonetheless, the variety of interpretations that have been made by state courts with state ERAs is evidence of the potential variability of Supreme Court interpretations. A cursory review leads one to believe that the single best predictor of how a state ERA will be interpreted is the public's attitude towards women's rights in that state at the time the decision is made, modified somewhat by the most current Supreme Court doctrine.

This interpretation is given some support by the fact that two states have declared sex to be a suspect class without benefit of a state ERA, and one of them, California, did so a few months before *Reed*.[73] Its analysis was quoted approvingly by the four justices in *Frontiero* v. *Richardson* who said sex should be considered suspect. Nonetheless, the California Supreme Court found its statutory rape law applying to men constitutional on the grounds that prevention of teenage pregnancy was a compelling state interest only *after* three federal circuit courts had struck down gender-based statutory rape laws in other states on the basis of the lesser standard of intermediate scrutiny. Although the Supreme Court had declined to review the circuit court decisions, it granted certiorari to the California case and upheld the law's constitutionality.

Oregon did not even rely on the federal Constitution; in 1982 its state supreme court interpreted a long-standing state constitutional prohibition against granting any citizen or class of citizens special privileges to invalidate legal classifications by sex.[74] Several other states have followed the Supreme Court's lead in finding many sex-based statutes to be unreasonable, even though they have not adopted the most recent intermediate scrutiny standard. Yet even these states have found statutes to be rationally related to reasonable goals such as those permitting wives to share in their husband's property after divorce, but not vice versa, and prohibiting girls from having paper routes before age eighteen.

The biggest danger in using the courts to make substantive changes in the law, whether with or without an ERA, is the lack of predictability. While legislative history can provide a guide to the courts as to what Congress intended, there is simply no guarantee that the courts will interpret a state law or practice the way proponents of equality wish it to be interpreted. Past cases may be a guide to future decisions, but cases which reach the Supreme Court are clearly ones on which there is disagreement as to the meaning of past decisions. This is complicated by the fact that the composition of the Court, or the courts, is not stable. As of this writing, five justices are seventy-five years of age or older.[75] Would a new Court appointed largely by President Reagan interpret an ERA liberally or narrowly? There is an enormous amount of legislative history on the ERA which would guide the Court, but that history does not disclose complete agreement on what its impact would/should be.

The biggest asset of the courts is that should they give the preferred interpretation, they set a standard which makes further changes easier. Once the circuit courts interpreted Title VII as preempting state protective laws, it was unnecessary to challenge each state law in court. Often the state attorneys general simply ruled them invalid. In other states they simply ceased to be enforced. An ERA would have a similar effect. It too would more easily reach "state actions" not incorporated into law and common law interpretations found only in judicial interpretations. There are many practices of state agencies which are never voted on by the legislature. All actions of the state are subject to constitutional scrutiny, whereas the same actions performed by private entities are not. There are many discriminatory conventions found in the common law inherited from pre-revolutionary England (e.g., the husband's obligation to support the wife and the wife's obligation to provide services) that would require revision with the ERA. (However, although these are peculiar to each state, none to this author's knowledge have been reinterpreted as a result of state ERAs.)

Nonetheless, unless a law uses discriminatory language, a court's ability to affect it is limited. Court decisions regarding race make a clear distinction between what must be shown to establish that a practice is unconstitutional, and what must be shown to render it invalid under a particular statute. Proof of a racially discriminatory intent or purpose is necessary to show that an employment practice is a violation of the Fourteenth Amendment. Establishment of a violation of Title VII only requires demonstration of a disparate impact.[76] Assuming the ERA would receive a similar interpretation, decisions such as that in *Personnel Administrator of Massachusetts* v. *Feeney*,[77] which upheld an absolute preference for veterans over non-veterans for state civil service jobs, even though one consequence was to virtually eliminate women from the better jobs, would remain in force because the statute was facially neutral.

Thus, achieving legal equality via the courts would not eliminate the need for legislation. Neither would it preclude it. As long as one's goal is to *eliminate* sex-specific laws, the failure of the Court to give the desired interpretation still leaves legislative action as an alternative route of political action. This is not the case should the courts choose to declare unconstitutional a sex-specific law or practice that is perceived as desirable. Under a Fourteenth Amendment interpretation, affirmative action on the basis of sex would no doubt receive similar treatment to that based on race. But if the courts were to interprete the ERA as strictly as Washington and Pennsylvania have done, it might well be used to eliminate state practices conducive to affirmative action for women. (This is speculative as those states have not done so.)

The one conclusion that can safely be reached about the costs and consequences of the alternative routes to legal equality is that none provides any guarantees. A constitutional amendment would establish a national standard, but exactly what that standard might be would still have to be interpreted by the courts. Sex might eventually be declared a suspect class without an ERA, or the intermediate standard might well be expanded to achieve the same effect. Much legislation would still be necessary to achieve real changes in the status of women even with an ERA. Courts are as much affected by political climates as are legislatures, but at different rates and in different ways. A conservative court might well interpret an ERA as narrowly as some of the states have done, or so broadly as to preclude affirmative action programs. The one thing that is certain is that if one does not agree with the Court's constitutional interpretation of a law or state practice, it takes much longer to change it than to change the law. Thus the judicial route to political change is preferable only if one is reasonably certain one is going to like the outcome or if the legislative route is blocked.

Symbolic Changes

The one characteristic which differentiates the ERA from all other routes to legal equality is its symbolic nature. Both opponents and proponents admit that it is a symbol of equality, though exactly what equality means, let alone whether it is desirable, is not agreed upon. Proponents would no doubt agree with Eleanor Smeal that the ERA "would empower women as full and equal citizens."[78] Opponents describe the anticipated effects of the ERA in such broad language that it is clear that they identify it with the whole pantheon of fundamental social, economic and political changes which would be necessary to achieve a radical feminist utopia.[79] Neither side views it as having purely legal consequences. Both would agree that the ERA is one of those public policies that "derive their salience and meaning less from their instrumental effects upon resource allocations than from the cues they generate that particular social groups occupy a changed status in relation to each other and will continue to do so."[80]

Conflicts of this nature have been labeled by Joseph Gusfield as "symbolic crusades." He argues that they reflect clashes not between classes with contrary economic interests but between rival social systems, cultures or status groups. What is at stake is not the specific issue over which they apparently fight, but the relative prestige of the values which each group represents.

> Since governmental actions symbolize the position of groups in the status structure, seemingly ceremonial or ritual acts of government are often of great importance to many social groups. Issues which seem foolish or impractical items are often important for what they symbolize about the style or culture which is being recognized or derogated. Being acts of deference or degradation, the individual finds in governmental action that his own perceptions of his status in the society are confirmed or rejected. . .
>
> If we conceive of status as somehow an unfit issue for political controversy, we are simply ignoring a clash of interests which generate a high order of emotion and political action in the United States. When a society experiences profound changes, the fortunes and the respect of people undergo loss or gain. We have always understood the desire to defend fortune. We should also understand the desire to defend respect. It is less clear because it is symbolic in nature but it is not less significant.[81]

If a particular proposed governmental action is infused with certain values, then its attainment suggests that those values and their proponents "have a legitimate claim to greater respect, importance, or worth in the society than have some others."[82] Amending the Constitution is the single most profound governmental action that can be taken. Thus its achievement is important not purely for its instrumental effects, but for the prestige which is thereby conferred on the values it represents. Small wonder then that those who fear the implications of the women's liberation movement also fear the ERA. What they are actually afraid of is destruction of the patriarchal nuclear family, degradation of full-time homemaking as the preferred lifestyle for adult women, and the elimination of sex roles. The fact that the ERA would not cause any of these outcomes is, to them, irrelevant, as is the fact that the legal effects of the ERA could be achieved by other means. In the eyes of its opponents the ERA symbolizes a loss of prestige for the patriarchical way of life.

Although most of the opponents as well as the proponents of the ERA are white, and not identified with any particular ethnic group, understanding that the fight over the ERA is basically a status conflict makes it possible to analyze its implications for racial and ethnic groups. These implications are not uniform, because different racial and ethnic groups do not have the same lifestyles or family configurations. Essentially, any racial or ethnic group for whom the patriarchal family structure and a sexual division of labor are desired norms and part of its basic identity will find the ERA inimical to its interests. If achievement of the ERA is perceived as resulting in a loss of prestige to patriarchy, then racial and ethnic groups who value patriarchy or the patriarchal family will also lose prestige.

Conversely, those groups which have been derogated for being matriarchal will gain in prestige. Considered as a group, blacks most closely fit this description. Black society is hardly matriarchal in any abstract sense of the word, but it has been labeled as such because black women are more likely to be the sole supporters of their families than are white women.[83] Compared to black men, black women have also exercised more power and responsibility within their own communities than white women have compared to white men. Because the institutions and values of white middle-class society, particularly the patriarchal family, are held up as the norm, "deviant" forms of social and family organization have been held to be undesirable. A governmental action which confers status on women, and enhances the prestige of those values associated with the women's movement, should undermine this degradation of the black family structure.

To the question of what difference does it make which route to legal equality is taken, the answer is: It depends on what is desired. Pragmatically, one has more control over the outcome of legislation than over court decisions. While one cannot always obtain the exact legislation one wants, that which is amended unfavorably in the middle of the process can oftentimes be killed. Court cases based on the Fourteenth Amendment are more predictable than those based on the ERA, and are likely to be simply because legal precedents based on race, religion and national origin are presumably to be followed. While legislative history would certainly guide the courts in any ERA decisions, it would still be virgin territory for legal interpretation and thus likely to depend, at least initially, on the composition of the Supreme Court and the general political climate in which its interpretations were made.

Politically, however, not all states are as receptive to the feminist position as is the U.S. Congress, and court cases require fewer resources than do lobbying fifty legislatures. Thus, absent a federal ERA or a declaration that sex is a "suspect" class, sole use of the legislative route to legal equality is likely to give checkered results. More important, indeed most important, the ERA has a symbolic weight that the other routes do not have, and this symbolic weight is most significant. It is the symbolic impact of the ERA which will be felt within different racial and ethnic communities. The ERA will confer governmental approval on improving the status of women and create expectations about their treatment. Whether this change is viewed as salutary or deleterious depends on the group and how it feels about patriarchy.

NOTES

[1]J. Stanley Lemons, *The Woman Citizen: Social Feminism in the 1920s* (Champaign-Urbana, Ill.: University of Illinois Press, 1973), p. 49.

[2]*Lochner* v. *New York*, 198 U.S. 45, 53 (1905).

[3]*Muller* v. *Oregon*, 208 U.S. 412, 422 (1908).

[4]Lemons, op. cit., p. 187.

[5]Cynthia Ellen Harrison, "Prelude to Feminism: Women's Organizations, the Federal Government and the Rise of the Women's Movement, 1942-1968" (Ph.D. Dissertation, Columbia University, 1982), p. 21.

[6]See *West Coast Hotel* v. *Parrish*, 300 U.S. 379 (1937).

[7]Susan Ware, *Beyond Suffrage: Women in the New Deal* (Cambridge, Mass.: Harvard University Press, 1981), pp. 79-82. The 1936 GOP platform stated the party's opposition to legislation which discriminated against women in federal and state governments.

[8]Lemons, op. cit., p. 204.

[9]Ibid., pp. 199-200.

[10]Harrison, op. cit., p. 38.

[11]Ibid, p. 62.

[12]Ware, op. cit., pp. 125-126.

[13]Harrison, op. cit., pp. 32-33.

[14]Ware, op. cit., p. 121. Harrison, ibid., p. 70.

[15]Harrison, ibid., pp. 58-60.

[16]Harrison, op. cit., pp. 71-87.

[17]Ibid., p. 88.

[18]Ibid., pp. 94-98.

[19]96 *Congressional Record* 872-873 (1950).

[20]99 *Congressional Record* 8954-8955 (1953).

[21]She did not assume her post until November, after the Senate vote. Harrison, op. cit., p. 121.

[22]Ibid., p. 124.

[23]Leila J. Rupp, "American Feminism in the Post War Period," in Robert H. Bremner and Gary W. Reichard, eds., *Reshaping America: Society and Institutions, 1945-1960* (Columbus, Ohio: Ohio State University Press, 1982), p. 30.

[24]Harrison, op. cit., p. 268.

[25]Ibid., p. 378.

[26]Margaret Mead and Frances Bagley Kaplan, eds., *American Women: The Report of the President's Commission on the Status of Women and Other Publications of the Commission* (New York: Charles Scribner's Sons, 1965), p. 65.

[27]President's Commission on the Status of Women, *American Women: Report of the President's Commission on the Status of Women* (Washington, D.C.: Government Printing Office, 1963), pp. 44-45.

[28]Jo Freeman, *The Politics of Women's Liberation* (New York: Longman, 1975), chapters 2 and 3.

[29]Edith Green (Democrat of Oregon) was the sole woman to vote against the sex provision. She later became the principal sponsor of another key piece of legislation for women, Title IX of the 1972 Education Amendments Act.

[30]Herman Edelsberg, at the New York University 18th Conference on Labor, cited in *Labor Relations Reporter* 61 (August 25, 1966): 253-255.

[31]*EEOC Guidelines* (April 22, 1966).

[32]*EEOC Guidelines* (November 22, 1965). The guidelines were eventually changed to bring them into compliance with court decisions on Title VII.

[33]Citizen's Advisory Council on the Status of Women, *Women in 1970* (Washington, D.C.: Government Printing Office, 1970), p. 2.

[34]The vote was not along party lines.

[35]Material for the preceding paragraphs was taken primarily from Freeman, *The Politics of Women's Liberation*, op. cit., chapter 6, and Catherine East, "The First Stage: ERA in Washington, 1961-1972," *Women's Political Times* (September 1982): 7-10.

[36]Freeman, *The Politics of Women's Liberation*, op. cit., pp. 220-221. See also Susan E. Marshall, "Keep Us On the Pedestal: Women Against Feminism in Twentieth-Century America," in Jo Freeman, ed., *Women: A Feminist Perspective*, 3rd ed. (Palo Alto, Cal.: Mayfield Publishing Co., 1984), p. 569; Nancy E. McGlen and Karen O'Connor, *Women's Rights* (New York: Praeger, 1983), pp. 373-374; David W. Brady and Kent L. Tedin, "Ladies in Pink: Religion and Political Ideology in the Anti-ERA Movement," *Social Science Quarterly* 56:4 (March 1976): 564-575. There is no evidence that the latter groups contained more than a few members.

[37]Janet K. Boles, "Building Support for the ERA: A Case of 'Too Much, Too Late,' " *P.S.* 15:4 (Fall 1982): 572-577; and "Systematic Factors Underlying Legislative Responses to Woman Suffrage and the Equal Rights Amendment," *Woman & Politics* 2:1/2 (Spring/Summer 1982): 14.

[38]Eleanor Smeal, *Why and How Women Will Elect the Next President* (New York: Harper & Row, 1984), p. 78.

[39]*Muller* v. *Oregon*, 208 U.S. 412 (1908).

[40]The legal history and analysis of this section is largely an adaptation of Jo Freeman, "Women, Law and Public Policy," in Jo Freeman, ed., *Women: A Feminist Perspective*, op. cit., pp. 381-401.

[41]*Slaughter House Cases*, 83 U.S. (16 Wall.) 36 (1872).

[42]Laurence H. Tribe, *American Constitutional Law* (New York: Foundation Press, 1978), pp. 994-1002. "Strict scrutiny" is also employed where fundamental rights, such as voting, travel, procreation, criminal appeals, or those protected by the First Amendment, are involved.

[43]President's Commission on the Status of Women, op. cit., p. 45.

[44]*Hoyt* v. *Florida*, 368 U.S. 57, 62 (1961).

[45]Pauli Murray and commission staff member Mary Eastwood later published this analysis in a law review. Pauli Murray and Mary Eastwood, "Jane Crow and the Law: Sex Discrimination and Title VII," *George Washington Law Review* 34 (December 1965): 232.

[46]President's Commission on the Status of Women, op. cit., p. 45.

[47]*Reed* v. *Reed*, 368 U.S. 57 (1971).

[48]Phone interview with Ruth Bader Ginsberg, now a judge on the D.C. Circuit Court of Appeals, on April 16, 1984.

[49]*Frontiero* v. *Richardson*, 411 U.S. 677 (1973).

[50]*Frontiero*, 411 U.S. at 692, concurring opinion. Judge Ginsberg does not believe that activity on the ERA actually preempted a majority opinion declaring sex to be a suspect class. She feels that this rationale was merely a convenient excuse as the Court was not yet ready to make such a gigantic departure from past decisions. Interview of April 16, 1984.

[51]*Craig* v. *Boren*, 429 U.S. 190, 197 (1976).

[52]*Craig*, 429 U.S. at 204.

[53]*Califano* v. *Webster*, 430 U.S. 313, 318 (1977).

[54]*Kahn* v. *Shevin*, 416 U.S. 351, 355 (1974).

[55]*Schlesinger* v. *Ballard*, 419 U.S. 498 (1975).

[56]*Schlesinger*, 419 U.S. at 508.

[57]*Michael M.* v. *Superior Court of Sonoma County*, 450 U.S. 464, 472 (1981).

[58]*Rostker* v. *Goldberg*, 453 U.S. 57 (1981).

[59]*Rostker*, 453 U.S. at 74.

[60]*Rostker*, 453 U.S. at 76.

[61]*Rostker*, 453 U.S. at 77.

[62]Harrison, op. cit., p. 155. The National Women's Party opposed the Equal Pay Act and the Business and Professional Women supported it.

[63]"50 States Project - Brief Outline," unpublished leaflet available from the White House, Washington, D.C.

[64]U.S. Department of Labor, Women's Bureau, unpublished "Working Paper on Studies of Sex Discrimination in State Codes" (October 1981), p. 4.

[65]Executive Order 12336; Republican National Committee, *Talking Points*, III:13(September 1983): 3. This idea was not conceived by the Reagan administration, however, but by the Nixon administration. It was put into existence under Presidents Ford and Carter. See Lavinia Edmunds, "Reagan Defector Barbara Honegger's Real Story," *Ms.* (November 1983), p. 89.

[66]U.S. Congress, Senate, Committee on the Judiciary, Report No. 98-390 on S-501, "Sex Discrimination in the United States Code Reform Act of 1983," 98th Congress, 2nd Session (April 11, 1984), p. 4. The report identifies as examples of controversial laws those involving the Selective Service and combat limitations, those involving separate rules for promotion for men and women among Naval and Marine Corps Reserve officers (see *Schlesinger* v. *Ballard*, supra), and "statutes requiring affirmative action that advantages women, which some oppose as constituting an unlawful form of reverse discrimination, and some support as a means of compensation for past inequities." Ibid., p. 6.

[67]See, for example, Eleanor Smeal, op. cit.

[68]Ibid., p. 28.

[69]*Singer* v. *Hara*, 11 Wash. App. 247, 522 P.2d 1187 (1974).

[70]*Mercer* v. *Board of Trustees*, 538 S.W.2d 201 (Tex. Civ. App. 1976).

[71]*Holdman* v. *Olin*, 581 P.2d 1164 (Hawaii 1978).

[72]See Comment, "Equal Rights Provision: The Experience Under State Constitutions," *California Law Review* 65 (September 1977): 1086-1112; Paul M. Kurtz, "The State Equal Rights Amendments and Their Impact on Domestic Relations Law," *Family Law Quarterly* 11 (Summer 1977): 101-150; Dawn Marie Driscoll and Barbara J. Rouse, "Through a Class Darkly: A Look at State Equal Rights Amendments," *Suffolk University Law Review* 12 (Fall 1978): 1282-1311; Philip E. Hassman, "Construction and Application of State Equal Rights Amendments Forbidding Determination of Rights Based on Sex," 90 *American Law Reports 3d*, pp. 158-216 (1979).

[73]*Sail'er Inn* v. *Kirby*, 5 Cal.3d 1, 485 P.2d 529, 95 Cal. Rptr. 329 (1971) invalidated a state statute prohibiting women from tending bar.

[74]*Hewett* v. *State Accident Insurance Fund Corp.*, 294 Ore. 33, 653 P.2d 970 (1982).

[75]Justice Brennan was born in 1906, Justice Powell and Chief Justice Burger were born in 1907, and Justices Marshall and Blackmun were born in 1908.

[76]*Washington* v. *Davis*, 426 U.S. 229 (1976). See also *Village of Arlington Heights* v. *Metropolitan Housing Development Corp.*, 429 U.S. 252 (1977).

[77]*Personnel Administrator of Massachusetts* v. *Feeney*, 442 U.S. 256 (1979), reversing 451 F.Supp. 143 (D. Mass. 1978).

[78]Smeal, op. cit., p. 28.

[79]Phyllis Schlafly, *The Power of Positive Woman* (New Rochelle, N. Y.: Arlington House, 1977).

[80]Murray Edelman, *Politics As Symbolic Action* (Chicago: Markham, 1971), p. 9.

[81]Joseph R. Gusfield, *Symbolic Crusade* (Urbana, Ill.: University of Illinois Press, 1963), p. 11.

[82]Ibid., p. 172.

[83]Daniel Patrick Moynihan, *The Negro Family: The Case for National Action* (Washington, D.C.: U.S. Department of Labor, Office of Policy Planning and Research, 1965). This is primarily true of lower-class families. Generally, two incomes have been necessary for black families to join the middle class. Furthermore, since the jobs women occupy rarely pay enough for even white women to support a family in a middle-class lifestyle, black women are highly unlikely to be the sole supporters of middle-class families.

WOMEN AS AN EMERGING POWER BLOC: ETHNIC AND RACIAL CONSIDERATIONS

Toni-Michelle C. Travis

George Mason University

Introduction

The 1984 presidential election was considered an historic event in the continuing battle of women to attain full equality in American society. Since 1920 American women have been able to vote, yet their potential power at the polls has only recently made a significant impact on candidates and veteran political observers.

Betty Friedan's 1963 publication, *The Feminine Mystique*, called attention to white suburban housewives who felt isolated and complained about a problem which was difficult to define. Since then the consciousness of women has been rising as the onetime housewife has become integrated into the work force and frequently taken on the role of political activist. Through the efforts of the National Organization for Women and the National Women's Political Caucus, a growing number of women have become an integral part of the electoral process. No longer are women merely spectators who leave the issues of politics and government to men.

Since 1981, President Ronald Reagan's budget-cutting policies have elicited negative reactions from a number of constituencies, including women. Funding cuts in federal programs which provided low-income assistance, job training, and child welfare programs particularly incensed women. Women began to exhibit a sense of group consciousness when they spoke of asserting themselves against Reagan's policies through electoral politics.

Women were not alone in their criticisms of Reagan's policies. Black civil rights advocates criticized the Reagan administration's neglect in enforcing civil rights laws. Prominent among the critics was Jesse Jackson, who launched a voter registration drive which was designed to promote his presidential candidacy and the Democratic party. As Reagan moved toward running for a second term, women and blacks became two of the most vocal groups opposing his administrations's policies.

The 1984 election raised the question of the future role of blacks and women in national politics and especially in the Democratic party. Blacks have been increasing their electoral strength and visibility since the 1965 Voting Rights Act. Women, however, are just beginning to assert their full political potential. Because women constituted 52.8 percent of the registered voters in 1983,[1] they clearly had the possibility of playing a pivotal force in voting against President Reagan. Election results show that Reagan received the women's vote, while the majority of blacks voted for the Democratic ticket.[2] Women voters did not present a united front across racial lines. Black women remained with the Democratic party and its historic vice-presidential candidate, Geraldine Ferraro, but a greater number of women in general joined the majority who voted for the Republican ticket.

The electoral potential of American women did not successfully unseat an incumbent president. Yet, women exhibited political clout by pressing the Democrats and Walter Mondale to consider females as suitable vice-presidential candidates. Many women activists felt that a major victory had been won for women when Geraldine Ferraro was chosen as Mondale's running mate. The victory, however, was short-lived, because it had negative consequences for those women who urged that the Democrats nominate a female but did not deliver the women's vote to the Democratic party. The primacy for women activists of a female candidate over a black vice-presidential candidate irreparably harmed the possible development of a formidable coalition between black women and white women.

It is likely that future attempts at electoral cooperation between black women and white women will again hinge on the issue of priorities. Black women still see race as a priority over gender considerations. White women have now put themselves in a difficult position because they were wrong in the 1984 election on electoral strategy, candidate selection, and the implications of the gender gap in presidential elections.

Historical Cooperation

Black women and white women, although not without dissension, have been working together to improve the condition of women since the abolitionist societies of the nineteenth century. The 1830s saw the establishment of anti-slavery societies led by white women, some of whom were workers, although the majority were housewives.[3] As these women fought against slavery they gained insight into their position in American society. Women were basically confined to the home, while men were expected to handle the political and social issues of the day. Middle-class white women began to understand that in the public sphere they were excluded from the political process, while in the home they were degraded and relegated to the roles of wife and mother. The anti-slavery movement offered these middle-class women a way to increase their self-esteem. By leaving the home to devote time to the anti-slavery effort, women felt that they were engaged in meaningful work. This chance to escape housework also afforded an opportunity to develop skills in protest politics. As abolitionists, white women developed fund-raising techniques, learned how to advertise their cause, and gained practice in public speaking.[4] Although they were political amateurs who were outsiders to the political system, the women adopted the petition as a principal weapon and began to seek sympathetic men and women as converts to their cause.[5]

Abolitionist women soon learned of the extent of their subordination when they went to London to represent the United States at the 1840 World Anti-Slavery Convention. American women had fully expected to participate in the proceedings. To their dismay, women were confined to a fenced-off area behind a curtain. Separation of the women from the main proceedings was an indication of their true status in the eyes of men who controlled public issues.

Black women made a concerted effort to work with white women in integrated anti-slavery societies. Records indicate that four black women joined the Female Anti-Slavery Society of Philadelphia and that Susan Paul, a black female, joined the Boston Female Anti-Slavery Society.[6] Black females also attended the first two national female anti-slavery conventions held in 1837 and 1838. However, their attendance created tension and raised the unsettling issue of whether black members could be admitted.[7] For white women, it was easier to accept black males such as Frederick Douglass, William C. Nell and Charles Lenox Remond as supporters, than the black women.[8]

Elizabeth Cady Stanton and Lucretia Mott, women who had been a part of the abolitionist movement, used their newly acquired political skills to call together those interested in the condition of women at the Seneca Falls convention. The 1848 convention became significant because it marks the beginning of the women's suffrage movement. Although a number of issues were considered, the suffrage resolution was the only one not unanimously accepted by the convention.[9] Frederick Douglass, a former slave and a supporter of equality for women, was instrumental in seconding Elizabeth Cady Stanton's controversial motion on the right of women to vote.[10] A black man thus played a key role in the early stages of the suffrage movement, while no black women were present at the Seneca Falls convention. In addition, the status of black women was ignored in the statements of the Seneca Falls Declaration.[11]

Historically, the Seneca Falls Declaration marks an important point in the fight for women's rights. It may be seen as a reflection of the consciousness of white middle-class women who conveniently ignored the issues confronting white working-class women in the New England textile mills and black women.[12] This glaring failure to mention the condition of black women is noteworthy because the organizers of the Seneca Falls convention had considerable involvement in the abolitionist movement.[13]

The Suffrage Movement

As the focus of the women's organizations shifted from abolition to suffrage, black women met discrimination. The conclusion of the Civil War and the onset of Reconstruction brought with them the enactment of the Thirteenth, Fourteenth and Fifteenth Amendments. The Thirteenth and Fourteenth Amendments were not controversial with women because they freed the slaves and granted them citizenship. However, the Fifteenth Amendment was problematic because it granted the right to vote to uneducated black males who were former slaves, while women were not mentioned. Again, Frederick Douglass played a role because he found it "vital" for black men to have the vote, but only "desirable" for women.[14] Douglass was not successful in convincing white women of the need to support black suffrage. The issue of black suffrage caused a split among the women as many withdrew from the Equal Rights Association to form the National Woman Suffrage Association. The newly organized NWSA clearly divorced itself from the issue of black suffrage.[15]

Leaders of the suffrage movement had hoped to persuade the Republicans in Congress to reward their demand for suffrage after the Civil War. These early feminists, however, did not understand the political priorities of the Radical Republicans. When the congressmen responded to the demands of women with "This is the Negro's hour," they were proposing legislation on the basis of political expediency.[16] As pragmatic politicians they were looking ahead to the approximately two million votes they would create for the Republican party.[17]

For black males the ability to vote was crucial in their daily battle for life and liberty against their former masters. Blacks faced the possibility of physical harm, unlike the white women who were pressing for their rights. From Frederick Douglass' perspective, black males needed the vote as a key weapon in the continuing struggle against racism after the Civil War.[18]

The suffragists lost in the crucial battle to enfranchise women under the same amendment which enfranchised black men. Their political defense, which hinged on arguments of white supremacy, reveals how tenuous their ties were to the issue of black equality. With trepidation, middle-class white women saw that former slaves were being elevated in status—they were free men, they were citizens, and now they could vote. As Angela Davis points out, white women began to feel that perhaps blacks had gained too much in the outcome of the Civil War.[19] Consequently, the priorities of black women and white women began to diverge as black women put the struggle for basic rights, which were already assured to white Americans, before the demands of the white feminists.

The Women's Club Movement

In the second half of the nineteenth century, women came together in what is called the women's club movement to advocate social reform on issues such as temperance, education for women, and dress. Black women also felt that these social issues were important, but their priorities were based on their status as women in a segregated society. As Rosalyn Terborg-Penn points out, the social and economic situation of black women was significantly different from that of white women:

> White women had no need to vindicate their dignity in the midst of national cries that they were wanton, immoral, and socially inferior. White women did not have the severe problems of racial discrimination, which compounded the black woman's plight in employment and education. Moreover, race consciousness was evident among Afro-Americans in general as civil rights organizations, business groups, and self-help societies emerged with names signifying race.[20]

Black activists originally sought to join white women's reform organizations. The white organizations, however, were so intent on maintaining support from their southern members that they rebuffed the black women, who subsequently established all-black organizations with similar goals.

Some black club leaders did not give up easily and made a concerted effort to work with their white counterparts. Josephine St. Pierre Ruffin, the wife of a judge and a prominent member of the Boston black community, attended the Milwaukee meeting of the General Federation of Women's Clubs in 1900. Initially, Mrs. Ruffin was assumed to be white by the other delegates. Subsequently, it was learned that she represented the New England Federation of Women's Clubs, as well as the Woman's Era Club, a black club which she had established. Mrs. Ruffin's credentials were reviewed. The resolution of this sensitive racial matter was to admit Mrs. Ruffin as a certified delegate from the General Federation of Women's Clubs, while rejecting her claim to represent the black women's group. This affront to Mrs. Ruffin caused the Woman's Era Club of Boston to issue a statement which anticipated the future state of black-white efforts. The Era Club announced that it now felt "that colored women should confine themselves to their clubs and the large field of work open to them there."[21] A rift along racial lines had definitely occurred.

Another prominent black club woman, Mary Church Terrell, president of the National Association of Colored Women, spoke at various times before the General Federation of Women's Clubs and the American Woman Suffrage Association on behalf of the social concerns of black women. However, her appearances were met by controversial comments from representatives from the southern delegations.

In general, leaders of women's clubs in the black community such as Ida B. Wells-Barnett, Frances Harper and Fannie Barrier Williams sought to work with the national women's organizations to insure the rights and improve the social conditions of all women. Their efforts sought to communicate that black women shared the same concerns of the white club women. The problem was that in a segregated society, black women had to pursue their goals in isolation, which relegated them to a footnote in this period of the women's movement. Consequently, there is a distorted view which underestimates the level of interest that black women had for major social concerns such as suffrage, temperance and educational reform.

This era of the women's movement culminated with the passage of the Nineteenth Amendment giving women the right to vote in 1920. Two analysts of the women's movement, Judith Hole and Ellen Levine, note that feminists thought that with

the passage of the Nineteenth Amendment the majority of women activists as well as the public at large assumed that having gained the vote women's complete equality had been virtually obtained.[22]

This was certainly true for white women who supported only a limited number of social reform organizations over the next forty years until the resurgence of feminism.[23] For black women, however, racial discrimination remained as they continued to fight the battles against lynching, segregation in employment and housing in the North, and

Jim Crow laws in the South. Black women continued in their struggle without the benefit of white organizational support, although on an individual basis white women were among the founding members of the National Association for the Advancement of Colored People and the National Urban League.

The Civil Rights Movement

The 1960s was the setting for a new stage in political activism. Beginning slowly with sit-ins in Greensboro, North Carolina, and bus boycotts in Montgomery, Alabama, the scattered protests grew to be a massive movement in support of civil rights for blacks. This was a major social movement led by such blacks as Martin Luther King, Jr., James Farmer, Stokely Carmichael, Roy Wilkins and Whitney Young, all demonstrating that no longer were blacks going to remain second-class citizens. Black men received most of the media attention, but black women were no less a part of this critical social revolution in American society.[24]

At the local level, community leaders such as Daisy Bates in Little Rock, Arkansas, and Gloria Richardson in Cambridge, Maryland, guided blacks through racial crises. Black women in the National Council of Negro Women, the NAACP, the Urban League and the black sororities enhanced their political skills by participating in the movement. In the civil rights era black women learned how effective it was to mobilize masses of people in a peaceful demonstration, how to utilize the media to bring attention to the civil rights movement, and how to lobby for legislation to enforce civil and political rights.

White community support for the civil rights movement came primarily from students, clergy and labor unions. For the most part it was a movement led by blacks with the help of white allies. In this movement black women were subordinate to black males, but not to white females. Unlike earlier social movements involving black women, this one reversed the roles played by black women and white women. Black women were no longer merely subordinate to the interests of white women. Middle- and upper middle-class white women who went south between 1963 and 1965 returned home feeling "stronger, angrier, more committed."[25] Many white women began to feel that they were coming into their own as they returned to their own turf and began to employ their new political skills. This experience helped reactivate the women's movement in the 1960s. As with the abolitionist movement, white women gained political acumen by having participated in a social movement which focused on the condition of blacks.

Women's Movement of the 1960s

The civil rights struggle of blacks caused white women again to become vividly aware of their subordinate position in American society. Key events which fostered the women's movement were: President Kennedy's establishment of the President's Commission on the Status of Women with subsequent commissions in each state; the publication of Betty Friedan's *The Feminine Mystique* in 1963; and the inclusion of sex in Title VII of the 1964 Civil Rights Act prohibiting discrimination in employment.[26]

The 1960s phase of the fight for women's rights began to take on a political focus. Again, white women wished to free themselves from the lowly position of housewife. Because few white women were wage earners and only a tiny number had ever held political office, white women found that their initial efforts lacked sufficient power to command serious media or legislative attention. White women who had been active in party politics began to see how little progress women had made within the political system in their struggle for equal rights.

The student sit-ins and protest marches of the civil rights movement and the demonstrations against the Vietnam War reactivated the consciousness of women. A new political woman began to emerge with the founding of the National Organization for Women in 1966, the National Women's Political Caucus in 1971, and the battle to reform the Democratic party rules in 1972. Women were no longer passive political pawns of the system; they were now active participants with their own agenda.

White women saw the 1960s as a time to reassess their identity. Women who had given up college aspirations to help pay for their husband's education and devote their lives to their families found that they were unfulfilled. They wanted more than a comfortable suburban lifestyle. White women had become trapped by the housewife's syndrome,[27] a never-ending domestic routine which did not allow them time or room to assert their individual identity. These economically secure, middle-class white women had never been career women. After finishing their housework they were overwhelmed with boredom because they had sufficient "free time to play bridge, attend club meetings, or stay home and read, listen to Beethoven, or just plain loaf."[28]

According to Friedan's analysis, women needed to break out of the confining housewife mold and grow in order to assert their own identity. To find this identity which had been suppressed by marriage, motherhood and housework, white women needed to enter the labor market. Referring to how society defines men according to their work, Friedan says,

Thinkers of other times put forth the idea that people were, to a great extent, defined by the work they did. The work that a man had to do to eat, to stay alive, to meet the physical necessities of his environment, dictated his identity.[29]

Consequently, women were to follow men and find their identity in work, which would utilize their full capacities. "Women, as well as men, can only find their identity in work that uses their full capacities. A woman cannot find her identity through others—her husband, her children."[30]

Friedan's identification of a problem facing middle-class white women and her pleas for changes eventually received attention. White activists who agreed with Friedan worked to establish the new women's organizations such as the the National Organization for Women (NOW), the National Women's Political Caucus, Federally Employed Women and the Women's Equity Action League. Black women played a role in founding these organizations, but for the most part remained on the sidelines. Black activists clearly remembered how black community leaders had been forced to play subordinate roles in the women's organizations at the forefront of the suffrage movement. The issues of such established organizations as the General Federation of Women's Clubs, the Women's Christian Temperance Union and the National American Women's Suffrage Association no longer dominated the agenda of these women activists. While white women were shifting their focus from the general complaint of a female identity crisis to political issues, black women were solidifying the social and economic gains of the civil rights movement.

Black Women's Organizations

A different set of historical events distinguished the lives of black women from those of the white women who formed the new organizations in the 1960s. Black women did participate in the battle for the passage of the Nineteenth Amendment, but the majority of black activists at the beginning of the twentieth century found it imperative to turn their attention inward to address the pressing and immediate problems which plagued rural and urban blacks in a segregated society.

Black women had sought to work with white club women on issues other than suffrage, but usually found that they were separated into segregated chapters for black women. This was the case with the growing Young Women's Christian Association, an organization which established black chapters under the direction of the secretary "for colored work."[31]

Black resources to establish and sustain national organizations have always been limited. During the early twentieth century numerous black women's organizations devoted their efforts to the uplift of blacks.[32] It was through these social, religious and civic organizations that black women gained experience in leadership, social reform and political protest.

Although a number of black civic, social and fraternal organizations made significant contributions during this period, only three organizations, the National Council of Negro Women and the two oldest black sororities, Alpha Kappa Alpha and Delta Sigma Theta, will be considered here. These three are notable because of their early and continuing role in promoting better conditions for black women.

Women who founded and built these organizations were the leaders in their communities fighting for day-care facilities, night schools, libraries, recreational facilities, vocational guidance and civil rights for blacks. These women were not bored housewives. They were black women who had graduated from Oberlin College and Howard University; they were the educated and acculturated members of their community who felt that they should lead the masses of blacks.

Black women have always faced a double burden of sexism along with racism. Racism severely limited the resources available for the development of black organizations. Black women's organizations thus differed from their white counterparts in goals, the time frame for achieving these goals, the range of issues addressed and the perspective of the political system.

In the last half of the nineteenth century as white women were concentrating on the suffrage issue, black women were sympathetic and supportive of this worthy goal. However, black women were keenly aware of the increasingly repressive political system which flourished in the South after federal troops, which had provided some measure of insurance for black rights, were ordered withdrawn by President Hayes in 1877. Black women found it imperative to make anti-lynching measures a priority among their many goals. As the southern states systematically stripped blacks of their franchise and instituted segregationist Jim Crow laws, which promoted the "separate-but-equal doctrine" in education, police, fire and health services, black women were compelled to form social service organizations which served the entire black community, not just black women. The pool of activist women who could devote time to activities outside the home was so small that black women could not afford to concentrate their limited resources on a narrow, single objective such as suffrage, birth control or promoting higher education for women. Instead, black women set sweeping goals as the purpose of the African Methodist Episcopal

(AME) Missionary Society shows: ". . . To spread the gospel at home and abroad and to succor those who were oppressed."[33] The church was primarily interested in promoting religious education, yet through its missionary societies it offered aid to both rural and urban blacks. In many cases it was the black church (Baptist, AME and Methodist), through its women's organizations, that offered the psychological and financial support desperately needed by the newly arrived southern migrant to the urban north. To promote youth membership in the church, recreational and social activities were organized for children. This helped working mothers who were trying to rear families in urban areas where municipal recreational or club facilities for black youngsters were few.

Because of the greater resources available to white women, they were able to establish numerous organizations with narrow goals that primarily benefited women, rather than the entire community. The names of the older women's organizations reflect this specialization— American Association of University Women, the National Federation of Business and Professional Women's Clubs and the League of Women Voters. In contrast, the goals of black women's organizations tended to be multi-purpose.

From the perspective of black women, the objectives of white women were important but not life-threatening. While white women were fighting for the right to vote, black women were combating violence against black men who tried to vote. Blacks were trying to improve basic living conditions in communities which often lacked hospital facilities and had only inadequate, segregated public schools. Black women desired immediate changes, but were realistic given the limits of their resources and their subordinate position viz. white women in the American social system. If possible, black women would have preferred to end lynching, as well as segregated facilities in education, health, housing and public accommodations. Yet, black women clearly understood that although they were citizens, they lacked a number of basic civil rights which were available to white women both before and after suffrage was granted. It was useless for black women to bring suit in the South against injustices such as rape perpetrated by whites. It was, for example, a common practice for white women to charge black men with rape as in the 1931 Scottsboro case involving nine black men. Black women did not view the political system and especially the judiciary as an effective way to redress their grievances.

For white women, the electoral system held hope as a way to improve their condition. It was thought that if women could only get the vote, they could affect policy and even run for public office. Black women could see the political system as a potential source of benefits for all blacks, but only in the distant future. They were aware of the limitations of the electoral system in changing conditions for blacks. White women only had to fight for the right to vote, while black women often had the additional obstacles of the poll tax and literacy tests.

Aside from the electoral process, white women had access to the judicial and legislative processes. Although judges and members of Congress were not overwhelmingly sympathetic toward the issues of concern to white women, they only had to fight a gender issue. Black women had to overcome the racial issue as well as the gender issue when seeking redress in the legislative or judical system.

The political arena was dominated by white men. However, after 1920 white women were able to penetrate the membership of this exclusive club by temporarily gaining congressional seats upon the deaths of their husbands. These women, such as Hattie Caraway, the first woman elected to the U.S. Senate, were usually the political pawns of the senior members of their congressional delegation or the party bosses back home. Nevertheless, white women were at least able to seek the aid of female members of Congress, even though they were usually not in a position of sufficient power to influence legislation.

Unlike white women, black women could not realistically look to Congress or the courts in the hope of finding a sympathetic black in the early twentieth century. In the Congress, black representation was sporadic after the peak period immediately following the Civil War and before the Compromise of 1877. George White of North Carolina, considered the last of the Reconstruction congressmen, ended his term in 1901. Early twentieth century black representation consisted of three congressmen from Chicago, Oscar De Priest, Arthur Mitchell and William Dawson, whose term began in 1943. Adam Clayton Powell came from New York City in 1944 to represent Harlem. These few blacks provided visibility and symbolic importance to issues which primarily affected blacks. In their early years in office they could offer little legislative assistance to black women because they lacked power in the committee system of Congress and in the Democratic party. Dawson and Powell served simultaneously and both finally attained sufficient seniority to become committee chairmen. Their ability to assist blacks, however, was limited, unless it involved legislation directly under the committee's jurisdiction.

The court system offered even less hope for addressing the issues of concern to black women. Blacks were excluded from becoming judges in the federal court system and were rarely able to rise to judgeships at the local or state level. Not until 1949 was William Hastie nominated to a judgeship on the U.S. Circuit Court of Appeals for the Third Circuit. It was 1961 before a black was appointed to a federal district court.

Because of the limitations of the legislative and judicial processes, black women found it necessary to use their organizations to bring pressure on the political society. The National Council of Negro Women (NCNW), founded in 1935, typifies the wide range of community problems that black women's organizations sought to address. Founded by Mary McLeod Bethune, NCNW now consists of twenty-nine black women's religious and pan-Hellenic organizations. Originally established as an umbrella organization, the NCNW clearly found it necessary to state that one of its purposes was to fight discrimination based on race and sex. The NCNW vowed

> to promote unity of action among women's national organizations and among all women in matters affecting the educational, cultural, economic, social, and political life of America.
>
> To work for the complete elimination of any and all forms of discrimination and segregation based on race, religion, color, national origin, or sex.[34]

As a pivotal organization among black women, the NCNW has been a pioneer in promoting civic education (later voter registration) among blacks during segregation, providing employment training for women, and fighting economic and political discrimination. Today, the NCNW is led by Dorothy Height who continues to promote the original goals through collaborative efforts with the established white organizations such as the American Association of University Women, the League of Women Voters and the National Federation of Business and Professional Women's Clubs.

During segregation, black women were without question excluded from white social and Greek letter organizations. Consequently, black sororities were founded at Howard University between 1900 and 1915 to address the social and intellectual needs of black women. Alpha Kappa Alpha, founded in 1908, set as its membership standards, "high scholarship, leadership, service, and character".[35] The sorority quickly expanded to other black college campuses. Although it functioned primarily as a social organization at the undergraduate level, it quickly grew to become a national organization with a service orientation. Because its members were among the better educated in the black community, they readily tackled political, economic and health issues which affected the entire community.

The Alpha Kappa Alpha sorority encouraged involvement in political activities, although it was limited in many ways because southern blacks could not participate in the political process. Marjorie Parker's history of the sorority shows that in the 1930s the sorority continued its interest in the passage of anti-lynching legislation, the elimination of segregated education, the plight of sharecroppers and tenant farmers, and supported the scholarly activities of the Association for the Study of Negro Life and History.

The sorority was keenly aware of the need to fight discrimination, and to keep the issue of racial injustice before Congress and before the public. To achieve these policy changes it decided in the 1930s to create

> a committee of members, preferably those living in the District of Columbia, to "work with the National Association for the Advancement of Colored People and inter-fraternal groups" to keep all the chapters of the organization informed of the situation surrounding the progress in Congress of legislation in which the group was interested.[36]

According to Parker, the sorority was especially interested in monitoring anti-lynching bills and fair employment legislation.

The underlying principles of the sorority stressed citizen participation. During segregation the sorority sought to participate in policy decisions that affected racial and religious minorities who were seeking to achieve integration.[37] To further citizen involvement the sorority established the Non-Partisan Council on Public Affairs. During the 1940s the Non-Partisan Council cooperated with national black organizations such as the NAACP, the Urban League, the National Association of Colored Women, the American Federation of Churches and the Brotherhood of Sleeping Car Porters in an effort to strengthen the fight for civil liberties and present the viewpoint of blacks in congressional hearings.[38] The council decided that its targets would be "discrimination in public life, disenfranchisement, lynching, and inequities in federal housing and hospitalization programs."[39]

Clearly, black sorority women were interested in improving the status of American women. However, because black women had to work with the handicaps of segregation, their priorities were the elimination of racial barriers and the enactment of legislation which would benefit blacks in general.

The Delta Sigma Theta sorority, founded in 1913, was also started at Howard University. Although originally thought of as a social organization, the Deltas saw their sorority as "a means of serving first the immediate community and, ultimately, the larger communities of race, region, and nation."[40] Even today, the Delta sorority "now lists herself as Public Service Organization rather than a 'social' sorority."[41]

Delta women were soon involved in contributing time and money to a number of organizations which promoted the causes of black women and the black community. Deltas served on the National Pan-Hellenic Council and the National Non-Partisan Council, the latter established by AKA women. Close ties were maintained with the National Council of Negro Women. Support was given to the American Council on Human Rights, a cooperative venture between AKA and the Deltas, which evolved out of the Non-Partisan Council. In addition, the sorority continued to monitor civil rights legislation.[42]

The history of the National Council of Negro Women and the Alpha Kappa Alpha and Delta Sigma Theta sororities reveals the seriousness with which black women worked for social and political causes during the early years of the twentieth century. Black women, however, found it necessary to give priority to issues which affected the general welfare of blacks, rather than to the narrower issues of women's rights that were of primary importance to white women. Operating under the double burden of racism and sexism, black women felt that it was necessary to establish broad-based, all-black organizations. Cynthia Neverdon-Morton's work on the black woman and interracial cooperation in women's clubs between 1895 and 1925 reaches a similar conclusion. She found that

> the combined efforts of black and white women working for common concerns would not become a reality until after 1925. The period 1895-1925 witnessed, however, the beginning of cooperation among the races and sexes. Black women had attempted to work with whites, but found it easier to work alone, to develop and strengthen their own organization, and, in later years, to merge with whites when necessary.[43]

Since black women retreated to form their own organizations at the turn of the century, the conditions of black women and white women have changed considerably. The civil rights movement of the 1950s and 1960s finally abolished the segregationist laws of the South and eliminated many of the de facto segregation practices in northern cities. However, women regardless of race benefited from the civil rights laws which were enacted primarily to insure the rights of blacks. Legislation of critical importance to all women were Title VII of the 1964 Civil Rights Act, the Equal Pay Act of 1963, and Title IX of the 1972 Education Amendments. For the first time legislation clearly spelled out a number of types of discrimination. Now that sexual discrimination had been identified, it highlighted the fact that all American women shared a common bond based on sexism. The removal of segregation as a potential issue separating women served to magnify the deep-rooted nature of sexism in this society.

The civil rights movement also left as its legacy the concept that the electoral system was truly a potentially powerful tool for redirecting policy and setting priorities on the political agenda. Blacks were trying to implement their long-held belief that the power of the vote would enable them to fight effectively discriminatory policy.[44] Once the organizational skills, along with the techniques of formulating political strategy, had been learned from their apprenticeship in the civil rights movement in such organizations as SNCC and CORE, white women found that their energies could be focused on women's issues.

New Political Women

In the 1980s women have entered a new political era. Twenty years since the women's movement of the 1960s, black women have been elected to the U.S. House of Representatives while white women sit in the U.S. Senate and on the Supreme Court. Women have served as cabinet members, governors and mayors. Although women are not a commonplace in all political settings, they are no longer an oddity in public office. The 1984 election had the potential of bringing together American women—black, white, Hispanic, Asian and Native American—in a massive electoral effort. There was heightened political involvement as women organized voter registration drives, served on presidential campaign staffs, and ran for municipal, state and national office.

By the summer of 1984 women had reached a new stage of political sophistication, which was characterized by a cooperative effort across racial lines. The goal was to get women to vote and to elect candidates, male or female, who supported women's issues. Three factors influenced this political development: the creation and sustained electoral efforts of women's organizations, the increased role of women in party politics, and the policies of President Reagan which adversely affected women across class and racial lines. Tangible results of the 1960s women's movement can be seen in the establishment of the National Organization for Women, the National Women's Political Caucus and the Women's Campaign Fund. These organizations are significant because of their longevity, their ability to politically educate the female population, and their continuing efforts to promote female political candidates. While these organizations have not always been successful in achieving their goals, they have inspired female political participation through their support for passage of the ERA, for reform in delegate selection in the Democratic party, and for female candidates seeking public office.

The National Women's Political Caucus exemplifies these new organizations. Founded in 1971 after the ERA amendment was defeated,
female activists decided to establish a

> national organization dedicated exclusively to increasing
> women's participation in all areas of political and public life—as
> elected and appointed officials, as delegates to national party con-
> ventions, as judges in the state and federal courts, and as lobby-
> ists, voters, and campaign organizers.[45]

Therefore, these women set as their task the election of women to Congress, state legislatures and city halls in their effort to insure that legislation was introduced and enacted which would eliminate sex
discrimination.

Psychologically, the NWPC provided a support network to women
who wanted to become more involved in politics and run for public
office. As an interest group the NWPC provided a legitimacy for
women who were amateur politicians, who were just learning how to
run a campaign and seek serious financial supporters. Although the
NWPC may have initially been dismissed as another strident women's
group, it quickly served notice on the political establishment that it
was a serious newcomer on the national political scene.

The NWPC played a major role in making women a significant political factor. Over the years the caucus has built an impressive record
of political successes and increased the number of women in the political and policymaking process. The NWPC can point to a number of
political accomplishments in helping to bring about delegate selection
reforms within the Democratic and Republican parties, helping to defeat candidates who did not favor women's issues, and assisting women
to build effective political action committees and coalitions.[46] Within
the political parties, women have sought to become more full-fledged
members of the policymaking process. The greater number of women
attending national conventions and serving on standing committees
has increased the role of women within the parties.

The NWPC has brought continued pressure on candidates to support the appointment of more women to policymaking positions.
Through the creation of the Coalition for Women's Appointments in
1976, the NWPC has joined forty-nine women's organizations in its
ongoing efforts to increase the number of female political appointees.
The Coalition for Women's Appointments has been able to show that
within a three-year period the number of women in full-time appointed
positions increased by 10 percent.[47]

Judicial appointments have been equally important to the objectives of the NWPC. After the passage of the Omnibus Judgeship Act,
pressure from women helped push the number of women in federal

judgeships from five to forty-one in 1980. Legislative priorities stressed the defeat of anti-abortion amendments in the U.S. House and Senate in 1979. Simultaneously, the NWPC continued its efforts to secure passage of the ERA amendment. By 1981, the NWPC had joined with other groups in a one million dollar media campaign to target four key states in the ERA campaign.

The NWPC continues to work to elect women to public office. Through the formation of political action committes and its 1982 "Win with Women" campaign, the NWPC could point to a record number of 1,666 women who filed as candidates. This push to get more women elected resulted in a 10 percent increase in the number of women state legislators throughout the country.[48]

Through the caucus politically active women, regardless of race, were able to gain political skills and experience, learn firsthand about the politics of running for office, and become more active members of their respective political party as convention delegates.

New Black Organizations

While the NWPC and NOW were growing and attaining momentum, primarily among white women, black women were reevaluating their position in American society. A new, younger generation than the women who built the sororities and the older established organizations felt that it was necessary to form a new network among black women, one which emphasized political participation and economic development. Of these new organizations which focused on the concerns of black women, the Coalition of 100 Black Women founded in New York City in the mid-1970s has become a national organization with chapters in major U.S. cities.[49] The coalition was formed because black women felt that economic and political empowerment were the cornerstones of a black women's advocacy group.[50] Composed of professional women, businesswomen, government workers and community activists between the ages of twenty and sixty, coalition chapters focus on a number of issues including teenage pregnancies, criminal justice, political action and scholarship development. The coalition stresses voter registration and mobilization because it is considered a "basic program initiative of the national network of women's organizations."[51]

In the last five years, other organizations have been started by black women which stress political issues rather than the social concerns of the earlier groups. The formation of the Black Women's Agenda, the National Institute of Women of Color and the Black Women's Roundtable on Voter Participation indicates that black women have reached a new stage of political sophistication. These new organizations attempt to solve problems which are of primary importance to the black community. However, in this post-civil rights movement era, black women also seek to work with women across racial and ethnic lines. Unlike the sororities and black professional associations which were established during segregation, these new groups did not form as a response to their exclusion from white organizations. Unlike the turn-of-the-century activists, these women came together to form networks not based on church affiliations or school ties. These organizers sought to mobilize black women from a wide range of backgrounds to tackle the persistent political and economic problems that undermine the social and economic health of the black community.

One example of these new organizations is the National Institute for Women of Color (NIWC), founded in 1981 as a non-profit organization. The NIWC seeks to bring together groups of women who have traditionally been isolated in order to "enhance the strengths of diversity and to promote educational and economic equity for women of color (Black, Hispanic, Asian American, American Indian, Alaska Native, and Pacific Islander)."[52] Unity is sought by employing the all-encompassing phrase, "women of color," rather than the narrower and potentially divisive term "minority." Among the NIWC's many objectives is to function as a network which

> links women on various issues and programs, promote[s] women of color for positions on boards and commissions, and to promote [sic] cooperative efforts between general women's organizations and women of color, while raising awareness about issues and principles of feminism.[53]

The NIWC was not conceived as a membership organization which would compete with the many existing groups demanding the attention of women; instead it was designed as a support structure that would complement the efforts of existing organizations.

Clearly, the emergence and continued growth of women's political organizations attest to the fact that black women and white women have come a long way in their struggle to reach political maturity. No longer amateurs, women have made some significant political gains— they have lobbied Congress, they have established political action committees, they have achieved equal delegate representation in the Democratic party, and they have campaigned in support of ERA state-by-state. Yet women have not reached their full potential in electoral politics. In order to influence national policy, women must elect more women to key offices, promote legislative issues of priority to women, and lobby to purge the statute books of antiquated laws which are discriminatory toward women.

The Political Potential—1984

The 1984 presidential election provided an opportunity for women to bring their collective efforts together to fulfill the suffragists' dream of women becoming a real force in politics. Bella Abzug and Eleanor Smeal, senior strategists and longtime activists, wrote that women could determine the outcome of the presidential election.[54] This optimistic outlook was based on the fact that women constituted a majority of the voters in every age category, and that polls from the 1980 election showed that women perceived political issues differently from men, thus constituting a gender gap. These two factors, coupled with the increased voter registration drives among women spearheaded by the Women's Vote Project, were supposed to be sufficient to defeat Ronald Reagan and his anti-female policies.

This voting potential is obvious from the population data which show that women constitute approximately 53 percent of the voting-age population. *The Women's Vote Beyond the Nineteenth Amendment*,[55] published by the League of Women Voters Education Fund, gives a breakdown of women by voting age based on census data, revealing that women constitute a majority in every age category.

- 18-20-year-old voters are 50.5% female
- 35-44-year-old voters are 51.4% female
- 45-54-year-old voters are 51.8% female
- 65-74-year-old voters are 56.6% female
- Over 74-year-old voters are 63.4% female

Not only do women have the strength of raw numbers, but they also have an additional potential of influencing elections because of the significance of the gender gap.

During the 1980 presidential campaign, the gender gap was officially recognized by Democratic presidential contenders and belatedly acknowledged by Republicans as a potential source of female power. An examination of Gallup poll data shows that "women have voted differently than men in every presidential election since 1952."[56] What has changed is that this difference in voting behavior has "only recently been measured, tracked, fostered, and generally christened by the political powers that be."[57]

When President Reagan won by a wide margin, the differences in attitudes between men and women created a significant gap across "all education, economic, geographic, and occupational borders."[58] In analyzing the 1980 election, the pollsters noted the largest gender gap ever recorded.[59] Reagan's budget-cutting policies heightened the significance of the gender gap, which persisted through the 1982 mid-term election. President Reagan's popularity polls showed a gender gap between four and seventeen points, with an average of nine points.[60] Undoubtedly, women continued to be dissatisfied with Reagan's position on the ERA, pay equity, affirmative action, insurance equity, comprehensive child care, and pension reform.[61] Women could see and feel the continued economic discrimination when studies showed that college-educated women still earned only sixty-one cents for every dollar earned by a male.

The passage of the ERA remained a priority issue among women in white-dominated political organizations. Election day 1980 exit polls conducted by CBS/New York Times showed that "eleven percent of the women ranked ERA/abortion as their two top priorities compared to five percent men."[62] Louis Harris polls taken in 1982 supported the view that women constituted a solid bloc on the ERA/abortion issue. The war/foreign policy issue also consistently separated men from women. When asked are you afraid Reagan will get us into war, women showed a gender gap maximum of twenty-two points in September 1983 and a minimum of eight points in March 1982.[63]

Black women too exhibited a gender gap. The Joint Center for Political Studies noted that "more black women than black men vote, both in absolute numbers and as a percentage of the population."[64] The Joint Center added,

> Between the 1976 and 1980 presidential elections, the percentage of eligible black men voting increased slightly, from 42.7 percent to 47.5 percent. The proportion of eligible black women voting increased from 49.9 percent to 52.8 percent.[65]

Gender gap issues are real to women. To translate political power into action, women in over sixty-five national organizations came together in the Women's Vote Project. This unprecedented, non-partisan coalition effort exhibited political sophistication and emphasized the potential strength of a united effort. The project sought to register women who were

> lower-income, less educated, single head of households, young working women, White, Black, Hispanic, Asian and Native American—all traditionally under-registered and under-voting.[66]

Each organization was committed to registering new voters, beginning with their own members.

The Women's Vote Project demonstrates a concerted effort on the part of black women and white women to work together for a common goal. Now that segregation is no longer an issue, black women and white women find that their political goals are quite similar, although their priorities may still differ. Black women, especially those in the sororities, have been involved in the Voter Education Project since 1962.[67] Now black women are helping white, Hispanic, Asian-American and Native American women learn these same political skills.

The Reagan political climate has fostered the formation of the Black Women's Roundtable on Voter Participation, composed of representatives from national black women's organizations. The group holds discussions on "important objectives and concerns of their collective memberships." In addition, they work to bridge "the 'gap' between the political views of black and white women."[68]

Black women are acutely aware of the irony of a national voter project led by white women's organizations, especially since blacks have suffered more from discriminatory policies and have extensive experience in voter registration due to previous exclusion from the electoral process.[69] Although a sizable number of black women and white women are opposed to Ronald Reagan's policies, black women are still worse off. Today black women are still at the bottom of the economic scale, especially those who head almost one-half of black families.[70] Over 70 percent of these female-headed families live in poverty.[71] Rates of unemployment remain high for black women, while "their average salaries are the lowest for any group."[72]

An underlying tension between black women and white women was present in the Women's Vote Project. By the summer of 1984 when the Democratic convention was to take place in San Francisco, this tension had mounted considerably as black women and white women clashed over the issue of Geraldine Ferraro as the vice-presidential nominee. White women pushed the gender issue, while blacks saw the selection of a black candidate as the priority.

Early in the 1984 presidential campaign, Jesse Jackson had made race a factor in Democratic party politics. Jackson's candidacy for the presidency raised questions of the seriousness of party support for a black candidate, the fairness of Democratic party rules, and the viability of a black candidate on the national ticket. As the convention was about to open, white women activists achieved their goal of securing a white female as the vice-presidential nominee. This triumph only exacerbated the tenuous relationship with black women and served to heighten the long-standing issue of gender versus racial priorities in candidate selection.

Blacks and the Democratic Party

Since Franklin D. Roosevelt was elected president in 1932, blacks have solidly supported the Democratic party. Although Mondale had critics among the black delegates, he retained a strong core of loyal black supporters. In some cases blacks favored Jackson's candidacy, but this had been primarily a political move which was limited to convention politics. The plan was to insure that in the convention, Jackson had delegate support which he could use as a bargaining tool.

Jackson's candidacy had focused media attention on blacks as a special interest group within the Democratic party and as a potential voting bloc during the election. The general assessment was that since Jackson could not win the Democratic nomination, he might try to use his influence over black delegates as a tool to obtain concessions from Walter Mondale. The possibility that Jackson might make demands on Mondale created uncertainty for women and other interest groups because Jackson's role was unique. No previous black had been such a serious contender for national office and won such substantial electoral support from blacks and whites in the primary contests.

Although Jackson's overall strategy was not clear, women felt assured long before the convention that he would not seek the vice-presidential slot and that Mondale would be unlikely to offer him the position. With Jackson eliminated as a possibility, women pressed Mondale to review local and national level, female elected officials as possible running mates. The review process included black and Hispanic males but no black females as potential running mates. This oversight was criticized by black female delegates who saw white feminists pressuring Mondale by threatening a fight on the convention floor if a women was not selected as his running mate.[73]

Female strategists thought that a women would be an asset on the Democratic ticket. Veteran political observers took a dimmer view. They viewed a female candidate as only adding fuel to the charges that the Democrats were held captive by special interest groups. Indeed, columnist George Will was led to see Mondale "as the wimp who was bullied by the National Organization for Women."[74]

Women won their battle for a female vice-presidential candidate, but it was costly. This tactical move was part of an overall strategy for women to use their voting potential to achieve their rightful place in American politics and society. This effort was based on a number of false assumptions that resulted in damaging the coalition efforts between black women and white women, and in diminishing the role of women within the Democratic party as a special group which deserved attention.

Those women who lobbied for Mondale to select a female vice-presidential running mate did not understand the mood of the American electorate. Mondale or any Democratic presidential candidate was considered to be fighting an uphill battle against a popular president.

Consequently, to add a female to the ticket, rather than to follow the traditional route of adding a white Protestant male to the ticket, was a calculated risk. The women were betting that a sufficient number of voters could be attracted to the Democratic ticket on the basis of factors such as Ferraro's gender, Catholicism, and Italian-American heritage. This assumption rested on the flimsy idea that voters, especially females, were so dissatisfied with Reagan's policies that they would vote Mondale, and that Ferraro would attract a number of voters strictly based on gender. The factors of gender, religion and ethnic heritage were assumed to be stronger than Reagan's popularity.

The advocates of a female candidate misunderstood the potential negative reaction from white males, particularly southerners, as well as women who were more family- rather than career-oriented. Yes, there were women who were elated to see Ferraro become the Democratic vice-presidential nominee. There was a gender gap between how these women felt about issues and how men perceived issues. The problem was that the gender gap was shallow; it only made a difference in a few Senate races, not in presidential politics.[75] The depth of the gender gap was sorely overestimated. East Coast women did not understand the more politically conservative outlook of southern and midwestern women, who saw no urgency for a female candidate.

Early in the primary season several political analysts questioned the electoral base of Mondale's support, since it appeared that the New Deal coalition had been splintered by Reagan's 1980 victory. Would the urban ethnic groups and southern whites give the Democrats their support in 1984? Labor leaders had decided to support Mondale and blacks had remained with the Democratic party. Mondale's ability to attract the traditional southern vote was in doubt. Two factors, Jesse Jackson's candidacy with his emphasis on racial issues and the selection of a female Catholic as a running mate, dearly cost Mondale voters among southern white males. Jackson was a detriment to Mondale's efforts because he had been so telegenic. Jackson had a flair for capturing media attention, demonstrated in the politically risky venture of rescuing Lieutenant Goodman. By injecting himself into this issue, Jackson became involved in foreign affairs and captured the attention of the international press. Jackson's flamboyant rhetoric with its racial overtones drove some southern male Democrats to vote Republican.

Ferraro's candidacy in no way increased Mondale's appeal among southern voters. Southern women still saw themselves in traditional roles centered around the home and family. Geraldine Ferraro represented a fast-talking, abrasive female from a northern city. Southerners thought that she might be a capable congresswoman from New

York City, but they did not feel it was time for the nation to elect a female vice-president.

Reaction of Black Women to Ferraro's Candidacy

The Ferraro candidacy caused a break in the pre-convention coalition among black women and white women. The drive to have a female on the ticket, as a priority before the selection of black candidate, pushed black women to form a new political organization. Black women at the Democratic convention felt that they had been overlooked by the Democratic party and by those who had worked to get Ferraro on the ticket. Not only were black women excluded from consideration as vice-presidential candidates, but they were also initially excluded from policymaking positions on Ferraro's campaign staff.

Black women felt strongly that their position within the Democratic party had been minimized to such an extent that they needed to form a new organization which "focused solely on the political power of black women."[76] Leaders of this strictly political organization were: C. Delores Tucker, vice-chair of the Democratic National Committee; Shirley Chisholm, former congresswoman; Dorothy Height, president of the National Council of Negro Women; Mary Berry, a member of the U.S. Commission on Civil Rights; Eleanor Holmes Norton of Georgetown Law School; Addie Wyatt, a labor leader; Jewel Jackson McCabe, president of the Coalition of 100 Black Women; the presidents of the black sororities; and numerous black females who were elected officials. Jesse Jackson also pledged support for this black women's organization.

The establishment of the Black Women's Political Caucus, which is now known as the National Political Congress of Black Women, marks a turning point in black political development. Black women, many of whom were civil rights activists, had long felt the need to separate themselves from white women's organizations. As Shirley Chisholm, the chair of the Congress of Black Women, pointed out, it was time for black women to stop being mere appendages, trying to get a little input into the decision-making process.[77] Again, as had happened so often in the past, black women found it necessary to establish an organization led by themselves that would set the priorities on the political agenda. No longer were black women to play the role of political broker between the white power structure and the black community. Black women were now to be a part of the political process as peers, not subordinates, to white women.

The necessity of establishing an all black women's organization at this time points to the failure of the white women's organizations to accept black women as their equals in leadership positions. Black women also found that existing organizations were inadequate for meeting the political priorities of black women.

The Congress of Black Women sees the political process as the route for achieving full participation in American society. The congress outlines its mission as follows:

- To encourage every Black women to engage in political activity beginning with registering to vote.
- To train Black women to understand the political process and how to operate effectively within it.
- To develop and encourage Black women to run for office at all levels.
- To endorse and support candidates for public office.
- To provide financial support for candidates for public office.
- To encourage the appointment of Black women at all levels of government and political parties.
- To develop and advocate public policy positions.[78]

Ferraro's candidacy had again raised the prickly issue of political priorities among women activists.

The Unused Potential

What are the implications of this split between black women and white women for the future of women as an emerging power bloc? The potential remains for American women to decide the outcome of future presidential elections because women constitute a majority of the voters. However, perhaps the more important question is, what is the prospect of black women and white women cooperating to achieve political power?

The formation of the Congress of Black Women serves notice on white women and both political parties that black women realize their potential electoral power and that they intend to use it. The unity of black women is greater than ever before because politically-based organizations now attract black women across all class lines. Black women remain keenly aware of their status, which is still circumscribed by racial and gender discrimination.

The future role of women in American politics will be shaped by both black women and white women. Black women, however, are now going to take a more aggressive position because they wish to remove the "disparity between the numerical voting strength of black women and the low percentage of public offices they hold."[79] Results of the

1984 election show that "nearly sixty percent of black women voted, the highest turnout among any group in the country."[80] Yet, black women can point to only one black female in Congress and account for less than one percent of elected officials.[81]

This sorry state of black female representation is not due to apathy, but rather to a previous lack of political mobilization led by black women. Black women have been politically involved since the pre-Civil War abolitionist societies. Only since the civil rights movement of the 1960s, however, have black women made a concerted effort to seek elective office. In the 1980s black women have really begun to assert themselves in electoral politics.

Prior to the 1984 election, black women were "vot[ing] more than any other sex/race group in the population."[82] This startling finding runs contrary to the generally accepted theories of voting behavior which contend that the higher the socioeconomic level, the greater the participation rate. These findings have confounded the researchers of female voting behavior. Marjorie Lansing concluded her study on the note that:

> Overall, a key finding is that black Americans, and especially black female Americans, do not fit the model of voting from the predictions developed over several decades. The themes of alienation, interest theory, mass participation theory, feminist theory—all relate to the mosaic of voting as described in this presentation. A deeper understanding of the specific relations among these factors will become feasible only when more extensive data become available—data designed specifically to explore black culture and not the white superculture.[83]

The 1983 Baxter and Lansing study[84] of women and politics attempted to go beyond the usual factors of education, occupation, income, age and marital status. Baxter and Lansing looked at black women in terms of their relationship to feminism. It became important to have a greater understanding of how black women perceived themselves when they are subjected to both racial and gender discrimination.

The economic situation for black women has always been different from that of white women. A key difference has been the fact that since slavery black women have had to work outside the home, which has made them far more economically independent than white women. They are also more likely to be the sole support of their families.

The most plausible hypothesis for the high voting rates for black females is that their unique position as victims of gender and racial discrimination spurs political participation. According to Baxter and Lansing, "increased awareness of discrimination should be associated with higher voting rates among black women."[85] In conclusion, Baxter and Lansing admit that they could not pinpoint one "explanatory theory which totally account[s] for the unique voting record of black women and their recent political activism."[86] Part of the problem is a lack of adequate research on voting patterns of black women. Most of the U.S. Census data only show a male/female breakdown for voting. Rarely do the census studies specify females by race.

Citing sociologist Joyce Ladner's work on black women, Baxter and Lansing suggest "that black women have filled roles almost the reverse of those held by white women."[87] It appears that black women—the young, well-educated, those who are members of the new black women's organizations—are keenly aware that their position is hampered by dual discrimination.[88] In response to their situation, Baxter and Lansing found that black women "have begun to join together in an effort to promote their own interests in a political system, which in the past, has excluded them almost entirely."[89]

Black women are not about to be left behind in running for public office. Again, the numbers show that black women are outstripping white women. According to the Joint Center for Political Studies, "the number of black elected officials nationwide rose by 8.6 percent between July 1982 and July 1983. As of July 1983, there were 5,606 black elected officials, up from 5,160 in July 1982."[90] The Joint Center found that

> the increase in the number of female black elected officials was larger than the overall increase: 13.1 percent. As of July 1983, some 22 percent of all black elected officials—1,223—were women. By contrast, only about 10 percent of all elected officials are women.[91]

To place the total number of black elected officials in perspective, the Joint Center noted that even with the increase in the number of black officeholders, "blacks hold only 1.1 percent of the elective offices in the country."[92]

Women are running for political office more and more often. The Center for the American Woman and Politics reported that as of 1984, women held 13.4 percent of the seats in state legislatures. Of the 993 women in state legislatures, blacks constituted 6.2 percent (sixty-two out of 993). Hispanic women accounted for less than 1 percent or only seven of the 993. In state government, three white women served as lieutenant governors, and Kentucky had a female governor. None of the governors, lieutenant governors or other statewide elective officeholders are black women.[93] Black women are participating in the political process, but to date they have fared poorly in electoral contests.

Conclusion

Ferraro's candidacy assured that future female candidates would be taken seriously by journalists, pollsters and party leaders. The potential of women as a voting bloc will no longer be ignored. Yet, this potential could become irreparably split into two camps, one of black women and one of white women.

Black women feel that, without question, they supported the Democratic party and Ferraro's candidacy. But the women who originally supported Ferraro's candidacy have shown little reciprocal support for black women and their political priorities. Longtime black activists are not likely to forget that Shirley Chisholm's 1972 campaign for the presidency, as well as Jesse Jackson's 1984 bid for the nomination, received no significant support from white women and their organizations.

Black women have clearly demonstrated their loyalty to the Democratic party. Election results, however, show that Reagan won such an overwhelming victory that a large percentage of white women had to have voted for the Republican ticket, showing that women who supported Ferraro's candidacy were unable to deliver the vote to the Democratic party. This is an expensive error which has caused white females to lose standing among Democrats. White female activists should now retreat to a lower level of visibility and take a less demanding position in the Democratic party.

Black women are in a completely different position because they have never pushed the Democratic party to take such a bold political risk as Ferraro's candidacy. Previous black demands have been a challenge to the Democratic party internally, rather than a challenge to American voters which tested the strength of party identification among longtime supporters such as Catholics, white ethnics and southern whites.

Under the dynamic leadership of Shirley Chisholm, black women are now ready to throw the support of their 69.5 percent registration rate and their 59.2 percent turnout rate behind black female candidates.[94] As a growing organization, the Congress of Black Women has attracted nearly two thousand members, held its first national convention where it drafted sixty-eight resolutions, and established a long-range fund raising plan.[95] These black women will stress developing an effective national network for political candidates, plan training sessions for potential candidates, and raise funds for political campaigns with the goal of achieving the political empowerment of black women.

Politically active black women have declared that they will no longer be subordinate to white female leaders, nor brokers for the black community. Those women who faithfully supported the 1984 Democratic ticket feel that although they have paid their dues, white women will not accept them as equals with legitimate polical priorities. Now that black women have stepped aside for the Ferraro candidacy, it remains to be seen to what extent white activists will cooperate with blacks to realize the full, but not adequately mobilized, potential of women in the electoral process.

NOTES

[1] Ethel Klein, *Gender Politics* (Cambridge, Mass.: Harvard University Press, 1984), p. 154.

[2] See Gerald M. Pomper, "The Presidential Election," in Gerald M. Pomper, et al., *The Election of 1984* (Chatham, N. J.: Chatham House Publishers, 1984), pp. 63, 66.

[3] Angela Davis, *Women, Race and Class* (New York: Vintage Books, 1983), p. 34.

[4] Ibid., p. 39.

[5] Ibid., pp. 46-47.

[6] Rosalyn Terborg-Penn, "Discrimination Against Afro-American Women in Women's Movement, 1830-1920," in Sharon Harley and Rosalyn Terborg-Penn, eds., *The Afro-American Woman* (Port Washington, N. Y.: Kennikat Press, 1978), p. 18.

[7] Ibid.

[8] Ibid., p. 19.

[9] Davis, op. cit., pp. 50-53. See also Judith Hole and Ellen Levine, "The First Feminists," in Jo Freeman, ed., *Women: A Feminist Perspective* (Palo Alto, Cal.: Mayfield Publishing, 1984), pp. 536-537.

[10] Davis, op. cit., p. 51.

[11] Ibid., pp. 53-54, 57.

[12] Ibid., p. 53.

[13] Ibid., p. 57.

[14] Terborg-Penn, op. cit., p. 20.

[15] Ibid., pp. 20-21.

[16] Davis, op. cit., p. 75.

[17] Ibid.

[18] Ibid., p. 77.

[19] Ibid.

[20]Terborg-Penn, op. cit., p. 21.

[21]Ibid., p. 23, quoting J. W. Gibson and W. H. Crogman, *Progress of a Race, or The Remarkable Advancement of the Colored American* (Naperville, Ill.: J. L. Nichols, 1902, 1912), pp. 181-182.

[22]Hole and Levine, op. cit., p. 541.

[23]Ibid.

[24]See Paula Giddings, *When and Where I Enter* (New York: William Morrow and Co., 1984); and Sara Evans, *Personal Politics* (New York: Vintage Books, 1980).

[25]Evans, op. cit., p. 82.

[26]See Jo Freeman, *The Politics of Women's Liberation* (New York: David McKay Co., 1975), pp. 52-53.

[27]Betty Friedan, *The Feminine Mystique* (New York: Dell Publishing, 1963), p. 16.

[28]Ibid., p. 57.

[29]Ibid., p. 321.

[30]Ibid., p. 324.

[31]Cynthia Neverdon-Morton, "The Black Woman's Struggle for Equality in the South," in Harley and Terborg-Penn, op. cit., p. 50.

[32]Some of these organizations and their founding dates are:

- Colored Women's League, 1892.

- National Federation of Afro-American Women, 1895.

    (The above two groups merged in 1896 to become the National Association of Colored Women.)

- Women's League of Lynchburg, Virginia, 1897.

- Neighborhood Union, Atlanta, 1911.

- Delta Sigma Theta, 1913.

- Alpha Suffrage Club of Chicago, 1914.

- School Teacher's League, 1916.

- Alpha Kappa Alpha, 1916.

- Women's League of Washington, D.C., 1982.

[33]Telephone conversation with Ms. Johanna Green, Director, Young People's Division of The Women's Missionary Society, African Methodist Episcopal Church (April 1984).

[34]Mary Elizabeth Vroman, *Shaped To Its Purpose: Delta Sigma Theta, The First 50 Years* (New York: Random House, 1965), p. 102.

[35]Marjorie Parker, *Alpha Kappa Alpha, 1908-1958* (AKA Sorority, 1958), p. 1.

[36]Ibid., p. 50.

[37]Ibid.

[38]Ibid., pp. 54-55.

[39]Ibid., p. 54.

[40]Vroman, op. cit., p. 5.

[41]Ibid.

[42]Ibid., p. 99.

[43]Neverdon-Morton, op. cit., p. 56.

[44]See Giddings, op. cit.

[45]National Women's Political Caucus, "About the Caucus," brochure (Washington, D.C.: National Women's Political Caucus, 1984), p. 1.

[46]Ibid.

[47]Ibid.

[48]Ibid., pp. 2-7.

[49]Interview with Julie Dade, member of the Washington, D.C. Chapter of the Coalition of 100 Black Women (March 1984).

[50]Telephone interview with De Vera Redman, president of the Washington, D.C. Chapter of the Coalition of 100 Black Women (April 1984).

[51]Ibid.

[52]National Institute for Women of Color, *Report of the 1982 National Strategies Conference for Women of Color* (Washington, D.C.: National Institute for Women of Color, 1982), p. 1.

[53]Ibid.

[54]See Eleanor Smeal, *Why and How Women Will Elect the Next President* (New York: Harper & Row, 1984); and Bella Abzug, *Gender Gap* (Boston: Houghton Mifflin Company, 1984).

[55]Mary Stone, Marlene Cohn and Matthew Freeman, *The Women's Vote: Beyond the Nineteenth Amendment* (Washington, D.C.: League of Women Voters Education Fund, 1983), p. 3.

[56]National Women's Political Caucus, "The Women's Vote: The Numbers, The Issues, The Impact," brochure (Washington, D.C.: National Women's Political Caucus, February 1984), p. 3.

[57]Ibid., p. 1.

[58]Ibid., p. 2.

[59]Ibid.

[60]Ibid., p. 3.

[61]Ibid., p. 5. For a detailed discussion of the issues, see Smeal, op. cit., and Abzug, op. cit.

[62]NWPC, "The Women's Vote," op. cit., p. 6. See also Klein, op. cit.

[63]NWPC, "The Women's Vote," op. cit., p. 8.

[64]"A Black Gender Gap?" *Focus* 12:10 (October 1983): 7.

[65]Ibid.

[66]The Women's Vote Project, "It's a man's world. unless women vote!" brochure (Washington, D.C.: The Women's Vote Project, 1984).

[67]Coalition of Black Voter Participation, Inc., "Black Women's Round-table on Voter Participation" (1984), p. 2.

[68]Ibid.

[69]Ibid.

[70]Ibid.

[71]Ibid.

[72]Ibid.

[73]Gerald M. Pomper, "The Nominations," in Pomper, et al., op. cit., p. 24.

[74]George Will, "Machiavelli from Minnesota?" *Newsweek* (July 16, 1984): 88, quoted in Pomper, "The Nominations," op. cit., p. 25.

[75]Ethel Klein, "The Gender Gap: Different Issues, Different Answers," *The Brookings Review* 3:2 (Winter 1985): 35.

[76]Dorothy Gilliam, "Womanpower," *The Washington Post* (August 6, 1984), p. 81, and "Women Upset Over Small Convention Role Regroup," *Jet* 65:22 (August 6, 1984): 55.

[77]Gilliam, "Womanpower," ibid.

[78]The National Black Women's Political Caucus, Statement of Purpose and Mission (1985).

[79]Dorothy Gilliam, "The Clout of Black Women," *The Washington Post* (June 13, 1985), p. C3.

[80]Ibid.

[81]Ibid.

[82]Ibid.

[83]Marjorie Lansing, "The Voting Patterns of American Black Women," in Marianne Githens and Jewel Prestage, eds., *The Portrait of Marginality: The Political Behavior of American Women* (New York: David McKay Co., 1977), pp. 392-393.

[84]Sandra Baxter and Marjorie Lansing, *Women and Politics* (Ann Arbor, Mich.: University of Michigan Press, 1983), pp. 102-112.

[85]Ibid.

[86]Ibid., p. 110.

[87]Ibid., p. 111.

[88]Ibid., p. 112.

[89]Ibid.

[90]"News from the Joint Center For Political Studies" (Washington, D.C: January 8, 1984), p. 1.

[91]Ibid.

[92]Ibid., p. 2.

[93]Center for the American Women and Politics, "Women in Elective Office," Fact Sheet (New Brunswick, N.J.: Eagleton Institute of Politics, Rutgers University, n.d.).

[94]Julie Dade, "Redividing the Political Pie," *Focus* 14:7 (July 1985): 6.

[95]Ibid.

FURTHER CONSEQUENCES OF DOUBLE JEOPARDY: THE RELUCTANT PARTICIPATION OF RACIAL-ETHNIC WOMEN IN FEMINIST ORGANIZATIONS

Elizabeth M. Almquist

North Texas State University

Racial-ethnic[1] women experience a unique situation in American life. They are dual minorities, but their particular situation is not simply the additive result of being both nonwhite and non-male. Instead, their dual minority statuses interact to produce distinct life conditions and perspectives. These conditions and perspectives are not precisely comparable to either those of their male counterparts or those of white women. These conditions influence the resources racial-ethnic women have available to commit to any social movement, the ideological/ value commitments minority women possess, the grievances they consider most pressing, the likelihood of participating in any social movements at all, and the specific probability of choosing to participate in some type of minority group movement rather than some type of feminist movement.

Placing the unique situation of racial-ethnic women in perspective requires taking a broad historical view of their lives in this country. Unfortunately, it also requires neglecting significant variations within individual racial-ethnic groups as well as brushing aside major differences among various groups. Nonetheless, it will be argued that several groups of minority women—blacks, Mexican Americans, certain Asian groups and Native Americans—have experienced broadly comparable historical and contemporary circumstances. These circumstances are sufficiently similar that, for purposes of understanding social movement participation, they can be described within one perspective.

Historical Perspective on Racial-Ethnic Groups

Among several possible social science perspectives, the internal colonial model provides the most useful interpretation of the unique situation of racial and ethnic groups in this country. Despite the fact that it focuses attention primarily on men, this perspective highlights the fact that racial-ethnic women have most of their significant social interaction within the confines of their particular racial-ethnic group. Indeed, the minority experience is a "crucible of identity." Identification with one's own ethnic group is both temporally and emotionally prior to identification with any other issue area. The experience of colonial domination and its associated racism has brought about this state of affairs.

The internal colonial model recognizes that the United States has practiced a number of policies which placed racial-ethnic minorities in roughly the same situation in which European powers placed the residents of the territories they conquered. England, France and Spain colonized external groups; the United States—formerly a colony itself—colonized groups within its own borders. In dealing with its internal colonies, the United States had a unique advantage. There were several racial-ethnic groups competing with each other; this competition kept labor costs so low that capitalists could reap huge profits. Internal colonial policies, both formal and informal, focused on admission, exploitation and control of racial-ethnic minorities. The formal policies were designed by a government which had been heavily influenced by the interests of capital. The informal, but no less oppressive, policies were designed and implemented by capitalists themselves. In all this, white workers were unwitting, but willing, participants.

Robert Blauner[2] identified five key features of internal colonialism which together led to economic (and, I would add, political) suppression of minorities. These features were applied with varying intensity to different groups. They are visible today in the lower socioeconomic status of minorities as compared to whites. How much lower is in direct proportion to the extent of colonization.

The first three features of Blauner's model involve political and social oppression which facilitate economic exploitation. These are involuntary entry of the minority into this country, attempts to suppress or strip away the native culture of the minority, and largely successful efforts to control the minority by establishing white-dominated bureaucracies. These features are most apparent in the harsh treatment accorded Native Americans, blacks and Mexican Americans. They are less apparent, but no less real, in the lives of Asian Americans, Puerto

Ricans and Cubans. These latter groups have higher socioeconomic status than the three larger groups mentioned previously.

The fourth element in Blauner's model, racist ideology, developed during and after the worst episodes of exploitation of racial-ethnic minorities. The primary function of racist ideology was to justify the exploitation. Racism may have originated among the powerful—southern plantation owners who found it necessary to declare slaves nonpersons, Anglo ranchers who used both forceful and "legal" means to wrest land away from Mexican ranchers in the Southwest and who found it convenient to keep Mexican peasants in virtual peonage status, capitalist agribusiness owners in the Far West who found it useful to keep minority groups abusing one another so that they would remain separate labor pools to be hired at the lowest possible cost—yet very quickly the non-powerful whites took up a racist stance. Poor southern whites raised their status by claiming racial superiority over blacks and giving their support first to slavery and later to exclusionary Jim Crow laws. Settlers everywhere perpetuated the stereotype of Indians as sneaking, thieving, heathen savages because it justified taking their land. White workers in the West demanded and got legislation excluding or severely limiting the rights of Asians. In these and other ways, non-powerful groups helped institutionalize racist practices. The rapid adoption and perpetuation of racist ideology provided perhaps the most enduring legacy of internal colonialism. The consequences for the mobilization of women in social movements will be explored later.

The fifth feature of Blauner's model is the direct effort to confine minority workers to discrete occupational niches. The examples are legion: allowing only tenant farming for blacks after the Civil War; importing Chinese laborers to dig mines and lay thousands of miles of railroad tracks; hiring Mexicans to clear the land and lay out irrigation systems for truck farming. Minority workers were used to develop the "agricultural base and the mineral-transport-communications infrastructure [necessary] for industrialization and modernization."[3] Thus these jobs were temporary. After the foundation for industrialization had been laid, increased competition among minority groups and with Anglo workers enabled employers to develop a dual, or segmented, labor market. Higher-paying jobs with better working conditions were reserved for whites; minorities were left to compete for the lower-paying ones. The racial segmentation of the labor market was the primary tool for the continued economic exploitation of minorities.

The Impact of Internal Colonialism on Women

Almost no one has sought to trace the impact of internal colonialism on women's lives. But it seems apparent that internal colonialism has overemphasized certain facets of women's roles, placed additional burdens on racial-ethnic women that white women have not had to shoulder, divided nonwhite women and white women ideologically, and led women to subordinate their interests as women to the interests of their particular ethnic group. Thus, operating largely through its influence on women's roles, internal colonialism has severely limited the resources minority women have had to commit to any social movement, encouraged them to consider racial grievances as far more pressing than sexual issues, and greatly enhanced the likelihood that women would support minority rights movements while at least postponing feminist activity.

In another publication,[4] I catalogued a variety of historical and contemporary effects of internal colonialism on women's lives, each of which influences the pattern of their participation in social movements. The first of these is poverty, which severely limits the resources—time, money and commitment—that can be used to attempt to redress grievances. Some groups, notably the Chinese and Japanese, have been able to make a long, slow climb out of poverty. This effort was facilitated greatly by female work, thrift and sacrifice.

For all groups, poverty enhanced the need for women to be employed. And, as was the case for men, the women were frequently confined to specific occupational niches: Chinese women in boardinghouses and laundries, black women in domestic service, Mexican-American women in field work, and many groups in canneries and garment manufacturing.[5] In the early days women encountered paternalistic dominance in their work, both from the Anglos who hired them and from the fathers and husbands who worked alongside them. A good deal of racial segregation in women's employment remains today, with minority women found less often as white-collar workers and more often as factory operatives, service workers and private household workers than Anglo women. However, the sexual barriers to minority women's occupational achievement and earnings are greater than the racial barriers.[6] Unfortunately, minority women and social scientists have consistently underestimated the sexual oppression minority women experience in the labor market, and have highlighted racial oppression instead. This is but one component in a whole constellation of forces which encourage minority women to focus their social activism on behalf of minority rather than women's rights.

Internal colonialism often meant that minority groups were left without ordinary political or social supports. Therefore, it required a defensive strengthening of the family. Colonized groups were forced to rely on their families for maintenance, support and protection. The need for a strong family often translated into a need for a strong mother. Women struggled to conserve precious resources, to make food, clothing and money stretch as far as possible. They worked to make the home a safe haven, a placed of respite from the rigors of a racist society. Betty Garcia-Bahne[7] has argued that this defensive strengthening played a pivotal role in the evolution of the Mexican-American subculture. The male worker faced a competitive, exploitative and authoritarian situation on the job; he tended to reproduce this relationship in his family. He had little reason to be certain that he could continue to fill the breadwinner role; the low wages that he did earn undermined his manliness. For these reasons he demanded extra obeisance and respect from his wife. Meanwhile, capitalism was devaluing the work traditionally done by women, thus reinforcing the view that women were unimportant. These elements combined to make women subordinate. Women were encouraged to sacrifice self-interest for the good of the family. This theme echoes among ethnic groups today. Many hold the view that the ethnic group cannot be strong unless the ethnic family is strong, and women should assume the primary responsibility for making it so.[8]

As part of a strategy for controlling minorities, the colonizers either deliberately or unwittingly destroyed much of the minority's original culture. But many groups resisted this onslaught and struggled to maintain a strong attachment to family and ethnic values. All these groups were patriarchal to a greater or lesser degree. Patriarchal values may have fit well with the dominant group's prejudices. In any case, they were among the few cultural elements that could be readily maintained.

Internal colonialism's insistence on the social segregation of minorities contributed to two further consequences that left an imprint on minority women's lives: rural origins with accompanying slow rates of urbanization and, once in the cities, ghettoization. Residing in rural areas and having few financial resources have meant that women lacked access to modern transportation, health care, contraceptive information, mass media and education. Each of these would contribute to women's ability to throw off the shackles of traditional sex-role stereotypes. These are resources that help women move toward free choice and self-determination. As minority groups slowly moved into the cities, they were residentially segregated. Confinement to ghettos meant that urban women were nearly as isolated from these resources as their rural sisters. Of course, many women leave the ghetto for vary-ing reasons. Nonetheless, the ghettoized woman has had less contact with the world outside, and fewer opportunities for emancipation and personal development.

Despite all these limitations, racial-ethnic women have supported a wide variety of minority group movements. They have been slower to embrace the feminist movement, and when they have taken it up, many have preferred to form their own feminist groups separate from those of Anglos. Before examining some aspects of their participation in organized action, it will be useful to survey contemporary theories about social movements.

The Resource Mobilization Perspective on Social Movements

The resource mobilization perspective (RMP) dominates the contem-porary study of social movements in the United States. There are actu-ally two versions of the RMP.[9] The first version (RM1 as articulated by Tilly,[10] Oberschall[11] and Gamson[12]) views social movement orga-nizations (SMOs) as very similar to rationally motivated interest groups which attempt to insert their concerns into the normal political process. In regard to strategies for achieving success, this version stresses the effect that external agents, especially the media, the gov-ernment, and opposition groups (countermovements) have on SMOs. The second version (RM2 as voiced largely by McCarthy and Zald[13]) likens social movements to businesses. SMOs are created by issue en-trepreneurs (leaders) who capitalize on discontent, and professionally organize the movement to capture resources ("raw materials" such as money, commitment, labor power, support from outsiders) that can be packaged and exchanged to achieve the goals the movement desires. In formulating strategies for success, RM2 stresses the value of using some resources to hire professional organizers, using tactics like direct mail campaigns to gain support from "conscience" constituents, and forming coalitions with other "like-minded" SMOs within the same so-cial movement sector. These differences between the two versions are matters of emphasis primarily; one can draw on both versions to gain insight into the mobilization and potential success of minority women in social movements.

Resource mobilization theorists stress the distinction between social movements and social movement organizations. A social movement is a "set of opinions and beliefs in a population which represent prefer-ences for changing some elements of the social structure and/or reward distribution of a society."[14] A social movement organization is a more or less formally organized group which establishes the movement's desires as its goals.

RM theorists then study the activities of the organization(s) rather than the movement. This is understandable, as organizations are more likely than movements to have offices, mailing lists, and identified leaders who can be studied. In addition, of course, SMOs are more likely than the inchoate mass to have developed a formal agenda of goals, to have designed some strategy, and to have vocalized an explicit ideology. Social movement analysts can then use the list of goals and assess whether alternative strategies are successful.

It should be pointed out, however, that there are a number of limits on the kinds of research on social movements that are feasible. Most studies are case studies of SMOs only; rarely if ever are the participants in a movement surveyed. Moreover, research tends to be conducted from an outsider's perspective; it is seldom possible for the social scientist to gain access to a movement organization in its early stages or to become privy to high-level strategic decision-making. Perhaps this is why some researchers study the movement by using primarily secondary sources such as newspaper coverage.[15] In addition, social movements often take action before they have mapped out a "grand strategy" and attempt to redress grievances before they have articulated a conscious ideology which would outline solutions to major problems. These tendencies frustrate efforts to determine which strategies will be successful, and incidentally cast doubt on the view that SMOs are directly comparable to rationally motivated interest groups.[16]

The study of social movements is a growth industry within sociology. Motivated perhaps by the very large number of social movements which emerged during the 1960s and 1970s,[17] a flood of new studies, articles and books has been produced. Within this new industry, there is a good deal of competition among ideas and their authors as well as a high degree of specialization in topics of study. The competition and specialization feed upon one another. What often happens is that the competitors emerge with a set of distinctions rather than a set of principles which explains the organization and effectiveness of collective action.

One set of distinctions that is useful for our purposes is that among three different aspects of mobilization. The three logically discrete aspects are mobilizing (founding or co-opting) an organization, mobilizing participants, and mobilizing resources. Each of these processes is costly to a movement, especially during the early phases of collective action. Each requires the expenditure of some time, energy and/or funds. If social movement organizers were totally rational actors, they would choose very carefully among these three areas of mobilization.

In fact, McCarthy and Zald[18] have argued that organizers should choose to co-opt existing organizations rather than to found new ones. They also suggest mobilizing conscience constituents (those who will reap no direct material gain if the movement is successful) rather than beneficiary constituents (those who experience a disadvantaged status or grievance and will benefit materially if the movement is successful). McCarthy and Zald also appear to be suggesting that organizers might bypass beneficiary constituents altogether; after all, if these are people who are sharply deprived, they will have few resources available to commit to the movement, therefore organizers should focus instead on mobilizing resources currently held by potential conscience constituents.

This view is rather remarkable; it ignores the needs and wishes of the people who most desire significant change, and discounts their abilities to speak and fight for themselves. Nonetheless there is some limited support for the idea. In a study of the state-level success of the women's suffrage movement, Keith Lance found that suffrage organizations which concentrated on attracting converts and holding rallies and conventions were ultimately less successful than those which emphasized lobbying state legislators and introducing bills into the legislature.[19]

Beyond their penchant for drawing distinctions, resource mobilization theorists emphasize structural rather than cultural antecedents and determinants of social movements. For the moment, let us focus on the question of mobilizing (primarily beneficiary) constitutents and the structural explanations proposed by resource mobilization theorists.

Structural Factors in the Mobilization of Constituents

The occasion for mobilizing social movements may be a single event which draws potential participants together, highlights long-standing grievances or introduces sharp new deprivations, crystallizes sentiments for change, and suggests at least the dim outlines of an effective strategy for responding.[20] Rosa Parks's refusal to move to the back of the bus is an outstanding example of such a precipitating factor. Immediately after hearing of the incident, E. D. Nixon began calling black ministers and other community leaders, asking them to meet in the Dexter Avenue Baptist Church and to bring as many other people as possible. Martin Luther King, Jr., was the nineteenth person he called.[21] That night, and in successive nights, many of the strategies for the civil rights movement were forged.

Precipitating factors become significant, however, only against a background of structural conditions which allow and foster social movement organization. One of these conditions is a lessening of social control of the aggrieved group. Potential participants must feel free to express grievances without fearing the cost of reprisal from those in authority over them. They must also be free to withdraw their energies and loyalties from existing commitments and redirect them along social movement paths.[22] Among all race-sex groups, minority women are least likely to have these freedoms, because they are much more tightly controlled than minority men, majority women or majority men. A variety of forces limits the options racial-ethnic women have. Minority women have the smallest financial resources of any race-sex group. If they are employed, minority women are much more likely than any other group to be employed by others who are unlike them. If they are receiving public assistance, they are controlled by the federal and state bureaucracies which govern the expenditure of funds. Within their families, women and girls are expected to be much more modest, unassuming and tolerant of deprivations than are men and boys.[23] In all these situations, reprisals for expressing grievances are likely to be swift and sure. In addition, racial-ethnic women are unlikely to be able to withdraw and recommit their energies because of their heavy responsibilities which amount to a situation of role overload.[24]

There are other conditions which enhance the likelihood that precipitating factors will generate a movement-formation response. These conditions, which Neil Smelser calls structural conduciveness, are generally more available for racial-ethnic women in recent years, as indeed they are for all groups. One aspect of structural conduciveness is the opportunity aggrieved groups have for issue aggregation and expression. The torrent of social movements that began or flourished during the 1960s provided just such an opportunity. New movements "fed off" prior movements, not just because they learned workable tactics from them, but also because the experiences of viable movements indicated the probable response that authorities would exhibit. Of course some authorities responded with violence, but others were at least neutral if not hospitable to movements. Jo Freeman[25] has pointed out that the younger branch of the feminist movement arose among women who were active in radical politics. These women were frustrated by the repression they experienced from male leaders, but simultaneously were inspired by their tactics. Similarly, many minority feminist groups arose among women who were already mobilized in moderate to radical minority group causes. Seeing male colleagues ridicule women's issues was just the sort of precipitating incident which led women to found their own separate movement groups.

Another type of structural conduciveness is any circumstance which will bring aggrieved groups together, increase communication among the aggrieved, and enable them to articulate their viewpoints. This aspect is particularly significant for minority women as they have increased their college enrollments more rapidly than any other group during the last decade. Bringing together a large number of "like-minded" people on college campuses is credited with being at least one factor in the development of the sit-in movement, the student power movement, and various groups within the feminist movement.[26] Finally, this aspect of structural conduciveness may be somewhat beneficial to minority women because of their changing employment patterns. They are increasingly moving out of the isolation of private household work, and into occupations (factory operatives) that are currently being mobilized into labor unions. They are also becoming more concentrated in all types of service work and in secretarial work, employment that is not noted for high levels of union activity.[27] Note, however, that the Coalition of Labor Union Women and other union groups are making significant inroads in organizing hospital service workers and secretaries.[28] Most important, perhaps, is that the number of minority women in white-collar employment is increasing, but that they are not advancing rapidly to the higher levels of white-collar jobs. This should work to produce "critical masses" of minority women who will join other work-related movements or organize their own.

Once precipitating factors occur in the context of conditions that are suitable for establishing an SMO, the incipient movement group grows and spreads along structural lines. Freeman,[29] especially, has described the critical significance of pre-existing organizations in establishing a new movement. Kathleen Tierney builds on Freeman's insight in describing the success of the battered women movement:

> Pre-existing social networks aided the movement in several ways. First, they provided common frames of reference and rationales for participation in the new movement. Second they provided co-optable networks—ongoing chains of interaction among persons likely to adopt and promote the idea of a movement to aid battered women. Pre-existing networks facilitate the growth of a movement because time, effort, and momentum do not have to be invested building consensus and establishing links among potentially interested parties. Third, the networks provided experienced people to act as movement leaders.[30]

Although he does not use the same terminology, Aldon Morris[31] has described the importance of churches and church members as providers of critical resources for the black southern sit-in movement. He has also indicated that the initiators of the earliest sit-ins were clusters of individuals who were geographically dispersed but linked together in informal communication networks. Successfully predicting the growth and spread of a social movement, then, requires knowing that pre-existing networks are present and available for co-opting.

Resource mobilization theorists have offered a number of hypotheses concerning how individuals and groups may be mobilized. Anthony Oberschall, who describes social movements as political protest groups (RM1), has stated several of them in formal terms. First,

> 1. . . . the greater the number and variety of organizations in a collectivity, and the higher the participation of members in this network, the more rapidly and enduringly does mobilization into conflict groups occur, and the more likely it is that bloc recruitment, rather than individual recruitment, will take place.[32]

This first hypothesis formalizes some of Freeman's insights and further points to the superior strategy of mobilizing clusters of persons rather than individuals. Note the significance of the term "collectivity" here. A collectivity is a quasi-group whose members have common latent interests, are dissatisfied with their situation, and share common grievances. Members of a minority group have seen themselves as a collectivity and recognized common interests for quite some time. Only recently have minority women begun to see themselves as having common interests that are separate and distinct from the interests of men in their group.

Oberschall's second hypothesis recognizes two further features of the collectivity. Other than exploitative ones, it may have few links with other collectivities that are above it in the stratification hierarchy, and the collectivity may be organized along either associational or communal lines. Associational ties are those of secondary groups based on occupational, religious, civic, economic, or other special interests. Communal ties refer to primary affiliations based on kinship and friendship. The degree of segmentation from power wielders and the type of organization affect both the type and extent of mobilization that can occur:

> 2. The more segmented a collectivity is from the rest of the society, and the more viable and extensive the communal ties within it, the more rapid and easier it is to mobilize members of the collectivity into an opposition movement.[33]

> 3. If a collectivity is disorganized or unorganized along traditional communal lines and not yet organized along associational lines, collective protest is possible when members share common sentiments of oppression and targets for hostility. These sentiments are more likely to develop if the collectivity is segmented

rather than vertically integrated with other collectivities of the society. Such protest will, however, tend to be more short-lived and more violent than movements based on communal or associational organization.[34]

The implications of these two hypotheses for racial-ethnic women are unclear. While minority women are rather obviously segmented from other collectivities, e.g., (largely male) white power holders, the nature and extent of communal and associational ties among minority women are unknown. The extent to which minority women have meaningful ties with other groups is also unknown. These ties are probably few in number because racism has effectively prohibited their development.

Oberschall offers a final hypothesis which is in opposition to the views of mass society theorists:

> 4. . . . activists in opposition organizations will be recruited primarily from previously active and relatively well-integrated individuals within the collectivity, whereas socially isolated, atomized, and uprooted individuals will be underrepresented, at least until the movement has become substantial.[35]

The message in this hypothesis is clear. Movement activists will be persons who are not integrated into dominant groups, but who are well integrated into the collectivity which seeks change.

Most of the foregoing ideas about mobilization refer almost exclusively to "bare bones" structural aspects of the collectivity. In a complementary view, Bruce Fireman and William Gamson[36] suggest that no movement will be effectively mobilized unless the collectivity exists as, or is transformed into, a constituency: a group with solidarity which recognizes that its interests lie in pursuing collective action. Solidarity, as interpreted here, is a slightly more inclusive concept than bare bones structure. Solidarity includes, of course, structural links among members of the constituency. But solidarity also means that members identify with each other and share a sense of common fate or destiny. This type of solidarity is enhanced in a number of ways: by having friends and relatives within the group, by participating in all types of organizations with other members of the group, and by sharing the same set of subordinate and superordinate relations with outsiders.

Two other features enhance solidarity as well:

Design for living. Groups frequently offer members a set of techniques for handling the problems they encounter in their daily lives—problems like finding and keeping good jobs and good spouses, making friends, raising children, staying out of trouble, and getting treated with dignity and respect. In trying to implement some design for going through life, a person may rely to a greater or lesser degree on support from other people and organizations in the solidarity group. To the extent that a person's design for living is shared and supported by other group members more than by outsiders, he has a basis for solidarity with the group.[37]

No exit. To the extent that a person is readily identified and often treated as a member of the group, so that exit from the group is difficult, he has a basis for solidarity with the group.[38]

These two aspects of solidarity are precisely the ones which limit the likelihood of minority women joining extensively with Anglos in feminist or other movements. They also limit the likelihood that specific groups of racial-ethnic women will join with each other in activist movements. Internal colonialism and racism practically guarantee that these groups would have no sense of solidarity with each other. Black women, Asian women, Native American women, Mexican-American women—all have little sense of sharing a common design for living with each other or with Anglos. At a minimum they are likely to regard any Anglo woman who has a husband and a decent job as part of the power structure. They may also see Anglos as direct oppressors. But they do have a strong sense of sharing within their own group and a belief that there is no exit from their racial-ethnic group membership.

Minority Feminist Organizations

A strong sense of solidarity within one's own group and apartness from other groups are expressed in this quotation from Consuelo Nieto:

It is difficult for the Chicana to forget that some Anglo women have oppressed her people within this society, and are still not sensitive to minorities or their needs. With Anglo women, the Chicana may share a commitment to equality, yet it is very seldom that she will find with them the camaraderie, the understanding, the sensitivity that she finds with her own people.

Anglo women sensitive to Chicanas as members of a minority must guard against a very basic conceptual mistake. All minorities are not alike. To understand the black women is not to understand the Chicana. To espouse the cause of minority women, Anglos must recognize our distinctiveness as separate ethnic groups.[39]

Because Chicana feminist organizations appear to exemplify many of the points that have been addressed, let us describe them in the context in which they occur. For the past several decades, Mexican Americans have been increasingly active in a variety of social movements to enhance their political, educational and economic opportunities. These activities have spawned an awareness of sexism and often have served as the springboard for feminist movements. The Chicana feminist movement also has strong roots in the working-class and union movements. Superficially, many Chicana activities resemble those of Anglo feminists. But they tend to concentrate on "safe" issues such as education and health care, issues that will not divide men and women. The writings of Chicana feminists express their separateness from Anglo feminists and their unity with Chicana males. Terry Mason points out that Chicanas dislike Anglo feminists because the Anglos appear to condemn all aspects of traditional femininity. She argues that the Chicana movement differs from Anglo feminism by depicting some aspects of the traditional female role—being a wife and mother—in a positive light. There is no overriding opposition between women and men; men are not depicted as the enemy or blamed for the limitations placed on women.[40]

Chicana feminism is shaped by the context in which it occurs. The Mexican-American population is quite diverse, with large segments highly acculturated to middle-class patterns and other segments relatively aloof from Anglo lifeways. In the face of this diversity, there is a strong need to stress Chicano solidarity to mobilize the population in pursuit of human rights goals. Many Mexican Americans see themselves as a colonized people. Maxine Baca Zinn shows that the main strategy for achieving decolonization and for forming the new La Raza is to use the family as the basic organizational unit of the movement.[41] In this "political familism," machismo is being redefined to mean active striving for the good of the Mexican-American people. All members of the family, young and old, male and female, are urged to contribute to the movement. Women are valued for their contributions to the family as well as for activities outside the home. Chicana feminism places little stress on liberation for women alone; it emphasizes instead the benefits that can be obtained for Chicanos as a group.

Other groups of racial-ethnic women have organized feminist groups, but they have not received much attention from researchers. However, Pauline Terrelonge has provided a very sensitive analysis of why black women have not adopted, or have not been allowed to adopt, a strong feminist consciousness. Terrelonge believes that a strong feminist consciousness is needed to overcome the problems black women face. She offers five reasons why the black community has not addressed the issue of sexism. The first "and most formidable is that many black intellectuals and spokespeople have [regarded sexism] as a racially divisive issue . . . a force that could generate internal conflict."[42] Thus the elevation of the race must be given first priority, as befits a colonized minority.

The second reason that blacks have avoided the issue of sexism, according to Terrelonge, stems directly from the ideology of racism. "Racism is so engrained in American culture and so entrenched among many white women, that black females have been reluctant to admit that anything affecting the white female could also affect them."[43]

Third, feminist awareness came in the context of the civil rights movement of the sixties. In that context, black women were told that the liberation of black men should take precedence over their own, and that attempts to establish priorities for black women would contribute to the emasculation of black men. This powerful message can be understood only in the context of the ideologies that social movements develop, not simply in the structural alliances members of collectivities have.

Fourth, policymakers and academicians have raised the specter of black matriarchy, a view that black women have somehow managed to dominate black men and to survive better in the white world than black men have. The acceptance of the myth of the black matriarchy virtually precludes recognition that black women are the victims of sexual oppression, especially in their subordination to black men.

Finally, the church delays the development of feminist consciousness. It is a deeply patriarchal institution. "[T]he church is the most important social institution in the black community and the one in which black women (in contrast to black men) spend most of their time and energy."[44] Black women can be mobilized through the church to support a variety of causes, but the cultural and ideological forces of the church delay the development of feminist consciousness.

Terrelonge's analysis calls attention to ideological and attitudinal forces which limit black women's participation as feminist activists. The authors who stress mobilization of constituents would suggest that these ideological and attitudinal forces stem from structural aspects of the black community. Thus the black community is segmented from the white community, and knit together by communal and associational ties which simultaneously heighten awareness of racial discrimination, produce black solidarity across sexual lines, and highlight the need for activism in pursuit of black causes. Others might argue that these ideological and attitudinal commitments are derived from cultural perspectives that are relatively independent of the structure and organization of the black community. Regardless of the outcome of such a potential dispute, what is most significant is that none of the materials reviewed here—Terrelonge's analysis, the resource mobilization perspective, empirical materials regarding minority feminist movements—suggests that feminist ideology is inappropriate for minority women. Instead, these materials explain why, in the past, racial-ethnic women have been unwilling to unite with Anglo-dominated feminist organizations. Numerous surveys[45] show that black women accept most feminist premises: the right to control one's body, the right to choose meaningful work and be appropriately compensated for it, the importance of women's participation in politics, and many others. Indeed, black women do not reject feminist ideology; they question only the prospect of free and equal participation with white women in an organized movement.

Strategies for Success

How are social movements able to be successful and thereby influence the course of public policy? Neither resource mobilization nor traditional perspectives provides more than hazy answers to this question. Apparently the success or failure of a social movement depends on complex interactions among several factors: the type of change the movement demands; effective mobilization of both the aggrieved group and conscience constituents; the resources and support received from all types of donors; the attitudes displayed by bystander publics; the ability of the movement to form coalitions with other movements, to insert their issues into the normal political process, to attract powerful supporters and to neutralize opposition; and, finally, just plain good luck.

The National Welfare Rights Organization (NWRO) illustrates these points.[46] Formed largely as a grass-roots movement among black neighborhoods with a high proportion of welfare recipients, the movement was successful in spurring many more women to demand all the benefits to which they were legally entitled. It was not so successful if one considers its failure to maintain a national organization and office for more than a few years, and its failure to affect basic policies regarding the distribution of welfare benefits. Mobilization of both beneficiary and conscience constituents was widespread, and limited changes which depended on beneficiaries demanding their rights and affecting local welfare offices were achieved, but more radical and far-reaching changes eluded the NWRO.

The organization had, temporarily, a number of supports that, had they continued over a period of time, might have led to the success members wanted. Local groups coalesced into a national organization which was able to establish a national office in Washington, D.C. The failure to maintain national leaders who could gain funds to do more than simply maintain an office appears to have been a critical problem. Alliances were formed with various anti-poverty and civil rights groups, but these tended to be coalitions on paper only, and to involve verbal support rather than strategic, active alliances which effectively joined programs, resources and battlelines. Certain churches supported the NWRO for a time, but their attention and support turned to other issues. Resource mobilization theorists would identify the failure of the group to package the issues and insert them into the normal political process as a key problem. Welfare rights simply did not become a powerful national issue, and it failed to attract enough powerful supporters. There was also the lack of an organized opposition to keep the issue alive on the political agenda. Bystander publics remained unmoved. Apparently, outsiders could sympathize with the plight of children who lacked adequate food, clothing and housing. They could perhaps perceive that welfare mothers deserved a decent living and to be treated with courtesy and respect. But they simply could not identify with the idea that poor black women deserved the same rights.

Another example highlights both the difficulties and the prospects for overcoming racial barriers to feminist organizing. Hospitals offer a paradigmatic case of racial and sexual segregation in the workplace. At the top, they are dominated mainly by white male administrators. At the bottom of the hierarchy are the service, food and cleaning workers, who are predominantly minority men and women. White female nurses and technicians are interposed between these separate groups. Thus, racial and sexual divisions correspond with job, authority and pay divisions. The various racial and gender groups are structurally separate from one another; they perceive no identity of interests, and may even view one another with suspicion or distrust. Yet, in some hospitals, union organizers have been able to mobilize disparate groups of workers by appealing to worker interests which transcend racial, sexual and job divisions.[47] Opportunities for pay and promotions, methods to improve the care given patients and thereby to take pride in a job well done, options for alleviating the concern parents have over the care of their children, and strategies for coping with shift work and eliminating the late posting of work schedules are examples of interests shared by nearly all hospital workers. The appeal involves persuading all groups that they have parallel interests, parallel designs for living, a common adversary, and at least minimal associational ties with each other. Only after disparate groups have come together over parallel issues that directly concern them all can they support each other on issues which affect them separately.

If female hospital workers who are so extremely segregated by race and by occupational divisions can be induced to join together on work-related issues, it will be much easier to organize women within the same occupations. This is precisely the logic used by the Coalition of Labor

Union Women in organizing blue-collar workers and by various groups of professional and secretarial workers. Minority women and white women who work at the same job can achieve a sense of solidarity that overcomes racial lines when their crucial and common interests are made salient. This solidarity is somewhat fragile though, and may dissolve as women leave the workplace and go home to their families, churches, and other institutions which are still racially segregated. Thus the prospects for feminist organizations which overcome racial barriers are still rather dim.

Conclusion

It has been argued here that the policy and practice of internal colonialism have had a number of specific consequences for racial-ethnic women, that these consequences have not been previously recognized, and that they are somewhat different for minority women than for minority men. Internal colonialism, and the accompanying racism, divided minority people from Anglos, erecting both structural and cultural barriers to open mingling across racial lines. These barriers exist for women and men alike. But for women, the consequences are even more severe. Colonialism increased the burdens that accompany women's roles, and exaggerated whatever patriarchal, male oppressive strains were present in minority group cultures. Therefore, minority women need women's liberation perhaps more than majority women, but at the same time are taught to view racial and ethnic issues as more important than women's issues.

In perhaps a circuitous way, the resource mobilization perspective explains why racial-ethnic women have been reluctant to join forces with Anglo feminists. The structural barriers between groups and the associational and communal ties within groups are simply too strong to permit rapid alliances across racial lines. Arguably, the resource mobilization perspective can also account for the partial success of some social movements (the NWRO), the formation of some minority feminist organizations, and the potential for workplace organization. But with its emphasis on spreading a movement along previously existing, cooptable networks, this perspective neglects the powerful part played by interests and ideas. A group with very limited financial resources—welfare mothers—can be mobilized when its interests are crucially affected and the idea of beneficial change is brought to the fore. Similarly, racial and occupational divisions can be overcome, as among hospital workers, when galvanizing ideas about possible changes are brought to bear on critical interests. A badly needed addition to the resource mobilization perspective, then, is an examination of how groups and individuals perceive their interests and how ideas of change can be targeted to reach the perceived interests of potential participants.

Minority women are currently assailed by a host of problem areas and bombarded with a number of ideas for potential social movement activism. They must choose carefully among these options. Because of the structural barriers imposed by racism, they perceive that their crucial interests lie more heavily in racial issues than in gender issues. Because of racism as well, they perceive little identity with majority women. Far from rejecting feminist beliefs and ideology, they nonetheless place lower priority on feminist activism than on racial activism. Workplace organizing holds high potential for increasing structural ties and for highlighting common interests, identities and issues that transcend racial lines. But there are limits.

White women began organizing the women's liberation movement when they realized that they were not being treated as individuals, but as members of the category "women." Minority women can rarely, if ever, perceive their treatment as being solely in the category of women. Their experiences are always received and interpreted as those of "black women" or "Hispanic women." This is the meaning of "double jeopardy." Those who would like to present a united, racially integrated feminist front will have to begin with those issues that are solely women's issues or, better, will have to mount a simultaneous assault on both racism and sexism. For double jeopardy there must be double solutions.

NOTES

[1]This chapter describes several groups including American Indians, blacks, Chicanos, Puerto Ricans, Cuban Americans, Chinese Americans and Japanese Americans. Some of these groups are culturally rather than racially distinct from the Anglo majority, but the treatment they receive is much more similar to that of racial minorities than to that of "white ethnics" such as Swedes, Poles or Hungarians. Thus the rather awkward term "racial-ethnic" is used. To avoid repetitious use of this term, I use the simpler term "minority" interchangeably with "racial-ethnic."

[2]Robert Blauner, *Racial Oppression in America* (New York: Harper and Row, 1972).

[3]Ibid., p. 62.

[4]Elizabeth M. Almquist, "Race and Ethnicity in the Lives of Minority Women," in Jo Freeman, ed., *Women: A Feminist Perspective* (Palo Alto, Cal.: Mayfield Publishing, 1984), pp. 423-453.

[5]For more details, see ibid., pp. 429-433.

[6]Elizabeth M. Almquist, *Minorities, Gender, and Work* (Lexington, Mass.: D. C. Heath, 1979); see especially chapter 6.

[7]Betty Garcia-Bahne, "La Chicana and the Chicano Family," in Rosaura Sanchez and Rosa Martinez Cruz, eds., *Essays on la Mujer* (Los Angeles: University of California, Chicano Studies Center Publications, 1977), p. 39.

[8]See, for example, Wynne Hanson, "The Urban Indian Woman and Her Family," *Social Casework* 61:8 (October 1980): 476-483; Shirley Fiske, "Rules of Address: Navajo Women in Los Angeles," *Journal of Anthropological Research* 34 (1978): 72-91; Irene Fujitomi and Diane Wong, "The New Asian-American Woman," in Stanley Sue and Nathan Wagner, eds., *Asian Americans: Psychological Perspectives* (Palo Alto, Cal.: Science and Behavior Books, 1973), pp. 236-248.

[9]Charles Perrow, "The Sixties Observed," in Mayer N. Zald and John D. McCarthy, eds., *The Dynamics of Social Movements* (Cambridge, Mass.: Winthrop, 1979), pp. 192-211.

[10]Charles Tilly, *From Mobilization to Revolution* (Reading, Mass.: Addison-Wesley, 1978).

[11]Anthony Oberschall, *Social Conflict and Social Movements* (Englewood Cliffs, N.J.: Prentice Hall, 1973) and "The Decline of the 1960's Social Movements," in Louis Kriesberg, ed., *Research in Social Movements, Conflict and Change* (Greenwich, Conn.: JAI Press, 1977).

[12]William A. Gamson, *The Strategy of Social Protest* (Homewood, Ill.: Dorsey, 1975).

[13]John D. McCarthy and Mayer N. Zald, "Resource Mobilization and Social Movements: A Partial Theory," *American Journal of Sociology* 82:6 (May 1977): 1212-1239.

[14]Ibid., p. 1217.

[15]See, for example, Perrow, op. cit.; and J. Craig Jenkins and Charles Perrow, "Insurgency of the Powerless: Farm Worker Movements, 1946-1972," *American Sociological Review* 42:2 (April 1977): 249-268.

[16]See Bruce Fireman and William A. Gamson, "Utilitarian Logic in the Resource Mobilization Perspective," in Zald and McCarthy, *The Dynamics of Social Movements*, op. cit., pp. 8-44, for an insightful critique concerning mobilization of interest groups versus mobilization of social movement participants.

[17]Charles Perrow, "The Sixties Observed," op. cit., and Jo Freeman, *The Politics of Women's Liberation* (New York: McKay, 1975).

[18]John D. McCarthy and Mayer N. Zald, *The Trend of Social Movements in America: Professionalization and Resource Mobilization* (Morristown, N.J.: General Learning Corporation, 1973).

[19]Keith Curry Lance, "Woman Suffrage in the States: An Analysis of Level and Timing of Success," (Ph.D. dissertation, North Texas State University, 1984).

[20]Neil Smelser, *Theory of Collective Behavior* (New York: Free Press, 1963). Much of Smelser's theory informs the following discussion.

[21]Bill Moyers, "A Walk Through the Twentieth Century," Public Broadcasting System (April 25, 1984).

[22]Smelser, op. cit.

[23]Lucy Jen Huang, "The Chinese-American Family," in Charles Mindel and Michael Habenstein, eds., *Ethnic Families in America* (New York: Elsevier North-Holland, 1976), pp. 124-147. See also Harry H. L. Kitano and Akemi Kikumura, "The Japanese-American Family," pp. 41-60 in the same book.

[24]Almquist, *Minorities, Gender, and Work*, op. cit., pp. 46-57.

[25]Jo Freeman, "Resource Mobilization and Strategy: A Model for Analyzing Social Movement Organization Actions," in Zald and McCarthy, *The Dynamics of Social Movements*, op. cit., pp. 167-189.

[26]Charles Perrow, "The Sixties Observed," op. cit. Perrow stresses, however, that the bringing together of students on college campuses cannot account for the total mobilization process.

[27]Almquist, "Race and Ethnicity in the Lives of Minority Women," op. cit.

[28]Patricia Cayo Sexton, *The New Nightingales: Hospital Workers, Unions, New Women's Issues* (New York: Enquiry Press, 1982); and Barbara M. Wertheimer, " 'Union is Power': Sketches from Women's Labor History," in Freeman, *Women: A Feminist Perspective*, op. cit., pp. 337-352.

[29]Freeman, *The Politics of Women's Liberation*, op. cit.

[30]Kathleen J. Tierney, "The Battered Women Movement and the Creation of the Wife Beating Problem," *Social Problems* 29:3 (February 1982): 207-220.

[31]Aldon Morris, "The Black Southern Sit-In Movement: An Analysis of Internal Organization," *American Sociological Review* 46:6 (December 1981): 744-767.

[32]Oberschall, *Social Conflict and Social Movements*, op. cit., p. 125.

[33]Ibid., p. 129.

[34]Ibid., p. 133.

[35]Ibid., p. 135.

[36]Fireman and Gamson, op. cit.

[37]Ibid., p. 36.

[38]Ibid., p. 38.

[39] Consuelo Nieto, "The Chicana and the Women's Rights Movement: A Perspective," *Civil Rights Digest* 6:3 (Spring 1974): 36-42.

[40] Terry Mason, "Symbolic Strategies for Change: A Discussion of the Chicana Women's Movement," in Margarita B. Melville, ed., *Twice a Minority: Mexican American Women* (St. Louis: C. V. Mosby Co., 1980), pp. 155-163.

[41] Maxine Baca Zinn, "Political Familism: Toward Sex Role Equality in Chicano Families," *Atzlan* 6:1 (Spring 1975): 13-16.

[42] Pauline Terrelonge, "Feminist Consciousness and Black Women," in Freeman, *Women: A Feminist Perspective*, op. cit., p. 562.

[43] Ibid., p. 563.

[44] Ibid., p. 564.

[45] Pamela Johnson Conover and Virginia Gray, *Feminism and the New Right: Conflict over the American Family* (New York: Praeger, 1983); Andrew Cherlin and Pamela Barnhouse Walters, "Trends in United States Men's and Women's Sex Role Attitudes: 1972-1978," *American Sociological Review* 46:4 (August 1981): 453-460; and Jean Lipman-Blumen and Ann R. Tickamyer, "Sex Roles in Transition: A Ten Year Perspective," *Annual Review of Sociology* 1 (1975): 297-337.

[46] Guida West, *The National Welfare Rights Movement: The Social Protest of Poor Women* (New York: Praeger, 1981).

[47] Sexton, op. cit.

TWICE PROTECTED? ASSESSING THE IMPACT OF AFFIRMATIVE ACTION ON MEXICAN-AMERICAN WOMEN*

Mary Romero

Yale University

Introduction

Critics of existing affirmative action legislation, executive orders and regulations[1] have continually sought to weaken federal requirements.[2] Opponents claim that anti-discrimination goals and employment strategies have resulted in "reverse discrimination" towards white males. In particular, correcting the practice and effects of discrimination by establishing goals and timetables has been perceived as "preferential treatment" or "protective status" given to minorities and women. The reverse discrimination viewpoint suggests that minority status within the marketplace is an advantage under affirmative action policies. It is argued that discriminatory hiring practices based on race, color, religion, sex and national origin have now become "preferential" hiring practices of persons previously denied equal opportunity. Such practices are identified as a violation of the meritocratic norm which assumes selection and advancement of the most meritorious, ambitious, hardworking and talented individuals.[3]

Most employers' adherence to affirmative action has revolved around two decisions: to hire and promote women and minorities; and not to hire white males. The second decision has come to be considered reverse discrimination since white males would have been hired had it not been for an employer's affirmative action program. The opposition of "neoconservatives" to affirmative action is presented as a moral dilemma: the employer either continues to discriminate against women and minorities or chooses to discriminate against white males.[4] Their opposition to affirmative action draws strength from traditional American principles of fair play and egalitarianism.

*I have profited greatly from my discussions with Dan McGovern and Teresa Peck. I should also like to express my thanks to Eric Margolis and Angie Zophy for their critical comments.

The reaction against affirmative action certainly suggests that there have been major shifts, or at least the potential for drastic changes, within the American occupational structure. As Nijole Benokraitis and Joe Feagin have commented:

Affirmative action must be heading in the right direction in attempting to eliminate institutionalized inequality because this is the first time a policy has elicited so much fear, hostility, antagonism, and virulent rhetoric from the otherwise complacent and condescendingly concerned dominant white group.[5]

In order to assess the validity of the criticism of affirmative action, one must discover if the programs have actually changed the relationship between white men and minority workers: Has affirmative action been successful in removing white male dominance in prestigious and high-paying occupations? Has affirmative action resulted in upward mobility for women and minorities by eliminating their concentrations within unskilled, low-paying white- and blue-collar occupations? Have white males had to suffer economically for advances made by minorities and women?

Assessing the effects of affirmative action legislation is not a simple matter because various factors have affected hiring practices. Women and minorities have increased their educational attainment as well as their participation in fields entered with post-secondary levels of education. Furthermore, the women's movement and various minority movements have continually kept employment issues at the forefront of their concerns.[6] However, while it is difficult to isolate a specific cause, the degree of representation of minorities, women and men in a variety of occupations can be analyzed statistically.

If the reverse discrimination viewpoint is correct, one would expect that the occupational distribution of white males has shifted downward, and that that of minorities and women has shifted upward. Minority workers and women would no longer be concentrated in low-paying, dead-end jobs, and would be improving their representation in higher-status occupations. Moreover, if minority status operates as an advantage in the labor market, it should follow that minority women (who "benefit" both by race and sex) would have made the most significant gains. In an attempt to address issues posed by the reverse discrimination viewpoint, comparisons were made between the occupational distribution of white males and Chicana[7] females. Comparisons between Chicana females and both Chicano males and white females were also made to assess the legitimacy of the claim that minority women operate in the marketplace with two advantages—race and sex.

Twice A Minority

Historical Situation

Before comparing the various groups, it is important to understand the historical basis for Chicanas' double-minority status. After the Mexican-American War, Mexican citizens were divided into those living in Mexico and those living in the area now occupied by the United States. Those remaining in the newly defined United States territory were forced to choose between losing their Mexican citizenship or losing their homes. After 1848, Mexican immigration expanded the Chicano presence in the Southwest and increased the number of Chicanas and Mexican women in the labor force. Immigration restrictions placed upon Asians through the Chinese Exclusion Act of 1882 and the Gentleman's Agreement with Japan in 1907 made Mexico an even more important source of cheap labor. As a result, one-eighth of Mexico's population crossed the border, not primarily for a dream of freedom and democracy, but for economic reasons.

Too often analogies and comparisons have been made between Chicanos and European immigrants which only serve to obscure and dissolve important differences. Carey McWilliams stated the differences succinctly:

> Living in a region which is geographically and historically a projection of their "homeland," and having struck deep roots in this region, the Spanish-speaking are not like the typical European immigrant minority in the United States. They did not cross an ocean; they moved north across a mythical border. They resemble, therefore, certain suppressed national minorities in Europe, although a closer parallel would be the French-Canadians in the Province of Quebec. There is this all important difference, however, that the border between the United States and Mexico is one of the most unreal borders in the world; it unites rather than separates the two peoples.[8]

The attempts to resist the fate of a conquered people were unsuccessful. Between 1854 and 1930, Chicanos lost two million acres of private land and 1,700,000 acres of communal or *ejido* lands.[9] Along with this loss of land went a loss of economic prosperity, which in this society has inevitably been followed by a decline in political power.

Scholars have documented the process by which land was enclosed and Chicano labor was "freed" for the industrialization of the Southwest. Numerous historical studies clearly illustrate the existence of a racially stratified labor force.[10] Mario Barrera has identified four aspects in the colonial labor system that affected Chicanos: labor repression; the dual wage system (sweetheart contracts); occupational stratification; and the need to maintain a reserve labor force and buffers for economic dislocation.[11] Although most labor history research on Chicanos has focused on the Mexican and Chicano men's experience in the colonial labor system, Chicanas worked alongside Chicano males in the fields, and were concentrated in low-paid service, laundry and garment industry jobs. Recently, several studies have been published on Chicanas that have documented their experience within the colonial labor process.[12]

As pointed out by Barrera, Anglos made no distinction "between the older Chicano settlers and the new arrivals."[13] Chicanas and Mexican women were a distinct segment of the labor force sharing similar economic relationships and the common experience of discrimination in the job market. The 1930 census listed 67,088 "Mexican" females over the age of ten as participating in the labor force.[14] During the 1930s, Chicanas and Mexican women were primarily employed as agricultural workers or in "traditional" female occupations, including domestic work, food service, laundry work, factory work in food processing plants and the garment industry.[15] Census data on Chicanas in 1930 show 44.8 percent in domestic and personal service, 20.7 percent in agriculture, and 19.3 percent in manufacturing. Mario Garcia's[16] study of the Chicano/Mexicano experience in El Paso documented the fact that Chicanas and Mexican women were the victims of occupational stratification and a dual wage system in local laundries and department stores. Other studies show that Chicanas, along with other women, were paid less than men in various occupations.[17] As Barrera has observed:

> Chicanas in the labor force generally find themselves in not one but two subordinate class segments, one based on race and another on sex. Their place in the occupational structure can be seen as representing a kind of intersection or overlap of the two kinds of class segments.[18]

The Current Situation

The 1980 census provides information on the current status of Chicanas.[19] The median age of Chicanas is 21.8, which is approximately eight years younger than the general population. Among Chicanas twenty-five years old and over, only 36.3 percent are high school graduates, whereas 65.8 percent of the total female population has completed high school. Within this same age range, approximately 9 percent of the Chicanas have completed between one to three years of college, and approximately 4 percent have four or more years.[20] Table 1 provides comparative data on educational levels for Chicano male and female populations and the total United States.

TABLE 1
YEARS OF SCHOOL COMPLETED BY CHICANOS
TWENTY-FIVE YEARS OLD AND OVER
(PERCENT)

Years of School Completed	Chicana Female*	Chicano Male**	Total U.S.
High School Graduates	36.3	38.9	66.5
College: 1 to 3 years	8.8	12.1	16.1
College: 4 or more	3.7	6.1	20.1

Source: U.S. Bureau of the Census, *United States Summary, General Social and Economic Characteristics*, Table 166, "Age, Fertility, Relationship, and Educational Characteristics by Spanish Origin, Type of Spanish Origin, and Race: 1980" (Washington, D.C.: 1980).
*n = 1,868,673
**n = 1,861,040

Census data[21] on female labor force participation display no significant difference between Chicanas and the general female population. This is an improvement because Chicana participation in the past has consistently been below white women. Forty-nine percent of Chicanas sixteen years old and over are in the labor force, and slightly over three-fourths of these work in the private sector, almost identical to the general female population. The second major employer of Chicanas is local government, followed by state and federal government. Only 2 percent are self-employed. Both married and single Chicanas participate in the labor force.[22] Approximately 46 percent of married Chicanas are in the labor force, and over half of the mothers with school-age children work.[23]

Methodology and Data

Annual reports from public and private employers, unions and labor organizations identifying the sex and racial/ethnic makeup of their work forces are required by the Equal Employment Opportunity Commission (EEOC). This is mandated by Public Law 88-352, Title VII of the Civil Rights Act of 1964, as amended by the Equal Employment Opportunity Act of 1972. This analysis is based on data from the 1971, 1975 and 1980 Employer Information Reports (EEO-1), subtitled "Job Patterns for Minorities and Women in Private Industry." EEO-1 reports are filed by

private employers with: (a) 100 or more employees, or (b) 50 or more employees and: (1) have a federal contract or first-tier subcontract worth $50,000 or more, or (2) act as depositories of federal funds in any amount, or (3) act as issuing and paying agents for U.S. Savings Bonds and Notes.[24]

Racial and ethnic identification were collected for nine job categories: officials and managers, professionals, technicians, sales workers, office and clerical workers, craft workers (skilled), operatives (unskilled), laborers, and service workers.[25] Occupational distribution and participation statistics were given by race/ethnicity and sex.

Two problems occur in assessing the changing occupational distribution of Chicanas: 1) the lack of available data, and 2) the lumping together of Hispanic groups as a single ethnic category.[26] The unique historical experiences of Chicanas in the United States that resulted in their minority status become lost in the Hispanic label. This is a critical observation, for it calls attention to the fact that empirical data pertaining to the work force status of Chicanas have been collapsed into data concerning Hispanic females, and thus remain undifferentiated. How this problem is addressed in this study will be explained shortly.

Differences between groups identified as Spanish origin or Hispanic can be observed in the 1980 census. For instance, the median age for Mexican Americans is 21.8 years and 22.3 for Puerto Ricans, whereas the median age is 37.5 for Cubans and 25.6 for other Spanish. Only 36.3 percent of all Chicanas and 39.1 percent of the Puerto Rican women, twenty-five years old and over, are high school graduates, while 53.3 percent of Cuban women and 54.9 percent of other Spanish women complete high school. Median years of school completed is 9.6 for Chicanas, 10.5 for Puerto Rican, 12.2 for Cuban and 12.3 for other Spanish women. Differences are also observable at the college level. As mentioned previously, roughly 4 percent of Chicanas twenty-five years old and over have four or more years of college, compared to 9.5 percent of Cuban women. Differences found in labor force characteristics between groups identified under Spanish origin are noted in Table 2. Chicanas and Puerto Rican women share more similarities than with Cuban or other Spanish women.

One now returns to the problem of undifferentiated data mentioned previously. In order to measure changes in the occupational status of Chicanas, three states with a significant Mexican population have been selected from the 1980 census. California and Texas have the largest populations of Mexican Americans. Illinois, with the fourth largest Chicano population,[27] was selected in order to include the Midwest. As alluded to earlier, EEOC data limit the researcher in that Chicanas are not disaggregated from the larger category of Hispanic females. By drawing conclusions and using statistics only from the three states

TABLE 2
FEMALE LABOR FORCE STATUS AND INDUSTRY BY TYPE OF SPANISH ORIGIN, 1980 (PERCENT)

LABOR FORCE STATUS[a]	Total of All Women	Chicana	Puerto Rican	Cuban	Other Spanish
16 and Over	(n = 89,482,168)	(n = 2,702,151)	(n = 675,370)	(n = 352,782)	(n = 1,156,600)
in Labor Force	49.9	49.0	40.1	55.4	53.4
With Children Under 6	15.2	28.5	26.3	11.1	20.8
(and in Labor Force)[b]	(45.7)	(43.8)	(31.0)	(51.3)	(46.1)
With Children 6-17	19.0	21.3	23.6	20.3	20.4
(and in Labor Force)	(63.0)	(55.8)	(42.1)	(67.0)	(62.2)
16 and Over, Married[c]	(n = 49,369,352)	(n = 1,506,869)	(n = 286,422)	(n = 189,410)	(n = 581,115)
in Labor Force	49.2	46.1	44.8	58.9	52.0
With Children Under 6	23.0	42.8	36.4	17.8	33.5
(and in Labor Force)	(43.9)	(42.5)	(38.9)	(50.5)	(45.7)
With Children 6-17	27.5	29.7	30.8	31.0	30.2
(and in Labor Force)	(60.1)	(52.7)	(47.7)	(65.9)	(59.6)
INDUSTRY					
16 and Over, Employed[a]	(n = 41,634,665)	(n = 1,189,458)	(n = 235,025)	(n = 180,987)	(n = 563,179)
Private Wage and Salary	75.0	77.7	77.9	84.9	79.9
Federal Government	3.6	3.6	4.6	1.8	3.8
State Government	5.7	4.6	4.3	2.8	4.9
Local Government	11.3	11.6	11.8	7.2	8.3
Self-Employed	3.7	2.0	1.2	2.6	2.6
Unpaid Family Workers	0.8	0.4	0.3	0.6	0.5

Source: U.S. Bureau of the Census, *United States Summary, General Social and Economic Characteristics*, Table 168, "Labor Force Characteristics by Spanish Origin, Type of Spanish Origin, and Race: 1980." (Washington, D.C.: 1980).
[a]"Labor Force" is defined as those employed and those unemployed and actively seeking work, whereas those "Employed" are only those who are currently working.
[b]Numbers in parentheses refer to the percentage of the number just above.
[c]Husband present

mentioned, an attempt is made to focus as much as possible on Chicanas only. The reader should be cautioned, however, that hereinafter the conclusions made and statistics given for Chicanas actually cover data that include all Hispanic females.

TABLE 3
PERSONS WHO REPRESENTED MEXICAN ANCESTRY
FOR SELECTED STATES, 1980

	Total Persons	Mexican	Percentage
California	23,667,902	3,361,773	14.20
Texas	14,229,191	2,495,035	17.50
Illinois	11,426,518	360,728	3.15

Source: U.S. Bureau of the Census, *Census of Population, Ancestry of the Population by State, 1980*. Supplementary Report PC 80-51-10, Table 3 (1980).

The analysis of occupational distribution and participation for Chicana workers in private industry in California, Texas and Illinois indicates the extent of occupational mobility Chicanas have experienced during the affirmative action era (see Table 4). Affirmative action was intended to change former recruiting patterns that excluded Chicanas and others as applicants. One would expect that guidelines providing equal opportunity for advancement within the work force would result in an increase in the number of Chicanas in managerial and professional positions. The period since affirmative action legislation was enacted has provided employers with time to implement affirmative action programs based on anticipated employee turnover rate and new vacancies, as well as time to promote and upgrade qualified Chicanas.

The question of reverse discrimination can be addressed by determining the degree of occupational shift among white males. If the reverse discrimination viewpoint is correct, one would expect to find that white males have experienced some shift from managerial and professional occupations to lower-paid positions, and are less dominant in managerial and professional occupations. Double protection under the law for minority women can be determined by comparing the advances made by groups protected only by sex or by race. If Chicanas do indeed experience double protection, advances into higher-income and prestigious occupations should be occurring at a faster rate than for either white females or Chicano males.

Occupational Stratification

The occupational distribution of Chicanas in private industry in 1971, 1975 and 1980 is presented in Table 4. Chicanas were primarily in blue-

TABLE 4

OCCUPATIONAL DISTRIBUTION OF CHICANAS IN PRIVATE INDUSTRY,
BY SELECTED STATES, 1971, 1975, 1980 (PERCENT)

	California			Texas			Illinois		
	1971	1975	1980	1971	1975	1980	1971	1975	1980
Total Employment	100.0	100.0	100.0	100.0	100.0	100.0	100.0	100.0	100.0
	(n=99,016)	(n=146,608)	(n=241,486)	(n=59,089)	(n=85,703)	(n=137,297)	(n=25,516)	(n=32,244)	(n=45,953)
Officials and Managers	1.4	2.1	2.7	1.1	2.1	2.4	0.5	1.2	1.6
Professionals	2.2	2.0	2.9	1.6	1.9	2.4	1.8	2.0	2.4
Technicians	2.3	2.4	3.4	3.5	4.0	3.8	1.6	1.9	2.5
Sales Workers	5.9	7.2	8.1	9.9	11.1	11.7	3.3	4.9	5.7
Office and Clerical Workers	32.1	30.1	26.9	20.6	23.8	23.8	19.1	22.0	21.6
Craft Workers	3.3	4.1	5.2	4.3	3.3	3.4	2.3	2.1	2.2
Operatives	24.8	23.1	22.9	32.7	28.9	26.3	37.0	32.3	29.8
Laborers	18.2	18.5	17.5	12.0	8.9	9.8	27.0	22.5	22.3
Service Workers	9.9	10.4	10.5	14.3	16.1	16.5	7.4	11.0	12.0

Source: U.S. Equal Employment Opportunity Commission, *EEO-1 Reports*, "Job Patterns of Minorities and Women in Private Industries, Occupational Employment in Private Industry by Race/Ethnic Group and Sex and by State and Industry, 1971, 1975, 1980" (Washington, D.C.: EEOC, 1980).

collar occupations in 1971. Over one-third of working Chicanas were
operatives, semi-skilled workers or laborers in California and Texas,
and almost two-thirds in Illinois fell within these occupational categories. Within blue-collar occupations, Chicanas were less likely to be in
highly skilled positions. Only 4 percent of the Chicanas in Texas were
craft workers, 3 percent in California and 2 percent in Illinois. Texas
had the largest percentage (14.3) of service workers, followed by California (9.9). Illinois had the least (7.4). Thirty-two percent of Chicanas
in California were office and clerical workers. That is 10 percent more
than found in Texas or Illinois. Very few Chicanas occupied managerial occupations. Approximately 6 percent of all official, managerial,
professional, and technical occupations were held by Chicanas in California and Texas in 1971. Only 3.9 percent were found to be in such
occupations in Illinois.

Occupational mobility over the decade has been minimal. Over half
of employed Chicanas in Illinois (54.3 percent), and approximately 40
percent in Texas and California, have continued to work in blue-collar
occupations. Approximately 50 percent of the blue-collar workers were
likely to be in operative occupations, a figure not much different from
that of 1971. There has been no more than a 3 percent increase in Chicanas employed in skilled occupations (craft workers). Although each
state has experienced an increase of Chicanas in white-collar positions,
most of these women have remained office and clerical workers.[28] There
has been only a 1.3 percent increase of Chicanas in official and managerial positions in California and Texas, and 1.1 percent in Illinois. Even
less progress has been made in professional occupations. Not one state
showed over a 1 percent increase in the number of Chicanas in professional occupations in ten years. Neither have Chicanas advanced in
technical occupations. The largest increase made by Chicanas has been
in California (1.1 percent). It is important to keep in mind that all
three states have recorded increases in the number of Chicana employees in private industry.

Another measurement of advancements made by Chicanas in private industry is occupational participation. Table 5 shows the share of
total employment and occupational categories held by Chicanas. Each
of the three states shows an increase in the proportion of Chicanas that
participate in private industry. Chicanas in Illinois made up 1.3 percent of the work force in private industry in 1971, 1.6 percent in 1975,
and 2.1 percent in 1980. Chicanas in Texas made up 2 percent more of
the work force in 1980 than they did in 1971. The largest increase in the
proportion of total employment occurred in California, where the Chicana participation rate increased from 3.8 percent to 7 percent.

TABLE 5
OCCUPATIONAL PARTICIPATION OF CHICANAS IN PRIVATE INDUSTRY,
BY SELECTED STATES, 1971, 1975, 1980 (PERCENT)

Share of:	California			Texas			Illinois		
	1971	1975	1980	1971	1975	1980	1971	1975	1980
Total Employment	3.8	5.2	7.0	4.5	5.3	6.5	1.3	1.6	2.1
Officials and Managers	0.5	0.9	1.6	0.5	1.0	1.3	0.1	0.2	0.3
Professionals	0.6	0.9	1.7	0.8	1.3	1.7	0.3	0.4	0.6
Technicians	1.6	2.4	3.9	3.2	3.6	4.2	0.5	0.6	1.0
Sales Workers	2.5	3.8	5.7	4.9	5.9	7.5	0.5	0.8	1.3
Office and Clerical Workers	5.8	8.0	9.9	5.4	7.6	9.7	1.4	2.0	2.7
Craft Workers	1.0	1.8	3.3	1.3	1.2	1.7	0.2	0.3	0.4
Operatives	6.3	8.1	11.1	7.4	8.0	9.5	2.1	2.4	3.1
Laborers	9.8	13.3	16.8	6.7	6.4	8.3	3.4	4.0	5.8
Service Workers	5.1	6.4	8.2	9.5	10.7	12.1	1.5	2.4	2.9

Source: U.S. Equal Employment Opportunity Commission, *EEO-1 Reports*, "Job Patterns of Minorities and Women in Private Industries, 1971, 1975, 1980," Table
2 (Washington, D.C.: EEOC, 1980).

The participation rate identifies occupations where Chicanas are concentrated. In 1971, Chicanas in Texas were concentrated in service occupations, unskilled blue-collar occupations and lower-paid white-collar occupations. Chicanas in California and Illinois were disproportionately distributed in similar occupations in 1971; however, the difference is higher in unskilled blue-collar positions than it is in service occupations. Chicanas are underrepresented in skilled and higher-paying positions in all three states. Chicanas did not have their proportional share of official, managerial, and technical positions in 1971. Chicanas were also underrepresented in sales occupations in California and Illinois.

The 1975 and 1980 occupational participation percentages show very little redistribution of jobs held by Chicanas. Both Illinois and California have a concentration of Chicanas in the same occupational categories as noted in 1971. Although Chicanas were only 7 percent of the labor force in California in 1980, they comprised 16.8 percent of laborers, 11.1 percent of operatives, 9.9 percent of office and clerical workers and 8.2 percent of all service workers. The same discrepancy can be noted in Illinois where Chicanas were only 2.1 percent of the labor force in 1980, yet comprised 5.8 percent of all laborers, 3.1 percent of operatives, 2.9 percent of service workers and 2.7 percent of office and clerical workers. Texas showed the largest concentration of Chicanas in service occupations.

The second major area of concentration of Chicanas in Texas is found among office and clerical workers (9.7 percent), followed by operatives (9.5 percent), laborers (8.3 percent) and sales workers (7.5 percent). Chicanas in California and Illinois differ from those in Texas in

TABLE 6
OCCUPATIONAL DISTRIBUTION OF CHICANAS AND WHITE MALES IN PRIVATE
INDUSTRY BY AVERAGE FOR CALIFORNIA, TEXAS AND ILLINOIS,
1975 AND 1980

| | Chicana | | White Male | |
	1975	1980	1975	1980
Total Employment				
Percentage	100	100	100	100
Number	264,555	424,736	3,144,274	3,296,314
Officials and Managers				
Percentage	1.97	2.47	18.05	19.34
Number	5,220	10,500	567,514	637,412
Professionals				
Percentage	1.99	2.66	12.89	13.8
Number	5,256	11,315	405,285	455,019
Technicians				
Percentage	2.89	3.42	6.37	6.63
Number	7,648	14,547	200,231	218,606
Sales Workers				
Percentage	8.19	8.97	9.55	9.37
Number	21,671	38,094	300,210	309,005
Office and Clerical Workers				
Percentage	27.09	25.33	5.54	4.9
Number	71,677	107,588	174,152	161,411
Craft Workers				
Percentage	3.59	4.3	19.7	18.34
Number	9,498	18,250	619,334	604,508
Operatives				
Percentage	26.1	24.76	17.61	17.12
Number	69,051	105,177	553,761	564,286
Laborers				
Percentage	15.86	15.51	5.63	5.41
Number	41,954	65,859	176,920	178,416
Service Workers				
Percentage	12.32	12.57	4.67	5.09
Number	32,580	53,406	146,867	167,651

Source: Composed from data in U.S. Equal Employment Opportunity Commission,
   EEO-1 Reports, "Job Patterns of Minorities and Women in Private Industries,
   Occupational Employment in Private Industry by Race/Ethnic Group and Sex
   and by State and Industry, 1975, 1980" (Washington, D.C.: EEOC, 1980).

that they were underrepresented in sales occupations in both 1971 and
1980. Chicanas in all three states did not have a proportionate share of
either official, managerial, professional, or technical occupations. In
1980 Chicanas held only .3 percent of the official and managerial positions in Illinois, 1.3 percent in Texas and 1.6 percent in California.

TABLE 7
OCCUPATIONAL PARTICIPATION OF CHICANAS AND WHITE MALES IN PRI-
VATE INDUSTRY BY AVERAGE FOR CALIFORNIA, TEXAS AND ILLINOIS,
1975 AND 1980

Share of:	Chicana		White Male	
	1975	1980	1975	1980
Total Employment				
Percentage	4.07	5.47	48.33	42.46
Number	264,555	424,736	3,144,274	3,296,314
Officials and Managers				
Percentage	0.72	1.18	78.29	71.56
Number	5,220	10,500	567,514	637,412
Professionals				
Percentage	0.87	1.41	67.25	56.57
Number	5,256	11,315	405,285	455,019
Technicians				
Percentage	2.25	3.59	58.8	53.9
Number	7,648	14,547	200,231	218,606
Sales Workers				
Percentage	3.4	5.0	47.1	40.62
Number	21,671	38,094	300,210	309,005
Office and Clerical Workers				
Percentage	6.08	7.9	14.78	11.85
Number	71,677	107,588	174,152	161,411
Craft Workers				
Percentage	1.14	2.02	74.62	66.75
Number	9,498	18,250	619,334	604,508
Operatives				
Percentage	5.91	7.98	47.37	42.82
Number	69,051	105,177	553,761	564,286
Laborers				
Percentage	8.3	11.18	35.01	30.28
Number	41,954	65,859	176,920	178,416
Service Workers				
Percentage	6.3	7.82	28.39	24.55
Number	32,580	53,406	146,867	167,651

Source: Composed from data in U.S. Equal Employment Opportunity Commission,
EEO-1 Reports, "Job Patterns of Minorities and Women in Private Industries,
Occupational Employment in Private Industry by Race/Ethnic Group and Sex
and by State and Industry, 1975, 1980" (Washington, D.C.: EEOC, 1980).

These data all indicate that the occupational distribution and participation of Chicanas in private industry over a ten-year period of
time has not shifted. Working Chicanas in California, Illinois and
Texas continue to occupy the lowest-paid, unskilled blue-collar and
white-collar occupations.

Preferential Treatment and Reverse Discrimination

In 1975 over 30 percent of all white males were in managerial and professional occupations, while fewer than 4 percent of employed Chicanas were in similar positions. In order to investigate whether a downward trend exists in the occupational distribution of white males in private industry as a result of the hiring and promotion of Chicanas and other minorities, the average of the three states was taken and occupational distribution and participation were calculated. The average for all industries in California, Texas and Illinois was computed for 1975 and 1980 (see Table 6). Where a downward shift in the distribution of white males in private industry occurred, it was less than 1 percent (with the exception of craft workers). More important, the downward shift occurred primarily within unskilled and lower-paid occupations. On the other hand, the distribution of white males in managerial and professional occupations actually increased. Chicanas made less than a 1 percent increase in any occupation during this period. Thus, the data do not indicate that white males have experienced a downward occupational distribution as a result of the entry or promotion of Chicanas or other minorities into managerial and professional positions; on the contrary, white males appear to have made continued progress.[29]

An average of the occupational participation within all industries in California, Texas and Illinois provides information on the price paid by white males for the hiring and promotion of Chicanas in private industry (see Table 7). Chicanas experienced a small increase in their proportion of total employment from 1975 (4.07 percent) to 1980 (5.47 percent). Even with this rise in total employment, Chicanas experienced little increase in their share of managerial, professional, technical, and craft worker positions in 1980. However, their concentration as office and clerical workers, operatives, laborers, and service workers did increase. In 1975 Chicanas not only were predominantly office and clerical workers, operatives, laborers, and service workers, but were underrepresented in higher-paying white- and blue-collar occupations. For instance, they were overrepresented by 4.23 percent in laborer positions and by 2.23 percent in service occupations, compared to their share of the total employment. Chicanas were underrepresented in higher-paid and skilled occupations. They had 3.35 percent fewer of the managerial positions and 3.2 percent fewer of the professional positions.

White males comprised 48.33 percent of the total work force in 1975 and 42.46 percent in 1980. White males were dominant in all the skilled and highly paid positions (officials and managers, professionals, technicians, and craft workers) in 1975. White males held almost 30 percent more than their proportional share of the managerial and nearly 20 percent more of the professional positions, and about 25 percent more of skilled blue-collar positions. The overabundance of white male representation in these jobs continued in 1980. As might be expected, white males were underrepresented in low-paid, low-status occupations in 1975. The most disproportionate distribution occurred in the "traditional female" occupation, office and clerical work, where white males were underrepresented by 33.55 percent. In 1975 white males were underrepresented by 19.94 percent in their share of service workers and 13.32 percent in the laborers category.

In short, white males have been able to maintain a disproportionate share of the higher-paying and skilled jobs in private industry despite affirmative action. The slight increases Chicanas have made into professional occupations have not been at the expense of the status quo.

Twice Protected?

The question of whether sex and/or race operate as advantages in the labor market can be investigated by comparing advances made by white women and Chicano males from 1975 to 1980 to those made by Chicanas. The averages for all industries in California, Texas and Illinois were used in this analysis in order to identify trends. Table 8 shows the occupational distribution among Chicanas, white females and Chicano males. Although women were primarily hired as office and clerical workers, white women were more likely to occupy this position than Chicanas in 1975, with 42 percent of white women in these positions as compared to 27 percent for Chicanas. Chicanas were more than twice as likely to be hired as operatives and laborers than white women. Over half of Chicano males were unskilled blue-collar workers in 1975 compared to about 40 percent for Chicanas. White females (17.02 percent) were more likely to be in managerial, professional, or technical positions than either Chicano males (10.16 percent) or Chicanas (6.85 percent) in 1975. Almost a fourth of white women were employed in these positions in 1980, while only one-tenth of the Chicanos were. White women experienced about a 5 percent decrease in their distribution as office and clerical workers from 1975 to 1980, whereas Chicanas dropped less than 2 percent. The largest changes in occupational distribution for Chicano males from 1975 to 1980 were an increase in their proportion of service workers and a decrease in their proportion of operatives.

The participation rates of each group provide more detailed information on the degree of representation in each occupational category

TABLE 8
OCCUPATIONAL DISTRIBUTION OF CHICANAS, WHITE FEMALES AND
CHICANO MALES IN PRIVATE INDUSTRY BY AVERAGE FOR CALIFORNIA,
TEXAS AND ILLINOIS, 1975 AND 1980

	Chicana		White Female		Chicano Male	
	1975	1980	1975	1980	1975	1980
Total Employment						
Percentage	100	100	100	100	100	100
Number	264,555	424,736	1,802,407	2,211,695	471,876	665,247
Officials and Managers						
Percentage	1.97	2.47	5.37	6.81	4.55	4.97
Number	5,220	10,500	96,862	150,547	21,462	33,084
Professionals						
Percentage	1.99	2.66	7.32	10.23	2.54	2.73
Number	5,256	11,315	131,854	226,220	11,990	18,153
Technicians						
Percentage	2.89	3.42	4.33	5.64	3.07	3.3
Number	7,648	14,547	78,108	124,697	14,485	21,929
Sales Workers						
Percentage	8.19	8.97	13.65	13.74	4.40	4.75
Number	21,671	38,094	245,953	303,945	20,770	31,614
Office and Clerical Workers						
Percentage	27.09	25.33	42.21	37.94	4.27	3.92
Number	71,677	107,588	760,863	839,066	20,151	26,054
Craft Workers						
Percentage	3.59	4.3	2.15	2.61	18.46	17.71
Number	9,498	18,250	38,692	57,828	87,064	117,828
Operatives						
Percentage	26.1	24.76	10.98	9.28	31.07	29.33
Number	69,051	105,177	197,860	205,209	146,615	195,111
Laborers						
Percentage	15.86	15.51	4.58	3.9	21.86	21.61
Number	41,954	65,859	82,610	86,222	103,172	143,754
Service Workers						
Percentage	12.32	12.57	9.41	9.85	9.78	11.68
Number	32,580	53,406	169,605	217,961	46,167	77,720

Source: Composed from data in U.S. Equal Employment Opportunity Commission,
EEO-1 Reports, "Job Patterns of Minorities and Women in Private Industries,
Occupational Employment in Private Industry by Race/Ethnic Group and Sex
and by State and Industry, 1975, 1980" (Washington, D.C.: EEOC, 1980).

(see Table 9). In 1975, white women were underrepresented in high-paying white-collar and blue-collar positions. Although white women comprised 27.71 percent of the total work force, they occupied only 13.36 percent of managerial, 21.88 percent of professional, and 22.94 percent of technical positions. White women did not hold their share of blue-collar positions either. However, white women occupied more

TWICE PROTECTED? 151

TABLE 9
OCCUPATIONAL PARTICIPATION OF CHICANAS, WHITE FEMALES AND CHICANO MALES IN PRIVATE INDUSTRY BY AVERAGE FOR CALIFORNIA, TEXAS AND ILLINOIS, 1975 AND 1980

Share of:	Chicana		White Female		Chicano Male	
	1975	1980	1975	1980	1975	1980
Total Employment						
Percentage	4.07	5.47	27.71	28.49	7.25	8.57
Number	264,555	424,736	1,802,407	2,211,695	471,876	665,247
Officials and Managers						
Percentage	0.72	1.18	13.36	16.9	2.96	3.71
Number	5,220	10,500	96,862	150,547	21,462	33,084
Professionals						
Percentage	0.87	1.41	21.88	28.12	1.99	2.26
Number	5,256	11,315	131,854	226,220	11,990	18,153
Technicians						
Percentage	2.25	3.59	22.94	30.74	4.25	5.41
Number	7,648	14,547	78,108	124,697	14,485	21,929
Sales Workers						
Percentage	3.4	5.0	38.59	39.95	3.26	4.16
Number	21,671	38,094	245,953	303,945	20,770	31,614
Office and Clerical Workers						
Percentage	6.08	7.9	64.57	61.61	1.71	1.91
Number	71,677	107,588	760,863	839,066	20,151	26,054
Craft Workers						
Percentage	1.14	2.02	4.66	6.39	10.49	13.01
Number	9,498	18,250	38,692	57,828	87,064	117,828
Operatives						
Percentage	5.91	7.98	16.92	15.57	12.54	14.81
Number	69,051	105,177	197,860	205,209	146,615	195,111
Laborers						
Percentage	8.3	11.18	16.35	14.63	20.42	24.4
Number	41,954	65,859	82,610	86,222	103,172	143,754
Service Workers						
Percentage	6.3	7.82	32.79	31.92	8.93	11.38
Number	32,580	53,406	169,605	217,961	46,167	77,720

Source: Composed from data in U.S. Equal Employment Opportunity Commission, *EEO-1 Reports*, "Job Patterns of Minorities and Women in Private Industries, Occupational Employment in Private Industry by Race/Ethnic Group and Sex and by State and Industry, 1975, 1980" (Washington, D.C.: EEOC, 1980).

than their share of the sales positions (38.59 percent), service jobs (32.79 percent), and office and clerical positions (64.57 percent). Chicano males lacked their share of all white-collar occupations, and were concentrated in all blue-collar and service jobs in 1975.

Chicanas and white women had modest increases in their share of the total employment from 1975 to 1980. Chicano males increased their

share of total employment by 1.32 percent. In spite of the similarity of
increases in the total employment over the five years, disparity exists
between the degree of advances made. White women were able to obtain a larger share of professional[30] (28.12 percent) and technical
(30.74 percent) occupations, while both Chicano males and females
continued to fall short of their share of these positions. Nor did either
group make substantial gains in obtaining its share of official and managerial positions. White women held a little over half of their share of
managerial positions,[31] and Chicano men held a little less than half.
Chicanas held less than a third of their share of managerial positions.
White women managed to reduce their overrepresentation within certain low-paying jobs (office and clerical workers, operatives, and service workers), but this was not the case for Chicanas and Chicano
males.

Conclusion

The incredibly slow pace at which Chicanas are moving into higher-
paying managerial and skilled positions and their concentration in
lower-paid white-collar and blue-collar occupations hardly legitimate
the claim of "preferential treatment." Analysis of occupational distribution and participation of Chicanas and white males clearly indicates
that white males have maintained their dominance in managerial and
professional positions. White males continue to be overrepresented in
the better jobs and fewer white males are relegated to the less attractive jobs—a rather odd effect of reverse discrimination or "affirmative
discrimination," as Nathan Glazer prefers to call it.[32] It appears to be
simply a continuation of racial and sexual inequality. William Ryan
urges that we clarify reality again by

> properly defining the discrimination issue as the continuation of
> old-fashioned, unreverse discrimination and preferential treat-
> ment of whites, affirmative action is providing merely the score-
> card with which to judge to what extent the old problem is being
> eliminated.[33]

Analysis of the occupational distribution and participation of Chicanas in private industry from 1975 to 1980 shows very little improvement. Chicanas are a long way from obtaining their fair share of
higher-income and prestigious occupations. The minuscule progress
made by Chicanas is not very encouraging when one considers that it
occurred not only during the affirmative action era, but also during a
period of rising Chicana labor force participation and increased educational attainment, and of pressure from Chicano and women's organi-

zations. It seems that instead of focusing research on the effects of affirmative action on minority and women's employment, we need to assess the impact of white male backlash on the composition of the labor force.

NOTES

[1]These statutes and orders include the Equal Pay Act of 1963, Executive Order 11246 as amended by Executive Order 11375, Title IX of the Education Amendments of 1972, and Title VII of the Civil Rights Act of 1964 as amended by the Equal Employment Opportunity Act of 1972. The Equal Pay Act of 1963 was the first legislation passed requiring equal pay for equal work regardless of sex. Later, coverage was extended to executive, administrative and professional employees in Title IX of the Education Amendment Act of 1972. Title VII of the Civil Rights Act of 1964 prohibits "discrimination on the basis of race, color, national origin, religion or sex in any term, condition or privilege of employment by unions and by employers." All public and private employers with fifteen or more employees were included under the amended law in 1972. Affirmative action activities are aimed at changing former recruiting patterns that tended to exclude women and minorities as applicants and to provide equal opportunity for advancement within the work force. Executive Order 11246 required that employers develop goals to include underrepresented groups. Timetables to achieve affirmative action goals were to be based on the "anticipated employee turnover rate, new vacancies, schedules for promotion and upgrading, and the availability of qualified women and minorities."

[2]The Office of Federal Contract Compliance (OFCCP) has proposed changes to alter requirements for federal contractors covered under Executive Order 11246 to apply only to contractors employing one hundred persons, rather than the existing fifty, and to contracts exceeding $100,000, rather than the existing $50,000. The seriousness of the proposed changes are pointed out by the National Council of La Raza in their publication, "Changes Proposed in Affirmative Action Requirements for Federal Contractors." "Presently, the federal contract compliance program covers nearly 29,000 contractors who hire 31 million persons, or one-third of the working population, and includes over $80 billion in federal contracts." Therefore, the proposed changes would apply to even fewer work sites than before.

[3]Critics of affirmative action have frequently claimed the lack of representativeness of minorities and women in particular occupations is due to their own deficiencies, such as lack of qualifications or the interference of family roles. This "blaming-the-victim" approach suggests that the remedy exists in programs aimed at changing the individual rather than the system. For specific examples, see Amitai Etzioni, "On Academic Blood Tests," *Science* (June 1971): 1087; Benjamin R. Epstein and Arnold Foster, *Preferential Treatment and Quotas* (New York: Anti-Defamation League of B'nai B'rith, 1974); Alan H. Goldman, "Affirmative Action," *Philosophy and Public Affairs* 6:2 (Winter 1976): 178-195; Richard A. Lester, *Anti-bias Regulation of Universities: Faculty Problems and Their Solutions* (New York: McGraw-Hill, 1974). Several studies show that minorities and women are overqualified for positions when compared

with their white male counterparts. See Morris Goldstein and Robert S. Smith, "The Estimated Impact of Antidiscrimination Programs Aimed at Federal Contractors," *Industrial and Labor Relations Review* 29:4 (July 1976): 523-543; Stanley H. Masters, "The Effects of Educational Differences and Labor-Market Discrimination on the Relative Earnings of Black Males," *The Journal of Human Resources* 9:3 (Summer 1974): 342-360; Dudley L. Poston, David Alvirez and Marta Tienda, "Earning Differences Between Anglo and Mexican American Male Workers in 1960 and 1970: Changes in the 'Cost' of Being Mexican American," *Social Science Quarterly* 57:3 (December 1976): 618-631.

[4]One of the most prominent neoconservatives is Nathan Glazer. See his book *Affirmative Discrimination: Ethnic Inequality and Public Policy* (New York: Basic Books, 1975).

[5]Nijole V. Benokraitis and Joe P. Feagin, *Affirmative Action and Equal Opportunity: Action, Inaction, Reaction* (Boulder, Col.: Westview Press, 1978), p. 211. It may not actually be the first time. One could compare the reaction of southern whites to the Civil Rights Act and court orders to integrate.

[6]Ibid., p. 193. Minority movements include Chicano, black, Native American and other political groups.

[7]The term "Chicano" refers to U.S. citizens, or persons of Mexican origin with long-term residency in the United States; frequently referred to as Mexican American, Spanish American or Mexicanos throughout the Southwest. Chicana refers to women.

[8]Carey McWilliams, *North from Mexico* (New York: Greenwood Press, 1968), pp. 207-208.

[9]Clark S. Knowlton, "The Impact of Social Change upon Certain Selected Systems of Spanish American Villages of Northern New Mexico," paper prepared for the Rural Sociological Society (Chicago, 1965).

[10]Rodolfo Acuña, *Occupied America* (San Francisco: Canfield Press, 1972); Thomas Almaguer, "Historical Notes on Chicano Oppression: The Dialectics of Racial and Class Domination in North America," *Aztlan* 5:1/2 (Spring/Fall 1974): 27-56; Mario Barrera, *Race and Class in the Southwest: A Theory of Racial Inequality* (Notre Dame: University of Notre Dame Press, 1979); David Montejano, "Race, Labor Repression, and Capitalist Agriculture: Notes from South Texas, 1920-1930" (Berkeley, Cal.: University of California Institute for the Study of Social Change, 1977), Working Papers Series 102.

[11]Barrera, op. cit., p. 40.

[12]Douglas Monroy, "La Costura en Los Angeles, 1933-1939: The ILGWU and the Politics of Domination," in Magdalena Mara and Adelaida R. Del Castillo, eds., *Mexican Women in the United States: Struggles Past and Present* (Los Angeles: Chicano Studies Research Center Publications, 1980); Mario T. Garcia, "The Chicana in American History: The Mexican Women of El Paso," *Pacific Historical Review* 49:2 (May 1980): 315-337; Paul S. Taylor, "Mexican Women in Los Angeles Industry in 1928," *Aztlan* 11:1 (Spring 1980): 99-131.

[13]Barrera, op. cit., p. 163.

[14]Cited in Barrera, ibid., p. 95. U.S. Bureau of the Census, *Fifteenth Census of the United States: 1930*, Vol. 5: General Report on Occupation, Table 4.

[15]Taylor, 1980.

[16]Mario T. Garcia, "Racial Dualism in the El Paso Labor Market, 1880-1920," *Aztlan* VI:2 (Special Issue, 1975): 197-218.

[17]Charles Hufford, *The Social and Economic Effects of the Mexican Migration into Texas* (San Francisco: R & E Research Associates, 1971, reprint of 1925 edition), pp. 58-59.

[18]Barrera, op. cit., p. 103.

[19]U.S. Bureau of the Census, *United States Summary, General Social and Economic Characteristics*, Table 166, "Age, Fertility, Relationship, and Educational Characteristics by Spanish-Origin, Type of Spanish Origin, and Race: 1980" (Washington, D.C.: 1980).

[20]Information on the Chicana population enrolled in school is limited to women twenty-five years and older. However, the percentages given of the total Chicano population are informative: 39 percent of eighteen to nineteen year olds are enrolled; 19 percent of the twenty to twenty-one year olds are enrolled; 11 percent of twenty-two to twenty-four year olds are enrolled. For the total U.S. population, the percentages are respectively 52 percent, 32.5 percent and 17 percent.

[21]U.S. Bureau of the Census, *United States Summary, General Social and Economic Characteristics*, Table 168, "Labor Force Characteristics by Spanish Origin, Type of Origin, and Race: 1980" (Washington, D.C.: 1980).

[22]For further discussion on working mothers and comparisons between Chicanas and white women and black women, see Rosemary Santana Cooney, "The Mexican American Female in the Labor Force," in Charles H. Teller, Leo F. Estrada, Jose Hernandez and David Alvirez, eds., *Cuantos Somos: A Demographic Study of the Mexican-American Population* (Austin, Texas: Center for Mexican American Studies, 1977), pp. 183-196.

[23]The 1970 census showed 28 percent of married Chicanas in the labor force. Forty-five percent of the married women had children under six. Twenty percent of mothers with children under six were in the labor force.

[24]Equal Employment Opportunity Commission, *EEO-1 Report*, "Job Patterns for Minorities and Women in Private Industry" (Washington, D.C.: EEOC, 1980), p. vii. Although data are collected from various industries, the term "employee" does not include temporary employees or employees hired for a specified period of time or for the duration of a specified job, which limits the data on the construction industry and agriculture.

[25]Officials and managers includes executives, middle management, plant managers, department managers and superintendents, purchasing agents, buyers, and kindred workers. Professionals includes accountants and auditors, airplane pilots, navigators, architects, artists, chemists, designers, dietitians, editors, engineers, lawyers, librarians, mathematicians, natural scientists, registered nurses, personnel and labor relations workers, physicians, social scientists, and teachers. Technicians includes occupations which require two years

of post-high school education. Sales workers includes insurance agents, brokers, real estate agents, sales clerks, grocery clerks, and cashier checkers.

[26]For a detailed discussion on differences between groups classified as Hispanic, see: Rosemary Santana Cooney and Vilma Ortiz, "Nativity, National Origin, and Hispanic Female Participation in the Labor Force," *Social Science Quarterly* 64:3 (September 1983): 510; Morris J. Newman, "A Profile of Hispanics in the U.S. Work Force," *Monthly Labor Review* 101:12 (December 1978): 3-14; and Lester Thurow, "Not Making It in America: The Economic Progress of Minority Groups," *Social Policy* 6:5 (March 1976): 5-11. For problems specific to use of census data, see Jose Hernandez, Leo Estrada and David Alvirez, "Census Data and the Problem of Conceptually Defining the Mexican American Population," *Social Science Quarterly* 53:4 (March 1973): 671-687; and Leo F. Estrada, Jose Hernandez and David Alvirez, "Using Census Data to Study Spanish Heritage Population of the United States," and Edward Fernandez, "A Comparison of Persons of Spanish Origin and Persons of Spanish Surname in the United States Using the March 1971 Current Population Survey," in Teller, et al., *Cuantos Somos*, op. cit. Another major problem with these particular data is the broadness of the categories used in the EEOC reports. This breadth may tend to hide important income differences within an occupation.

[27]Arizona has the third largest Mexican population, 368,259.

[28]This is not an unusual finding. Blumrosen noted that the bulk of new women workers have taken traditional female jobs. Ruth G. Blumrosen, "Wage Discrimination, Job Segregation, and Women Workers," *Employee Relations Law Journal* 61:1 (Summer 1980): 77.

[29]Morris Goldstein and Robert S. Smith found that affirmative action programs were helping white men but were having an adverse effect on women. Morris Goldstein and Robert Smith, "The Estimated Impact of the Antidiscrimination Program Aimed at Federal Contractors," *Industrial and Labor Relations Review* 29:4 (1976): 523-543.

[30]This increase in the participation of white women in professions does not necessarily guarantee equality. Cooney found in her study on female professionals in the United States, Canada, Australia and New Zealand that women tend to be concentrated in the lower-status positions within occupations. Rosemary Santana Cooney, "Female Professional Work Opportunities: A Cross-National Study," *Demography* 12:1 (February 1975): 107-120.

[31]The increase in the number of women holding managerial positions has been questioned because the category includes supervisory positions in fields that have low-paying jobs.

[32]See Glazer, op. cit.

[33]William Ryan, *Equality* (New York: Vintage Books, 1982), p. 207.

ETHNIC-MINORITY WOMEN IN THE PRIVATE CORPORATION: THE CASE OF OFFICIALS AND MANAGERS

Jeanne Prial Gordus and Marian M. Oshiro

University of Michigan

Public policy toward ethnic-minority women may have been reflected best in the attitude of those legislators who allowed "sex" to be added to the list of outlawed qualifiers in the Civil Rights Act of 1964. Sex discrimination was to have been the "reductio ad absurdum" of the entire bill, to demonstrate that discrimination, whether based on sex or race, was not a legitimate subject of legislation.[1]

But the act did become law, and the stage was set, not only for the casting of greater numbers of women into many roles previously denied them, but also for struggles among the racial and ethnic groups, and perhaps even between individuals who were members of more than one of the disadvantaged groups named in Title VII of that law—ethnic-minority women. It is a problem of identities—self-identity and legal identity—as well as a question of "discrimination" and what it means to be "disadvantaged." It belongs not only to these women, but to the federal agencies which write the rules defining compliance with the law, and the organizations, private and public, which must comply with them.

The complexity of the problem invites interdisciplinary research and detailed analysis. In this chapter we aim to present brief suggestive discussion of the following:

- Theoretical approaches to human resources development and to individual responses to social and economic problems;

- Changes in employment statistics and labor force participation of women, particularly minority women, from 1973 to 1980;

- Different patterns of minority women's participation in various job categories, with particular attention to officials and managers;

- Suggestion of some specific problems of career preparation and development to explain why access may be legislated, but upward mobility may not result;

- Trends in labor force and occupational growth; and

- Public policy implications of these findings.

Evidence of Discrimination

Discrimination is difficult to prove—it resides in the performer of the act of discrimination. There is, however, a general notion of what it is: an action resulting from an attitude born of one's own experience, or adopted from the generalized experience of others (in whose judgment we have more or less faith), which subsumes the individual human being into a sterotype by foregrounding certain attributes (the word is used advisedly—characteristics are *attributed*, validly or not) in order to differentiate one particular class of "things" from another. But while discrimination as a cause may be difficult to prove in individual cases, Lester Thurow and others have proven it in the aggregate and certain quantifiable effects clearly support the perception of its existence.[2]

Much of the research to date has compared women to men; less of it has focused on minority group members, and still less on minority women as a special group. The studies have been either in-depth interviews of a very small sample of women—and hence insufficient for generalizations—or aggregated data concerning such large numbers of women that the significant differences between ethnic groups are obscured. Both kinds of studies are, nevertheless, useful for raising questions and suggesting responses to the problems minority women encounter in the workplace.

The employment effects treated in this chapter can be found in or derived from the Equal Employment Opportunity Commission's EEO-1 reports for private industry. Use of these figures, though, must be cautious for several reasons. First, coverage is limited to employers of one hundred or more permanent workers, thus providing very limited coverage of industries such as construction and agriculture where employment tends to be of limited duration, and where women would be expected to fare poorly. On the other hand, if it is true that larger companies have better representation of women, but that women are more likely to achieve top positions in smaller companies, we may be overlooking an important group since only relatively large employers are included.[3]

Second, by EEOC requirement, coverage is limited to companies with financial ties to the federal government through contracts or handling of federal funds.

A third and very important limitation of the data is common to all such enumerations: determination of racial or ethnic group. In the first volume of the *Ethnicity and Public Policy* series, Ira Lowry discussed problems related to self-identification of race and ethnicity used by the Bureau of the Census, and the need for a more scientific approach.[4] In contrast, EEO-1 identification is determined by the employer. However, since our interest is in employer behavior as affected by employer *perception* of employee racial or ethnic identity, one may actually be at something of an advantage in using figures based on the employer's determination of the race/ethnicity of employees. Yet, since employers would wish to be perceived as complying with EEOC requirements, some numbers could be inflated.

The fourth consideration, designation of job categories, is more of a concern since we are focusing on minority women's representation in particular job categories. The category in which we are most interested, officials and managers (O & M), is especially problematic, since individuals who are trained for and begin their careers in other categories can continue to perform tasks specific to their entry positions while assuming additional kinds of tasks and responsibilities. Thus they might be counted in either job category. In addition, there are several levels of management jobs, and women and minorities have done better at the lower and middle levels.

In spite of these limitations, 75 percent of manufacturing firms covered by the Bureau of Labor Statistics' reports, as well as substantial portions of other major industries, *are* included, and offer a reasonable base for initial analysis. EEOC employment figures are given by gender, by five racial/ethnic categories and by nine job categories, for 162 industries.

Perusal of the EEOC figures shows that, in 1980, 41 percent of the 34,075,881 enumerated workers were women; 8.5 percent of them from ethnic/racial minority groups. Their distribution in the nine job categories is not surprising, and has remained essentially the same for the four reporting periods: women are overrepresented in the lower-paying jobs and underrepresented in the better-paying ones. For minority women, the situation is even more clearly defined in terms of economically preferable jobs. Equally predictable is the overrepresentation of women versus men of the same ethnic group in the lower-paying job categories, and underrepresentation in better-paying ones.

TABLE 1

PARTICIPATION IN JOB CATEGORY, 1980

All Women[a]		Median Weekly Earnings[b]			Minority Women[a]	
			ISDP	CPS		
82.8%	Office and Clerical	Service Workers	$165.02	$163.28	Service Workers	16.8%
55.1%	Service Workers	Laborers	$177.98	$187.20	Office and Clerical	14.3%
52.7%	Sales Workers	Clerical Workers	$185.51	$186.64	Laborers	11.0%
		Operatives[c]	$214.14	$221.72	Operatives	9.2%
41.0%	Workforce Rate	Sales Workers	$212.63	$239.20		
		Craft and Kindred Workers	$303.94	$293.32	Workforce Rate	8.5%
40.2%	Technicians				Technicians	7.5%
37.2%	Professionals	Professional, Technical and Kindred[c]	$325.65	$310.77	Sales Workers	7.1%
34.2%	Laborers				Professionals	4.6%
32.9%	Operatives	Managers and Administrators (Non-farm)[c]	$353.51	$335.51	Craft Workers	2.3%
18.5%	Officials and Managers				Officials and Managers	2.0%
9.6%	Craft Workers					

Source: U.S. Equal Employment Opportunity Commission, "Job Patterns for Minorities and Women in Private Industry, 1975," *EEO-1* (Washington, D.C.: EEOC, 1980); and U.S. Bureau of the Census, "Wage and Salary Data from the Income Survey Development Program: 1979," in *Current Population Reports*, Special Studies, Series P-23, No. 118 (Washington, D.C.: Government Printing Office, 1979), p. 5.

[a]Percentages based on data from 1980 EEOC report.

[b]Figures are from the census report. ISDP figures are the average of four weeks in January; CPS figures are "usual" weekly wages.

[c]The job categories are approximate matches only. In the category "Operatives," the figure shown is the average for non-transport and transport operatives combined (ISDP: $188.91 and $239.37; CPS: $199.66 and $243.78).

TABLE 2
WOMEN'S PORTION OF JOB CATEGORY
RELATIVE TO MEN OF SAME ETHNIC GROUP, 1980,
BY PERCENT

Job Category	Black Women	Hispanic Women	Asian/ Pacific Islander Women	Indian/ Alaskan Native Women	All Minority Women	White Women
Office and Clerical Workers	81.9	78.7	76.2	58.0	80.0	83.4
Service Workers	55.1	41.0	50.0	49.2	51.4	56.9
Sales Workers	61.4	54.1	51.6	45.2	57.9	52.0
Workforce Rate	47.1	39.3	48.3	34.9	44.7	40.1
Technicians	57.4	38.4	39.9	35.1	50.0	38.5
Professionals	55.7	37.2	39.0	29.9	45.6	36.2
Operatives	36.4	34.7	53.9	32.9	36.6	31.7
Laborers	33.5	31.4	46.0	32.9	33.1	34.7
Officials and Managers	31.0	22.9	25.0	19.0	27.3	17.8
Craft Workers	16.0	14.0	23.6	10.7	15.5	8.5

Source: U.S Equal Employment Opportunity Commission, "Job Patterns for Minorities and Women in Private Industry, 1975," *EEO-1* (Washington, D.C.: EEOC, 1980).

While there is some variation among the racial/ethnic groups, two observations seem clear: (1) Women, both white and minority, are *over*-represented in two of the lowest-paying job categories, service workers and office and clerical workers, both with reference to the work force as a whole, and with reference to men of the same race in that work force; (2) Women, both white and minority, are *under*represented among craft workers and officials and managers, both with reference to the work force as a whole, and with reference to men of the same race in that work force. Craft workers are the highest-paid blue-collar workers; officials and managers are the highest-paid of all workers.

Focus and Implications

Of the nine job categories, this study focuses on officials and managers (O & M) for several reasons. Minority women stand to make the greatest economic gains through O & M employment, and it has been indicated that minority women are poorly represented in the O & M category. Also, minority group members who have been in managerial positions for a number of years are experiencing discouragement at having reached plateaus in their careers.

O & M positions are likely to be found at a more uniform rate in a large number of industries, perhaps in all industries, than are the other job categories. Therefore, cross-industry comparisons may be more valid. Since O & M makes up an average 11.4 percent of each industry (ranging from 4.2 percent to 22.1 percent), a close study of this job category also puts one in a position to consider whether male-dominated industries appear more hostile to minority women. If so, further questions are raised: Does the hostility appear to seep down from top management? Or does it emanate upward from (male and/or female) workers who resent having to take orders from a woman and/or minority person? What can the willing do to mitigate the resistance?

Unlike the other eight job categories, O & M is a metacategory in that workers who begin their work lives in the other categories can move upward into O & M by adding managerial skills to those required for their previous work. Switching from one of the other job categories to another would more likely require a total replacement of one set of skills for another.

For the analyst, the variety and complexity of questions of discrimination are potentially greatest for the category of officials and managers. For example, although different studies have disagreed on what portion of salary differentials can be attributed to gender or racial differences, some part is always attributed to such differences; in the case of O & M, a significant additional source of disparity is the negotiability of salaries and perquisites which can substantially increase actual compensation. In contrast, craft and many other workers who are more often unionized receive set wages, according to job classification, with little or no room for individual negotiation or for productivity or merit differentials. The minority woman's main hurdle in such job categories is simply to get into the classification; but as a manager, not only does she have to get into the job category, but once in it must have considerable individual negotiating skill, as well as a sense of the "going rate" for certain levels of responsibility and kinds of contributions to the company.

The concept of ethnicity is the most delicate and, perhaps, the most crucial question raised by this inquiry. It has been said again and again that, in management, much of the reason for career advancement is the perception, not merely of a person's competence, but of her/his "belonging"—of sharing the same goals and values, employing the same methods and means to agreed-upon ends, and more. The outcome of this attribution of "sameness" in the hiring and promotion process is to reduce perceived risk. Those who are the "same" as the decision-makers are perceived, rightly or wrongly, as less risky choices since their future work performance and style are assumed to be similar to those of the people currently making personnel decisions. Are capable minority workers being held back because they are still perceived to be too different, perhaps "too ethnic," to be trusted with the most vital positions in a company? More important, is the minority worker's *self*-perception one of ethnic integrity and maintenance, and to what extent must these characteristics be set aside or even sacrificed entirely in order to attain the most rewarding positions in private industry?

The melting pot, some say, was a myth. Was it? Have earlier, white male immigrants—Italians, Poles, Irishmen and others—melted into the corporate pot? Was it a *functional* myth? Without such a faith, and where there is emphasis on ethnic pride, do pressures to be true to one's ethnic group create an unresolvable dilemma for those who could also operate effectively within the corporate culture?

The dilemma of maintaining ethnicity and succeeding in the corporate environment may be reflected in a major study of more than four thousand male and female managers from twelve major corporations.[5] The study identified 104 female and 144 male Native Americans and showed a striking correspondence between responses of white respondents and Native American respondents, but subsequent investigation showed that those identified as Native Americans were quite removed from their cultural sources. Is it necessary to sacrifice cultural identification in order to participate and succeed in corporate America?

For women, there are added questions of maintaining or sacrificing femininity, however each woman may define it for herself. The problems multiply (at the very least) geometrically as ethnic standards of femininity compete with those of the majority society, as well as with expected and acceptable standards of feminine behavior within the corporate environment in relation to subordinates and superordinates (male or female). This combination of demands can be especially hard on the minority woman if she attempts to satisfy all of them. The stresses of the management function compound the problem, especially if the woman is one of the first of her gender and/or race in a position of responsibility. She is a vulnerable target if a company wishes to fulfill its prophecy that women and/or minorities cannot do the job.

How Bad Is It?

Table 3 (see p. 164) presents women's percentage of the enumerated work force *by job category* for each of four years, with breakdowns by race, for each of the EEOC's nine job categories. Table 4 (p. 166) compares women's percentages for each racial/ethnic group to the percentage for the same group of women as a portion of the total work force. These statistics provide some comparability across racial/ethnic groups, showing large differences in their work force numbers as well as the degree that racial representation and distribution changed across

TABLE 3
WOMEN'S PERCENTAGE OF JOB CATEGORY EMPLOYMENT, 1973, 1975, 1978, 1980

Race/ Ethnic Group by Year	Partici- pation Rate	Officials and Managers	Profes- sionals	Techni- cians	Sales Workers	Office & Clerical Workers	Craft Workers	Opera- tives	Laborers	Service Workers
All Women										
1973	36.7960	12.8599	28.9445	31.8850	45.2958	79.3932	7.3536	30.7273	30.0632	51.8408
1975	37.1452	14.1576	29.9611	33.3484	47.7751	80.2237	7.1333	30.2733	30.7155	53.3656
1978	39.5906	16.9942	34.3499	37.9211	50.3725	82.0077	8.5713	32.3785	34.0214	54.6779
1980	40.9689	18.5205	37.1645	40.1650	52.7395	82.7599	9.5792	32.9416	34.1624	55.0567
White										
1973	30.5323	11.8544	26.0227	26.2353	40.9860	69.5167	5.9625	23.8552	21.5717	36.6255
1975	30.5058	12.8758	26.7989	27.4484	42.7257	68.8875	5.7763	23.2314	21.9410	37.9055
1978	31.7219	15.1731	30.3600	31.1061	44.0740	68.7746	6.6909	23.8428	23.5952	38.5442
1980	32.5160	16.4863	32.5966	32.7048	45.6534	68.4486	7.2695	23.7888	23.1259	38.3037
Black										
1973	4.3383	0.6660	1.6307	4.2410	2.6996	6.6304	0.8704	4.7870	5.3649	12.2429
1975	4.5336	0.8267	1.6075	4.3112	3.2043	7.5822	0.8395	4.8768	5.5945	12.0591
1978	5.2214	1.1374	2.0820	4.7513	4.0338	8.5999	1.1022	5.7965	6.2967	12.1450
1980	5.4497	1.2326	2.4032	5.0123	4.3671	9.1784	1.3474	5.9035	6.4900	12.3735

TABLE 3 (cont.)

Spanish-Surnamed (1973) / Hispanic (1975, 1978, 1980)

Year										
1973	1.4510	0.2220	0.4172	0.8590	1.2119	2.3129	0.4181	1.7366	2.7480	2.3403
1975	1.5664	0.2949	0.4714	0.9410	1.4041	2.7102	0.4175	1.7844	2.7988	2.6700
1978	1.9122	0.4366	0.6017	1.1883	1.7245	3.2416	0.6039	2.1666	3.5182	2.9508
1980	2.1251	0.4946	0.7085	1.3421	2.0799	3.5852	0.7241	2.4711	3.8292	3.2443

Asian American (1973, 1975) / Asian/Pacific Islander (1978, 1980)

Year										
1973	0.3394	0.0781	0.8192	0.4578	0.2489	0.7292	0.0627	0.1902	0.1923	0.4217
1975	0.4102	0.1139	1.0199	0.5281	0.2909	0.8640	0.0736	0.2479	0.2262	0.5096
1978	0.5933	0.1837	1.2330	0.7588	0.4172	1.1305	0.1385	0.4300	0.4224	0.8082
1980	0.7317	0.2395	1.3756	0.9738	0.5105	1.2917	0.1869	0.6230	0.5300	0.9130

American Indian (1973, 1975) / Amind/Alaskan Native (1978, 1980)

Year										
1973	0.1348	0.0393	0.0545	0.0917	0.1671	0.2037	0.0398	0.1581	0.1860	0.2131
1975	0.1290	0.0461	0.0631	0.1195	0.1499	0.2297	0.0261	0.1326	0.1549	0.2211
1978	0.1415	0.0633	0.0730	0.1163	0.1229	0.2608	0.0356	0.1424	0.1887	0.2295
1980	0.1462	0.0673	0.0804	0.1318	0.1284	0.2558	0.0511	0.1549	0.1870	0.2221

All Minority Female

Year										
1973	6.2636	1.0055	2.9218	5.6496	4.3277	9.8764	1.3911	6.8721	8.4914	15.2182
1975	6.6393	1.2818	3.1621	5.9000	5.0493	11.3862	1.3569	7.0418	8.7745	15.4600
1978	7.8687	1.8211	3.9899	6.8149	6.2985	13.2330	1.8803	8.5356	10.4262	16.1336
1980	8.4529	2.0342	4.5679	7.4602	7.0861	14.3112	2.3096	9.1527	11.0364	16.7530

Source: U.S. Equal Employment Opportunity Commission, "Job Patterns for Minorities and Women in Private Industry," *EEO-1* (Washington, D.C.: EEOC, 1973, 1975, 1978, 1980).

TABLE 4
WOMEN'S PERCENTAGE OF JOB CATEGORY COMPARED TO PERCENTAGE OF TOTAL WORK FORCE

Race/ Ethnic Group by Year	Partici- pation Rate	Officials and Managers	Profes- sionals	Techni- cians	Sales Workers	Office & Clerical Workers	Craft Workers	Opera- tives	Laborers	Service Workers
All Women										
1973	36.7960	34.9491	78.6620	86.6534	123.0997	215.7658	19.9847	83.5071	81.7023	140.8870
1975	37.1452	38.1142	80.6594	89.7784	128.6171	215.9732	19.2038	81.4998	82.6903	143.6675
1978	39.5906	42.9248	86.7627	95.7830	127.2334	207.1393	21.6498	81.7833	85.9330	138.1082
1980	40.9689	45.2062	90.7139	98.0377	128.7305	202.0066	23.3816	80.4063	83.3861	134.3865
White										
1973	30.5323	38.8257	85.2300	85.9263	134.1792	227.6824	19.5284	78.1310	70.6520	119.9467
1975	30.5058	42.2077	87.8485	89.9776	140.0576	225.6538	18.9350	76.1540	71.9240	124.2566
1978	31.7219	47.8316	95.7067	98.0587	138.9887	216.8047	21.0923	75.1619	74.3814	121.5065
1980	32.5160	50.7021	100.2478	100.5806	140.4028	210.5074	22.3566	73.1602	71.1216	117.7995
Black										
1973	4.3383	15.3516	37.5884	97.7571	62.2271	152.8340	20.0631	110.3427	123.6636	282.2050
1975	4.5336	18.2349	35.4574	95.0944	70.6789	167.2445	18.5172	107.5701	123.4008	265.9939
1978	5.2214	21.7834	39.8743	90.9966	77.2551	164.7048	21.1092	111.0142	120.5940	232.6004
1980	5.4497	21.6177	44.0978	90.9738	80.1346	168.4202	24.7242	108.3270	119.0891	227.0491

TABLE 4 (cont.)

Spanish-Surnamed (1973) / Hispanic (1975, 1978, 1980)

Year										
1973	1.4510	15.2997	28.7525	59.2005	83.5217	159.4004	28.8146	119.6829	189.3866	161.2887
1975	1.5664	18.8266	30.0944	60.0740	89.6386	173.0209	26.6534	113.9172	178.6772	170.4545
1978	1.9122	22.8323	31.4663	62.1430	90.1840	169.5220	31.5814	113.3040	183.9870	154.3144
1980	2.1251	23.2744	33.3396	63.1546	97.8730	168.7073	34.0736	116.2815	180.1891	152.6657

Asian American (1973, 1975) / Asian/Pacific Islander (1978, 1980)

Year										
1973	0.3394	23.0111	241.3671	134.8850	73.3352	214.8497	18.4737	56.0400	56.6588	124.2486
1975	0.4102	27.7669	248.6348	128.7420	70.9166	210.6289	17.9424	60.4339	55.1438	124.2320
1978	0.5933	30.9624	207.8206	127.8948	70.3185	190.5444	23.3440	72.4759	71.1950	136.2211
1980	0.7317	32.7319	188.0005	133.0873	69.7690	176.5340	25.5432	85.1441	72.4340	124.7779

American Indian (1973, 1975) / Amind/Alaskan Native (1978, 1980)

Year										
1973	0.1348	29.1543	40.4302	68.0267	123.9614	151.1127	29.5252	117.2848	137.9821	158.0860
1975	0.1290	35.7364	48.9147	92.6356	116.2015	178.0620	20.2325	102.7906	120.0775	171.3953
1978	0.1415	44.7349	51.5901	82.1908	86.8551	184.3109	25.1590	100.6360	133.3568	162.1909
1980	0.1462	46.0328	54.9931	90.1504	87.8248	174.9658	34.9521	105.9507	127.9069	151.9151

All Minority Female

Year										
1973	6.2636	16.0530	46.6472	90.1973	69.0928	157.6792	22.2092	109.7148	135.5674	242.9625
1975	6.6393	19.3062	47.6270	88.8647	76.0516	171.4969	20.4373	106.0623	132.1600	232.8558
1978	7.8687	23.1435	50.7059	86.6076	80.0449	168.1726	23.8959	108.4753	132.5021	205.0351
1980	8.4529	24.0651	54.0394	88.2561	83.8304	169.3052	27.3231	108.2788	130.5634	198.1923

Source: U.S. Equal Employment Opportunity Commission, "Job Patterns for Minorities and Women in Private Industry," EEO-1 (Washington, D.C.: EEOC, 1973, 1975, 1978, 1980).

the years. The resulting percentage figures show clearly the over and underrepresentation of women in the different job categories.

In only three instances are women represented in a job category at or near their representation in the work force as a whole, all in 1980: white female professionals, white female technicians, and Hispanic female sales workers. Although women as a group came close to parity among technicians in 1980, the different groups ranged from 63 percent for Hispanic women to 133 percent for Asian/Pacific Islander women.

Each and every minority group is underrepresented in sales, crafts, and officials and managers. For black women and Hispanic women, O & M shows the poorest proportions: 21.6 percent and 22.3 percent of work force rate, respectively. For Asian/Pacific Islander and American Indian/Alaskan Native women, proportions are 32.7 percent and 46.0 percent, respectively, second to craft workers (25.5 percent and 35.0 percent, respectively). White women have the same ranking, but better O & M representation: their worst proportion is in crafts at 22.4 percent, followed by O & M at 50.7 percent.

The disproportion in the clerical and service categories seems to have been mitigated slightly for some groups over the years. This *may* indicate that more minority women are entering a greater variety of jobs; however, since there has been much variation across ethnic groups and job categories, it may also mean that women of different groups are in different low-paying categories. For example, Asian/Pacific Islander women have become less overrepresented in the clerical category, but also less underrepresented among laborers, both low-paying job categories.

Industrial Perspective

Minority women are represented in many of the 162 industries at or above their representation in the total work force: black women in fifty-five industries; Hispanic women in sixty-two; Asian/Pacific Islanders in fifty-six; and Native Americans in sixty-one. However, they rarely do as well in representation in the O & M category: blacks are represented in three industries at or above their representation in the total work force; Hispanics in two; Asian/Pacific Islanders in five; and Native Americans in nine. Even white women's representation only reaches parity in eleven industries. In eighty categories, minority women make up less than one-tenth of 1 percent of O & M.

Interestingly, only three of the sixteen industries in which minority women do have O & M parity (listed in Table 5) achieve it for more than one minority group: social services, men's and boys' furnishings, and services to buildings.

TABLE 5
O & M MINORITY FEMALE PARITY INDUSTRIES, 1980

Industry	Size Rank	O & M % Minority Women	Minority Group	Group Women Norm %
Men's and	104	0.18	A/A Native	0.15
Boys' Furnishings		2.19	Hispanic	2.13
Footwear, except	314	0.15	A/A Native	0.15
Variety Stores	57	0.15	A/A Native	0.15
Banking	17	0.80	A/P Islander	0.73
Commercial and Stock Savings Banks	18	0.82	A/P Islander	0.73
Credit Agencies Other than Banks	81	0.16	A/A Native	0.15
Medical Service and Health Insurance	104	0.21	A/A Native	0.15
Real Estate	141	0.16	A/A Native	0.15
Hotels and Other Lodging Places	52	0.16	A/A Native	0.15
Hotels, Motels and Tourist Courts	53	0.16	A/A Native	0.15
Services to	88	2.19	Hispanic	2.13
Buildings		5.58	Black	5.45
Health Services	6	1.06	A/P Islander	0.73
Nursing and Personal Care Facilities	59	0.84	A/P Islander	0.73
Hospitals	8	1.10	A/P Islander	0.73
Social Services	94	8.69	Black	5.45
		0.27	A/A Native	0.15
Museums, Botanical and Zoological Gardens	162	5.60	Black	5.45

Source: U.S. Equal Employment Opportunity Commission, "Job Patterns for Minorities and Women in Private Industry," *EEO-1* (Washington, D.C.: EEOC, 1980).

At first glance, the sixteen industries listed in Table 5 may not appear to have much in common: industry size ranges from the smallest (museums, botanical and zoological gardens) to the sixth largest of the 162 (health services); percentage of O & M in the industries ranges from a low of 4.46 percent (services to buildings) to a high of 23.24 percent (credit agencies) of an industry's work force.

On the other hand, they do have several things in common: All but two may be considered "female-intensive," having 41 percent or more women employees (41 percent is the overall work force participation rate for women). Also, industries in which a particular group is parity-represented in O & M are even better represented in the industry overall.

But a closer look reveals characteristics which are discouraging for any women in those industries. Footwear, the sole manufacturing industry in the list, will be greatly affected by foreign imports once regulation is reduced. Banking and related activities, after experiencing a period of growth in the 1970s, are expected to decline, partly because of automation—ranging from "instant tellers" to new computerized loan offices—and deregulation. Perhaps excepting services to buildings, the other industries are also vulnerable to recessionary setbacks.

Why Is It So? What Can Be Done?

It is crucial here to consider how public policy can promote employment equality for women, particularly minority women. In order to do so, one must first consider the preparation of minority women for O & M positions and industry's response to them.

There is, of course, no "minority woman." The EEOC's four ethnic groupings constitute the most minimal recognition of differences. Within those four groupings are smaller and smaller subgroups, each quite unique. Among the broader lines of differentiation are national and/or geographical origin (e.g., Korean vs. Chinese, Alaskan Eskimo vs. Cherokee Indian, Cuban vs. Puerto Rican); current geographical location (e.g., urban vs. rural, southern vs. western); generation in the United States (the first three generations are probably as different from each other as any sequence of generations will ever be); conditions at entry (e.g., war refugee vs. technical specialist); and age at time of entry (e.g., child vs. middle-aged woman).

This chapter will not go into great detail about the strikingly different histories of the minority groups in the United States; that has been done by Elizabeth Almquist for the largest of the minorities.[6] As new groups increase their representation in this country, additional histories will no doubt be needed. Roy Bryce-Laporte has outlined the major sources of the new immigration, and it will be interesting to see how quickly and in what jobs and industries they will find acceptance.[7]

Suffice it to say that Native Americans are the only group to have preceded white men, have their numbers greatly reduced by them, and, along with Mexican Americans, have their lives increasingly circumscribed as whites have found reason to desire what was their land. Blacks were the only group brought in as chattel and encouraged to increase their numbers as long as they provided free labor. Asians were brought in, too, but as contract laborers; to perform specific tasks, but with the expectation of returning to their homelands. Most of the earliest Asian women were brought here through the efforts of men of their own group who had preceded them. More recent Asian/Pacific Islander immigrants largely have been of two distinct types: political refugees sometimes grudgingly admitted, and highly-trained technical specialists whose services were desired. Hispanics—the one ethnic, rather than racial, category—are as diverse as the various Asian/Pacific Islander subgroups, and have entered to some extent by choice. The different histories and the role of women throughout those histories have contributed to their preparedness (or lack thereof) for the roles newly opened to them. We thus now consider women at three stages of their careers: preparation, entry, and retention and promotion.

Preparation

Career Selection and Formal Education: Preparation begins as early as the first role model a child selects. Much of the child's eventual selection is affected by parents and school officials, who not only encourage or discourage him/her in the selection of subjects to study and help the child to master the subjects but, more importantly, broaden or narrow career expectations and aspirations. In the case of minority women who have fewer role models available, parental and school encouragement are particularly important.

One way in which public policy could contribute to broadening youthful horizons would be to encourage higher levels of scientific and technical education for girls as well as boys in every grade. We emphasize scientific and technical education because women have been grossly underrepresented in related careers, and a lack of technical expertise has often been mentioned as a barrier to movement to upper-level management positions. Greater numbers of minority women teaching in these areas and acting in school administrative roles would also promote children's aspirations in those fields, whereas it would be desirable but difficult for all school children to obtain meaningful exposure to corporate role models.

Informal Education: For the newest immigrants, a first priority may be bilingual education and/or special language learning assistance. With few exceptions, the language barrier must be overcome; how thoroughly may vary with the field chosen. Beyond the mechanics of the language, however, are the connotations of communication styles. How does one's manner of expression demonstrate confidence, trustworthiness, strength or weakness? The normative meanings of verbal and non-verbal messages are a significant part of the informal education important for career development.

Again, minority females have few role models from whom to learn or pattern their own behavior. Summer internship programs would offer an opportunity to observe and begin to understand business operations and managerial communication styles. For those younger, visits to offices or visits by managers into the schools could provide additional exposure. Particularly for those who live in ethnic communities, it is important to create opportunities to observe how people in other settings relate to one another.

The Informal Network: Even more subtle kinds of preparation are simply not attainable except by accident of birth or acquaintance. No "inside contacts" can be made without membership in the "right" country club. Lack of common experiences leaves a gap where one would like to show, "I am like you, and therefore can be trusted like you." Rare is the father with accumulated acumen, associations and wealth to pass on to daughters, the husband with the same to leave to a widow, or other relatives to help minority women as white women have sometimes been helped. Public policy in a capitalist political economy can do little to change this, but it cannot go without mention.

Entry

Qualifying through education—a degree in the appropriate field, perhaps some on-the-job training, part-time or during the summers while going to school—seems to have become more accessible to women. Women are also now beginning to choose fields previously so dominated by men as to have been near-monopolies. However, in spite of a higher *average* level of education, fewer women than men have the more advanced degrees (see Table 6), and while many more women are now in engineering and business schools, most of them are white.

TABLE 6
EDUCATIONAL ATTAINMENT OF MEN AND WOMEN, 1980
(IN THOUSANDS)

	Men	Women
4 years high school	21,485	27,237
1 to 3 years college	9,927	10,196
4 years college	7,322	6,070
5 years or more college	6,550	3,699

Source: U.S. Bureau of the Census, "Money Income of Households, Families, and Persons in the United States: 1981," in *Current Population Reports*, Series P. 60, No. 137 (Washington, D.C.: Government Printing Office, 1981).

Obviously, to change these statistics would require additional scholarship assistance throughout the extra years of graduate education. Individual and corporate tax write-offs of graduate education expenses for prospective or current employees would provide an incentive for both company and individual. Moreover, corporate write-offs for paid internships would encourage specific, relevant experience for individuals and provide an indirect subsidy for a company's in-house training programs. Again, subsidies for training programs would assist both company and individual by pre-screening applicants for long-term careers within a company, and by providing career-relevant experience for both those retained by a company and for those who will have increased their marketability within an industry. Thus, it would provide a "foot in the door" for all trainees.

Retention and Promotion

Specific Training: In discussing graduate education and internships, a distinction is being made between general and specific training. General training is usually acquired in classrooms, but specific training—the training that makes employees most useful to a firm—is acquired in various ways on the job. Most frequently it occurs in large companies and firms, and although occasionally it is firm-specific, more commonly it is industry-specific. Because an investment is made in the individual worker, it becomes in a training firm's interest to retain the trainee. A consistent drain of trained personnel, especially to competitors, is obviously undesirable; therefore, it is also in a training firm's interest to pay a somewhat higher wage than the employee could obtain elsewhere. In effect, firms choose the wage premium they will pay and the resignation rate they are willing to accept simultaneously. In fact, higher wage premiums are paid by firms which invest in training.[8] Therefore, it is important for minority women to acquire in-house training to increase their value to a corporation and hence a corporation's incentive to retain them.

A number of case studies have already indicated that women (not necessarily minority women) who have found opportunities blocked have moved to new jobs or have begun their own businesses. Obviously these departures are not cost-free, either for these women or for the firms from which they depart. At the very least, training costs are lost and a substantial price tag can be attached to the search for mid-level managers to replace the minority women, who no doubt were selected initially after extensive and expensive screening. This should be a particularly salient point for employers who provide in-house training—but it is another double-edged sword in that it can either encourage employers to provide incentives for trained minority workers to stay with the company, or discourage employers from investing in training those workers in the first place, for fear they will leave.

Career Track: In addition to formal qualifications, there are differences in career tracks: minority groups members have often been placed in staff, rather than line, positions. They are personnel directors, for example, rather than financial planning managers. The decisions with which they have been entrusted have not been linked with the company's profits or losses, yet it is the person who captures profits for the company who also captures promotions. Women and minority persons who may at one time have chosen the "safer" staff positions have become aware of the limitations that accompany security, and more are choosing technical, financial and other areas.

Relocation: Another problematic area is that of changing companies and/or geographic location in order to secure a promotion. For minority women, relocating with the same or a new company can be a special hardship because many minority communities are in specific geographical areas. Except for Native Americans, most are in urban areas; a move to company headquarters in a small town can mean total isolation.[9] Similarly, large numbers of Asian/Pacific Islanders are located on the Pacific Coast, Puerto Ricans in the Northeast, and Cubans in Florida. Moves to other parts of the continent can mean separation not only from family and friends, but from psychologically important traditions and social support as well. If the move is a temporary one, an opportunity to prepare for a higher-level position again near the ethnic community, this may be tolerable. If it is a permanent relocation, however, ethnic environment may once again lose to job requirement—or vice versa.

Future Industrial and Demographic Projections

Ethnic-minority women have, in fact, improved their representation in managerial and administrative positions during the past ten years. These gains have been concentrated in a few industries (health care, hospitals, social services) where legislation has worked effectively because of sanctions, or where representation may have fit in with a changing customer group. Many are industries where men traditionally have not wished to be employed because of low wage rates and poor benefit packages.

But will this trend toward improving representation of ethnic-minority women continue? If continuation depended exclusively upon supply factors, the increasing number of women, including minority women preparing for higher-level positions,[10] would provide the answer. However, the demand for minority female officials and managers depends heavily upon institutional response, enforcement of equal opportunity regulations, and labor market conditions, namely, the expected growth in the job category. At present, there is clearly a stasis, if not a reversal, of vigilance in enforcing affirmative action. As Table 7 shows, there appears to be a relatively limited amount of occupational growth, at least according to the moderate growth scenario developed by the Bureau of Labor Statistics.

Among the forty occupations expected to experience the largest job growth, only one managerial occupation, store managers, is projected to experience a substantial rate of growth, from a total of 292,000 in 1982 to a total of 301,000 in 1995.[11] In general, all managerial categories are expected to grow modestly over the next decade or so, no more than 35 percent for the total period, at a maximum rate of 2.8 percent per year but probably lower.

Demographic Factors

The "baby boom" generation now ranges in age from the early twenties to the early forties. Most of the young adults are now in the work force or trying to reestablish a connection with it. James Smith and Finis Welch, among many others, have noted that the enormous size of this cohort has depressed earnings and limited opportunities for its members.[12] Minority women managers and officials have been part of this cohort and have participated in the experience.

This large cohort size has had different implications for its members at different points. In the 1960s and 1970s it meant relatively restricted access and depressed wages. Through the 1980s and 1990s it will mean scarcer-than-normal promotional opportunities. This phenomenon has been called the career plateau, referring to that situation in which access to an entry-level position followed by moderate career progression leads to a long period of non-promotion, with upward mobility blocked by incumbent managers as well as by numerous peers competing for the same few positions.

This demographic context has ominous implications for the career progression of minority women managers. A concerted effort on the part of corporations to facilitate upward mobility for ethnic-minority women members of this cohort cannot be expected to be widespread. Litigation as redress for non-promotion is clearly not desirable except as a last resort. Moreover, hostility toward women, especially ethnic-minority women, can hardly be expected to abate among men whose careers will also be stalled.

There is a real possibility that those minority women who now occupy managerial positions may actually find their productivity and performance threatened. Without access to informal networks—and such access will surely not be easy in homogeneous organizations, or in those dominated by males—managers will find results harder to attain

TABLE 7[a]
FORTY OCCUPATIONS WITH LARGEST JOB GROWTH, 1982-1995 MODERATE-TREND PROJECTIONS

Occupation	Change in Total Employment (thousands)	Percent of Total Job Growth	Percent of Change
Building custodians	779	3.0	27.5
Cashiers	744	2.9	47.4
Secretaries	719	2.8	29.5
General Clerks, Office	696	2.7	29.6
Salesclerks	685	2.7	23.5
Nurses, Registered	642	2.5	48.9
Waiters and Waitresses	562	2.2	33.8
Teachers, Kindergarten and Elementary	511	2.0	37.4
Truckdrivers	425	1.7	26.5
Nursing Aides and Orderlies	423	1.7	34.8
Sales Representatives, Technical	386	1.5	29.3
Licensed Practical Nurses	220	0.9	37.1
Computer Systems Analysts	217	0.8	85.3
Electrical Engineers	209	0.8	65.3
Computer Programmers	205	0.8	76.9
Maintenance Repairs, General Utility	193	0.8	27.8
Helpers, Trades	190	0.7	31.2
Receptionists	189	0.7	48.8
Electricians	173	0.7	31.8
Physicians	163	0.7	34.0
Clerical Supervisors	162	0.6	34.6
Computer Operators	160	0.6	75.8
Accountants and Auditors	344	1.3	40.2
Automotive Mechanics	324	1.3	38.3
Supervisors of Blue-Collar Workers	319	1.2	26.6
Kitchen Helpers	305	1.2	35.9
Guards and Doorkeepers	300	1.2	47.3
Food Preparation and Service Workers, Fast Food Restaurants	297	1.2	36.7
Managers, Stores	292	1.1	30.1
Carpenters	247	1.0	28.6
Electrical and Electronic Technicians	222	0.9	60.7
Sales Representatives, Non-technical	160	0.6	27.4
Lawyers	159	0.6	34.3
Stock Clerks, Stockroom and Warehouse	156	0.6	18.8
Typists	155	0.6	15.7
Delivery and Route Workers	153	0.6	19.2
Bookkeepers, Hand	152	0.6	15.9
Cooks, Restaurants	149	0.6	42.3
Bank Tellers	142	0.6	30.0
Cooks, Short Order, Specialty and Fast Food	141	0.6	32.2

Source: George T. Silvestri, John M. Lukasiewicz and Marcus Einstein, "Occupational Employment Projections Through 1985," *Monthly Labor Review* 106:11 (November 1983): 37-49.

[a]Includes only detailed occupations with 1982 employment of 25,000 or more. Data for 1995 are based on moderate-trend projections.

without the power that access to informal channels provides. Deprivation of access to these informal associations will also limit internal labor market information and thus reduce further the probability of upward mobility.

If the progress made by minority women managers stalls, if individuals reach a premature plateau in their careers due to demographic factors external to the firm, and internal organizational issues complicated by those demographic realities, what course will be adopted by these managers?

Exit, Voice, or Psychic Disengagement

Few minority group members have been in management positions long enough to say much about plateaus and dead ends. Those who have, mostly black men, have expressed disillusionment;[13] equality appears to have its limits. Some may have contented themselves with the improved, though not optimal, situation. Others have moved to different companies or are starting their own firms. Both options can be fitted into basic types of individual responses to social and economic problems.

Albert Hirschman has noted, and Richard Freeman and James Medoff have recently extended the argument, that there are fundamentally two methods through which social and economic problems are approached.[14] One of these, the "entry-exit mechanism," emphasizes the degree to which individuals correct the difference between the ideal and the desired condition in the workplace by departing from, and thus penalizing, the bad employer. Another approach uses communication to bring the actual condition closer to that desired through discussion, participation, bargaining, voting and other institutionalized mechanisms. A classic example of the utilization of "voice" is the development of the labor movement, as well as of workplace-related legislation sometimes closely associated with union development.

In a few cases of frustrated O & Ms, collective action of some sort can be expected. The occasional company with commitment to minority recruitment may very well attempt to make changes in order to retain these managers. However, the caucus or employees' association is not likely to attract many ambitious individuals since any negative repercussions are likely to damage careers.

In reality, of course, there are many situations in which neither approach is considered feasible nor desirable. A third option—what is called here "psychic disengagement"—can result, producing behaviors which range from a minimal level of productivity to counterproductive action.[15]

Theoretical Perspectives and Public Policy Recommendations

Thus far this chapter has been applying one of two types of approaches to the current situation and future prospects for ethnic-minority women in O & M positions. Drawn from the literature of labor economics, this approach emphasizes human capital—the training and resultant skills that workers bring to the workplace and which are made specific and important inputs to the job and the firm. Another important school of thought shifts the emphasis subtly from the skills and knowledge possessed by an applicant or jobholder to the signal value of a credential validating this possession. That is, the degree, certificate or other credential signifies to a potential employer that its possessor has been prescreened by an educational institution and has been judged as trainable.

The data presented in this chapter have not been offered to support either variation of this economic approach, but currently data on groups of displaced workers generally support the idea that validated skills are more influential in determining labor market outcomes than other variables such as age, race or sex.[16] Therefore, an important theme of this chapter has been that personal and institutional investment in postemployment training and development are important for career development in all cases, especially when productivity signals such as sex and race are negative as in the case of minority women. When competition for scarce promotions is keen, the training investment pattern becomes even more crucial.

We draw now from a second approach, from the psycho-social literature on life cycles and the interaction between personal characteristics and life experiences which determine capacities, expectations and, to a significant degree, the outcomes of personal growth and development or stagnation and frustration. More specifically, we point to data taken at Empire State College on a large group of adult learners drawn from different demographic groups, different socioeconomic strata and different occupational groups. The "conventional wisdom" which has been confirmed often—namely that, in contrast to men, women tend to develop generally more positive views of their capacities as they progress through the life cycle—is validated once more in this study.[17]

Overall, women and men in the first phase of life (age less than twenty-three years, the "pulling-up-roots" phase) had nearly the same level of confidence in their academic ability. That level was lower for both groups through the second phase (age twenty-three to twenty-nine, the "getting-into-adult-world" phase), with the difference between the two groups remaining about the same. In the third phase (age thirty to thirty-six, "putting down roots"), women's confidence was slightly greater, while that of men was lower by about the same amount as between the first and second phases. In this phase, women's confidence first surpassed that of men, and remained above that of men throughout the remaining stages.

During the fourth phase, (age thirty-seven to forty-three, "mid-life transition"), women's confidence was slightly lower than in the third phase, while that of men was at its lowest. The difference between the two groups was greatest in this phase. In the fifth phase (age forty-four to fifty, "middle adulthood"), men showed higher self-perception than in the fourth, while women showed slightly lower self-perception. Into the sixth phase (age fifty-one to fifty-seven, "late adulthood"), both groups' self-perceptions were better, with men showing greater improvement over phase five than women, but women remaining about five percentage points above men. Finally, in the last phase (age fifty-eight and over, "early retirement"), the confidence level of women was again higher, while that of men decreased.

Women in high-level, white-collar occupations show the most confidence in both academic and leadership ability in phase three (age thirty to thirty-six), and significantly less confidence in all subsequent phases—presumably as their careers stall and their aspirations are frustrated. Men in the same occupational group also show a lower perception of their academic ability until phase six, but slightly higher perceptions of their leadership ability, peaking in phase six (age fifty-one to fifty-seven).

As indicated in employment forecasts and supported by the data presented here, the moderate success enjoyed by minority women managers may not continue at the same rate, and may even deteriorate. Responses to this situation in terms of investment in specific human resources and returns on that investment can be seen, in part, as a function of the positive self-perceptions of women in high-level, white-collar occupations.

To a great degree, this heightened self-esteem may reflect early low expectations combined with positive labor market experiences. What will happen as the labor market experience becomes less positive? Depending upon the individual answer to that question, in addition to a number of other factors such as personal and family situation and finances, a choice will be made between exit, voice, or psychic disengagement.

Already mentioned has been the low likelihood of exercising voice in a situation where to do so would be to become one of the "them" in the labor-management division. In many cases a kind of psychic detachment is much more probable, a variation of the much-described "burnout." This form of adaptation, like exit, entails costs to both the individuals and the firms involved. The greatest cost, however, may be that lost productivity resulting from discouragement and the perception of blocked opportunity could instead be interpreted as validation of old beliefs in those negative productivity signals—wrong race, wrong sex—as once-productive minority women managers succumb to the same mid-career blues that men experience without the same kind of long-term penalty. For women, it is not unlikely that this adaptation to blocked career aspirations could have adverse effects upon the next generation seeking entry-level positions, just as their predecessors provide the "evidence" to be used against them by those who wish to revert to more blatant discrimination.

What is suggested is that, just at the time the revised mid-career perceptions of women about their future prospects provide the basis for a bleak scenario, the other element, that is their heightened perception of academic and leadership ability, could point to a a partial solution. Whether it is the actual acquisition of learning as the human capital theorists claim, or the signal it provides the employer as A. Michael Spence[18] and others claim, that is most effective with employers, continued education will certainly be a major factor in facilitating the advancement of ethnic-minority managers into whatever higher positions are available. In this indirect way, public policy can help to stabilize and enhance present performance and achievement, and maximize progress within the limits imposed by demographic and other considerations.

Universities and public institutions, as well as private institutions with public assistance, should provide education that is specifically targeted and conveniently delivered to those who wish to advance. Opportunities may be limited in the few postgraduate managerial programs for those already identified as fast-track, but new programs can be set up with even more sophisticated content.

However, even if public policy initiatives to improve the position of ethnic-minority women managers are implemented, competing obligations may cause a low priority to be placed upon such external personal development programs. Facilitating mechanisms are needed. In large firms, particulary those which have already taken management development seriously, career development programs for all workers, and especially for minority and female workers, need to be put in place. With the rapidly shifting employment pattern in the American labor market, due in part to technological change and market shifts, such career development programs are crucial to the retention and enhanced performance of all workers.

What about small firms, those which seldom can even afford a personnel officer, let alone a management development specialist? The roving consultant is not a solution to this problem, but the local college or university may very well hold the answer. A viable educational response to this situation, subsidized in part by both universities and firms and supported by public policy, should be sought. For example, a consortia of small companies could be formed, and faculty-graduate student teams could provide a wide array of services, including career development. Besides the obvious benefits of helping develop linkages between business, industry and education, the programs and their evaluations would provide experimental situations in which research relevant to policy could be carried out.

This strategy could also be used to assist small companies started by those who decided to leave their corporations. Obviously, assistance from the Small Business Administration, plus some assistance with capital acquisition, would be essential for such new firms, but the subsidy could be provided on another level as local universities and colleges provided management training and development and personnel services to new companies, once again garnering the advantages of access for research projects.

Summary

Except during the 1973-1975 recessionary period, women of all racial and ethnic groups have been improving their representation in most job categories, both in numbers and in share of jobs; but the amount of improvement has varied by job category for the four different minorities, and by industry. Very few industries employ a representative proportion of minority women in official and managerial jobs, and a lack of detailed job descriptions may mask the low level of responsibility and power that these individuals actually have.

Women are being wiser in their choice of educational curriculum and career track, but there are prices to be paid on the way to the still largely unreachable top. Self-identity as a woman and as a member of one's race may be compromised along the way, and could lead to serious personal problems. Demographic considerations also limit the possibilities for continued career progress, as does an apparent relaxation in equal employment opportunity enforcement.

Nevertheless, there are a number of public policy developments which could aid both minority group members in mid-career who feel their progress has been halted, and those preparing for the future labor market. Government assistance could be provided jointly with academic or other training institutions to create a reciprocal relationship in which industry would benefit from the findings of academic studies, and simultaneously provide study material for improving our understanding of what is really happening to women and minorities in the world of the private corporation.

Time and funding permitting, we might then be able to do what we have yet to see done: investigate the coping mechanisms of the minority women who are already in the structure, as well as their patterns of access, mobility, achievement, compensation and overall career development. We might then be able to begin to change the way things are and move a step closer to that elusive ideal situation.

NOTES

[1] Even the editors' note preceding the record of congressional debate reflects a particular attitude: "The introduction by Congressman Smith (D., Va.) of an amendment prohibiting discrimination in employment because of sex . . . led to 'ladies' afternoon in the House." See Equal Employment Opportunity Commission, *Legislative History of Titles VII and XI of Civil Rights Act of 1964* (Washington, D.C.: Government Printing Office, 1968), pp. 3213-3228.

[2] See W. Lester Thurow, *Generating Inequality* (New York: Basic Books, 1975).

[3] See Ruth G. Shaeffer and Edith Lynton, *Corporate Experiences in Improving Women's Job Opportunities* (New York: The Conference Bureau, 1979).

[4] See Ira S. Lowry, "The Science and Politics of Ethnic Enumeration," in Winston A. Van Horne, ed., *Ethnicity and Public Policy*, Vol. 1 (Milwaukee, Wis.: University of Wisconsin System American Ethnic Studies Coordinating Committee, 1982), pp. 42-61.

[5] John P. Fernandez, *Racism and Sexism in Corporate Life* (Lexington, Mass.: Lexington Books, 1981).

[6] See Elizabeth M. Almquist, *Minorities, Gender, and Work* (Lexington, Mass.: Heath, 1979), Chapters 2, 3 and 4 on Indians and blacks, Spanish-heritage minorities and Asian minorities, respectively.

[7] Roy S. Bryce-Laporte, "The New Immigration: Its Origin, Visibility, and Implication for Public Policy," in Winston A. Van Horne, ed., *Ethnicity and Public Policy*, op. cit., pp. 62-88.

[8] See Donald O. Parsons, "Specific Human Capital: An Application to Quit Rates and Layoff Rates," *Journal of Political Economy* 80:6 (November/De-

cember 1972): 1120-1143; and John H. Pencavel, "Wages, Specific Training, and Labor Turnover in U.S. Manufacturing Industries," *International Economic Review* 13 (February 1972): 53-64.

[9]A *Wall Street Journal* article suggests that a large number of corporations have headquarters in very small remote towns where local people are not very receptive to company people of any race. Single women of any race can find activity highly restricted. See Susan Carey, "So You've Landed A Headquarters Job? Don't Smile So Fast," *Wall Street Journal* (April 10, 1984), pp. 1, 20.

[10]See Suzanne Bianchi and Nancy Rytina, "Occupational Reclassification and Changes in Distribution by Gender," *Monthly Labor Review* 107:3 (March 1984): 11-17.

[11]George T. Silvestri, John M. Lukasiewicz and Marcus E. Einstein, "Occupational Employment Projections Through 1995," *Monthly Labor Review* 106:11 (November 1983): 37-49.

[12]James P. Smith and Finis Welch, "Affirmative Action and Labor Markets," *Journal of Labor Economics* 2:2 (April 1984): 269-301.

[13]Two examples, both of which are about blacks (mainly men), are George Davis and Glegg Watson, *Black Life in Corporate America: Swimming in the Mainstream* (Garden City, N.Y.: Anchor Press/Doubleday, 1982), and a more recent article, "Progress Report on the Black Executive: The Top Spots Are Still Elusive," in *Business Week*, (February 20, 1984), pp. 104-105.

[14]See Albert O. Hirschman, *Exit, Voice and Loyalty* (Cambridge, Mass.: Harvard University Press, 1970); and Richard B. Freeman and James L. Medoff, *What Do Unions Do?* (New York: Basic Books, 1984).

[15]Rosabeth Moss Kanter, *Men and Women of the Corporation* (New York: Basic Books, 1977).

[16]Jeanne P. Gordus, Sean McAlinden, Robert K. Holloway, Karen S. Yamakawa and Marian M. Oshiro, "Labor Force Status, Program Participation, and Economic Adjustment of Displaced Auto Workers," Final Report to the Office of Automotive Industry Affairs, U.S. Department of Commerce, November 1984 (Ann Arbor, Mich.: Industrial Development Division, Institute of Science and Technology, University of Michigan, 1984).

[17]Timothy Lehmann, "Do Men and Women In Transition Have Different Educational Needs?," *Continuum* XLVII:4 (1983): 3-9.

[18]A. Michael Spence, *Information Transfer in Hiring and Related Screening Processes* (Cambridge, Mass.: Harvard University Press, 1974).

THE BLACK WOMAN: PERSPECTIVES ON HER ROLE IN THE FAMILY

Elmer P. Martin and Joanne Mitchell Martin

Morgan State University

Generally, social scientists have viewed the black woman as playing a matriarchal role in the black family. The matriarchal theme in social science literature paints a picture of the black woman as dominating the black family and the black community, and serving as an accomplice with the white male in emasculating black men. The alleged matriarchy in the black family is held to be not only the cause of black family instability, but the cause of the deterioration of the black community as well. The cure-all for stabilizing the black family and community, so the argument goes, is to establish a strong patriarchy where the black woman plays a subordinate role to the black man.

The matriarchy thesis has not just been confined to social science literature where it has generated much controversial debate,[1] but also has been the focus of public policy. As one black feminist scholar noted, "Those with a traditional bent . . . are often the shapers of social policy, to say nothing of public opinions (the 'Moynihan report' on the family being a case in point)."[2]

The purpose of this chapter is not only to revisit briefly the debate about whether black matriarchy is a myth or reality, but, more significantly, to demonstrate that this debate has obscured crucial roles black women have played in the black family and community. This overemphasis on matriarchy has overshadowed three important roles of black women: as survivalists, as achievers, and as agents of social change. It is argued that in these roles both a strong matriarchy (viewed by many scholars as the problem) and a strong patriarchy (viewed by these same scholars as the solution) have deleterious effects on the black family and community. Further, it is maintained that these three roles are rooted in black culture and serve as a counterbalance to a white racist, sexist society and to male chauvinist deviations in the black community. Moreover, it is suggested that public policy which seeks to actually stabilize the black family and community would be more effective if it sought, instead, to strengthen black women in these roles, rather than to destroy an alleged matriarchy and establish a black patriarchy.

Concepts Defined

Before examining four major perspectives of the black family as they bear on the matriarchal notion and shed light on the role of the black woman in the family and community, it is first important to define key concepts, namely the three roles so important to the well-being of the black family as well as the black community, and so distorted by a preoccupation with matriarchy.

In their classic study of urban black life, *Black Metropolis*, Horace Cayton and St. Clair Drake held that "the dominating interests" or "centers of orientation" around which individual and community life revolve are: "1) staying alive; 2) having a good time; 3) praising God; 4) getting ahead;" and 5) "advancing the race."[3] Three of these modes of adaptation—staying alive, getting ahead, and advancing the race— are of particular interest to our analysis.

These three highlight the major roles black women play in the black family and community—their roles as survivalists (staying alive), achievers (getting ahead), and agents of social change (advancing the race). The other two dominant features of urban black life and black culture, having a good time and praising God, are significantly related to the three. For example, many blacks see praising God as the basis of surviving, getting ahead, and advancing the race.

The survivalist role refers to those functions performed by black women for the purpose of family maintenance or well-being (in order to keep the family members alive). The achiever role pertains to those functions performed by black women to become successful in the mainstream of society (or to get ahead). The agent of social change role entails those functions performed by black women to break down barriers to black equality, opportunity and uplift (or to advance the race).

Perspectives of the Black Family

There are four major social science perspectives of the black family which in some way or another address the role of black women. These perspectives are: the pathology-disorganization perspective; the strength-resiliency perspective; the africanity perspective; and the extended family perspective.

The Pathology-Disorganization Perspective

The pathology-disorganization perspective is a commonplace in the social sciences. This perspective emphasizes black family disorganiza-
tion, maladies and deficits. As an outgrowth of racist literature viewing
black people as subhuman beings, the pathology-disorganization perspective sees the black family in a pejorative, condemning manner. Its
major thesis, as suggested earlier, is that the black family is a broken,
sick institution because it is dominated by black women or a matriarchy; or as its chief proponent, Daniel Patrick Moynihan, said, "In essence, the Negro community has been forced into a matriarchal structure which because it is so out of tune with the rest of the American
society, it seriously retards the progress of the group as a whole, and
imposes a crushing burden on the Negro male and, in consequence on a
great many Negro women as well."[4] Advocates of the pathology-disorganization perspective have attributed practically every social and
psychological problem imaginable to an alleged matriarchal family
system: divorce, desertion, crime, delinquency, self-hatred, the emasculation of men, illegitimacy, cultural deprivation, low I.Q. scores,
poverty, and so on.

The pathology-disorganization perspective was advanced several
decades ago by the black sociologist, E. Franklin Frazier, particularly
in his work, *The Negro Family in the United States*. Frazier went outside
the bounds of scholarly objectivity and waged a pejorative attack on
both men and women of the black lower class, viewing them basically
as immoral, irresponsible and promiscuous.[5] Frazier's studies became
so popular that for years afterwards social scientists merely parroted
his words. For example, Gunnar Myrdal in his "monumental," "classic" work, *An American Dilemma*, wrote that Frazier provides "such
an excellent description and analysis . . . that it is practically necessary
only to relate its conclusions to our context and refer the reader to it for
details."[6]

The pathology-disorganization perspective became so entrenched in
the social science literature that it is difficult to find one study before
the sixties that did not take this viewpoint; and the matriarchal thesis
became so prevalent that it was taken for granted as an acceptable,
undeniable truth. This school of thought reached its peak with "The
Moynihan Report." Moynihan put together copious statistics which
supposedly provided ample evidence that a black matriarchy made for
a "tangle of pathologies," which included illegitimacy, divorce, crime,
unemployment, female-headed households and poverty. As stated earlier, this report advanced the pathology-disorganization perspective to
the level of public policy in its call for the government to intervene in

black family life by breaking up the matriarchal structure of the black family and establishing black patriarchal, nuclear families.

Since the patriarchal, nuclear family for many years was seen as the norm for the American society, even those scholars not heavily influenced by the pathology-disorganization perspective tended to view a patriarchal, nuclear family as the most desirable family system for black people. For example, Mozell Hill, in his study of the All-Negro Society, wrote that the lower-class family, which is "predominantly matriarchal" and therefore has "a loose, elastic structure," is not "nearly so cohesive as . . . the compact, patriarchal upper class family."[7] Charles S. Johnson expressed views alleging the superiority of the patriarchal family when he said that: "One of the greatest threats to emotional security in the family setting . . . is the one-parent family, whether this irregularity is due to death, desertion, divorce, or failure of the mother to marry."[8]

Kate Millett is correct in writing that contemporary white sociology often operates under a "patriarchal bias when its rhetoric inclines toward . . . the implication that racial inequity is capable of solution by a restoration of masculine authority."[9] The exception to this statement is that many black social scientists, for example, Frazier, Hill, Johnson and even W.E.B. Du Bois,[10] all of whom tended more or less to give "black perspectives" to "white sociology," also advanced black patriarchy as the ideal.

The Strength-Resiliency Perspective

The strength-resiliency perspective is basically a reaction to the negative view of the black family in the pathology-disorganization perspective. It emphasizes the ability of the black family to survive and achieve in the face of overwhelming barriers to freedom and opportunity. Andrew Billingsley's *Black Families in White America* signaled the arrival of this perspective. Billingsley attacked the pathology-disorganization perspective and maintained that the black family must be viewed as a social system within the wider society, which depends largely upon that society for jobs, resources and opportunities to meet "instrumental functions."[11] Billingsley demonstrated that there are a variety of nuclear, extended, and augmented black family structures,[12] and not just the typical single-parent, female-headed family structure which garners most of the attention of proponents of the pathology-disorganization perspective. He found that some black families are matriarchal, some patriarchal, and some egalitarian.[13] Furthermore, Billingsley did not picture the black woman as an oppressive force crushing black men and occasioning all kinds of ills in the family and community. He not only looked at the black woman who in the midst of impoverished circumstances does all she can to survive, but also at the achievement-oriented black woman so sorely neglected in patho- logical-disorganization literature.[14]

The picture of the black woman which emerges from Robert Hill's strength-resiliency perspective[15] is one of a survivalist and achiever. Hill, who examined five black family strengths—strong kinship bonds, strong work orientation, flexibility of family roles, strong achievement orientation, and strong religious orientation—sees black families as ba- sically egalitarian units where men and women work together and have equally important roles in the survival and advancement of the family.

Joyce Ladner, another exponent of the strength-resiliency perspec- tive, devotes her entire study, *Tomorrow's Tomorrow,* to "depicting the strength of the Black family and Black girls within the family struc- ture."[16] Robert Staples, also a strength-resiliency scholar of the black family, presents an entire study of black women.[17] Both Ladner and Staples, like Billingsley and Hill, are highly critical of the matriarchal thesis. Ladner maintains that while black women are strong by neces- sity due to all they have encountered in America, they are not necessar- ily dominant or domineering.[18] Staples sees the perpetuation "of the myth of the Black matriarchy, cultivated by America's image makers" as "part of the divide-and-conquer strategy that ruling classes have used throughout history."[19] He writes:

> The system of racism and capitalism benefits from maintaining sexual differentials in income and status within the Black popula- tion. Blacks as a group would constitute a far more homogeneous and formidable antagonist if all discrimination and interior divi- sions were eliminated.
>
> Instead, Black men who accept the myth of the Black matriarchy act on the premise that they can gain their rightful place in soci- ety by subjugating Black women. They believe that in order for the Black man to be strong the Black woman must be weak.[20]

The Africanity Perspective

As the strength-resiliency perspective gained ground, certain varia- tions of it appeared. One such variation is the africanity perspective. This perspective criticizes the thinking that slavery completely de- stroyed the traditional African cultural heritage. The exponents of the africanity perspective maintain that the strength of black families is due to African survivalism. Wade Nobles, the chief advocate of this view, sees such elements as an emphasis on group survival and oneness, strong parent-children relationships, respect for the elderly and the extended family system as evidence of africanity in black family life.[21] Patriarchy and the concomitant subordination of women, which are characteristic features of traditional African family life, are not treated in his analysis. Therefore, Nobles does not provide a hint as to whether these aspects of africanity are carried over to black Americans from the African heritage. Instead, his africanity perspective counters the white nuclear family which social science traditionalists seek to impose on black Americans.

Niara Sudarkasa has also advanced the africanity perspective.[22] She sees the extended family network as a chief characteristic of the African family, and maintains that the most distinct feature of the African extended family is that consanguinity bonds or "blood ties" are more important than conjugal bonds or "marital ties."[23] In other words, the stability of the African extended family, according to Sudarkasa, does not depend on the stability of marriages, but instead on the nature of kinship ties. She sees this as also true of the Afro-American extended family. This means that so long as extended family members are cooperating for mutual survival, identity and advancement, a family can still be strong with the father absent, a child can be taken care of whether or not he or she is illegitimate, and "adult females have a right to motherhood if they choose it and to male companionship regardless of whether or not they are married."[24]

Clearly, this perspective maintains that instead of pondering over statistics showing high rates of illegitimacy, female-headed households and desertion, which conjure up images of black women as immoral, emasculating and promiscuous, women in the black family should be viewed in the context of black culture and the African cultural heritage.

The Extended Family Perspective

The nuclear family often has been posited in the social sciences as the ideal type to which American families should conform. Any other family system was apt to be seen as pathological or deviant. When compared to the nuclear family, the extended family was seen as an anachronism, a part of early American agrarian society or the family life of immigrants.

The extended family perspective is generally a reaction against the bias in social science literature toward the nuclear family. Martin and Martin[25] and other students of this perspective[26] view the extended family as the chief mechanism for the survival of millions of blacks over the generations. These researchers believe that black family life is grossly distorted when exclusively or predominantly seen from the nuclear family perspective. For example, what appears to be a "broken home" may really be an intricate part of a strong extended family network where the female head, if not receiving support from the father or fathers of the children, could be receiving a significant amount of aid from other males in the family such as her father, grandfather, brothers, uncles and male cousins. It is the so-called broken family, that is, the single-parent household, which is defined as constituting a matriarchy. But the fact is that the male is simply not in the household; matriarchy implies female dominance in crucial family decision-making whether men are present in the household or not. In the context of the extended family, a matriarchy is contrary to the female's interests. She may be strong; she may even be the chief economic provider for herself and her children. But in the extended family, mutual survival depends on give-and-take on the part of both sexes, and few women, especially when they are burdened with children, can emerge so domineering and emasculating as to alienate themselves from the help they may receive from or give to male members of the family.

Patriarchy is definitely at variance with extended family survival. Patriarchy implies that each black male is capable of providing economic independence for his own wife and children. But historically, as will be shown in more detail, many black men have been unable to become economically free of the need for aid from other kin, including black women. To cut themselves adrift from the help of relatives in an effort to present a bold display of black machismo would amount to economic suicide.

Historical Background

It can be seen that the traditional perspective on the black family is being vigorously challenged by new, emerging perspectives. It is being challenged on the grounds that it overemphasizes deficits instead of focusing on strengths; that it seeks to have black families live up to a white family type instead of looking at the African cultural heritage; and that it emphasizes the nuclear family while neglecting the extended family, the most powerful mechanism for black survival.

In light of these perspectives, the key question here is: What does history show? The study of black family history reveals that for black women, a matriarchy did not develop in slavery and become a dominant feature of the black family; and that patriarchy, far from being a cure for black family ailments, actually worked contrary to the best interest of the black family. What history also demonstrates is a remarkable equality between the sexes; first, an equality foisted upon them by slavery; later, an equality which was seen by black men as being in their own best interest and the best interest of the race generally; and, most significantly, an equality which was the product of strong black womanhood adamantly refusing to play subordinate roles.

Traditional African Family Life

So elaborate were African kinship systems that several extended families could form a clan and several clans could make up an entire tribe or community, placing the family as the cornerstone of traditional African society. This means that consanguinity and conjugal bonds were equal in importance since kinship ties were crucial to the African way of life and marriage was seen as a sacred affair. Both kinship and marital ties in traditional Africa were for the most part centered around an elaborate system of polygyny and patriarchy. Polygyny brought men as many wives as they could afford, gave them status and prestige in the community, provided them with a variety of sex partners, gave them a number of children to ensure the continuity of the family lineage, and guaranteed them a number of work hands. Patriarchy made men the unquestioned heads of the family. It made them leaders, authority figures and decision-makers in the African community. It also gave them dominant roles as chiefs, priests, healers, rainmakers, prophets, teachers, warriors, counselors and wielders of power.

Women generally played important but, nevertheless, inferior roles in the wake of a rigorous system of polygyny and patriarchy. They were expected to obey the authority of their husbands. They were expected to do much of the menial chores. More than anything, they were expected to have children. Bearing children gave them their greatest sense of respect and worth in a male-dominated society. Jomo Kenyatta said that once a man and woman are married, "they regard the procreation of children as their first and most sacred duty."[27] A barren woman, regardless of what other qualities she might have, was virtually seen as a failure, if not a curse or a disgrace. The emphasis placed on kinship, marriage and having children made it highly unlikely that a woman could choose to have babies out of wedlock, or even engage in sex out of wedlock, without great ostracism and rejection. Though divorce was sanctioned in most traditional African communities, spinsterhood, so-called illegitimacy and single parenthood were virtually nonexistent.

How much of the traditional African family was carried over to the New World? According to africanity proponents, the traditional African family virtually survived intact except for a few cultural adjustments or transformations. African Americans developed a strong sense of family as did their African forebears. Taking people from their families and homeland and bringing them motherless to a strange land made them long even more for their families or to be part of a family in the New World. But if the strong sense of family continued as an African survivalism despite slavery, it was no longer governed by the rituals, customs and beliefs which gave the African family meaning and durability. Instead, it was determined largely by the will of slaves to survive a hostile environment, to become in essence a new people, new Africans, part of, yet remote from the traditional African experience, part of, yet not fully in accord with the dominant white American society.

The Slave Family

John W. Blassingame was correct when he held that in slavery, "black men could no longer exercise the same power over their families as they had in Africa."[28] Slavery destroyed African patriarchy. It stripped black men of authority over their wives and children. The slave master was the chief patriarch, the authority figure and decision-maker. The black man was relegated to a position so out of character with the heritage of African patriarchy that he could not even "protect his wife from the sexual advances of whites and the physical abuse of his master."[29]

As cruel and as dehumanizing as slavery was, it ironically equalized the black man and the black woman in ways hardly dreamed of in traditional Africa. Eugene Genovese holds that "the slave families . . . rested on a much greater equality between men and women than . . . the white family."[30] Blassingame contends that "the transformation of African familial roles led to the creation of America's first democratic family in the quarters, where men and women shared authority and responsibility."[31] Merle Hodge writes that slavery bore a negative, de facto equality, "the equality of cattle in a herd."

> We became "equal" from the moment African men and women were clamped to the floor alongside each other for the horrifying middle passage. A slave was a slave—male or female—a herd of livestock, a unit of the power that drove the plantation. The

women worked equally hard out in the fields with the men, and were equally subject to torture and brutality.[32]

Angela Davis observes that blacks "transformed that negative equality which emanated from the equal oppression they suffered as slaves into a positive quality: the egalitarianism characterizing their social relations."[33]

Slavery equalized the black man and black woman in the most important world on the plantation, the world of work. Leslie Owens points out that the black man did not do any work that the black woman did not do also.[34] W.E.B. Du Bois suggested that if feminists need proof that women are the occupational equals of men, all they need to do is look at the black woman in slavery. He said "the fact that she could and did replace the white man as laborer, artisan, and servant, showed the possibility of the white woman doing the same thing . . . Moreover, the usual sentimental arguments against women at work were not brought forward in the case of Negro womanhood."[35] Sojourner Truth put the equality of the black women in the world of work in more illustrative terms. She said, "I have plowed, and planted, and gathered into barns, and no man could head me—and ain't I a woman? I could work as much and eat as much as a man (when I could get it), and bear de lash as well—and ain't I a woman."[36]

Part of the process of equalization of the black sexes was a conscious effort on the part of the slave master to defeminize black women This defeminization came not only by working black women as hard as males and subjecting them equally to punishment and brutality, but also by forcing black women in many instances to wear men's clothing and to treat them in a manner so crude and coarse as to leave them fully aware that they were not "placed on pedestals." As Sojourner Truth commented: "Nobody ever helped me into carriages, or ober mud puddle, or gives me any best place . . . And when I cried out with a mother's grief, none but Jesus heard."[37]

Not only were black women made equal to black men, but they also bore extra burdens which black men did not. In a certain sense, the black woman was a "special captive."[38] As such, women not only worked "side by side with men at nearly every task on the plantation,"[39] but also did so-called women's work as well. Leslie Owens writes:

[T]here were certain duties considered women's work that men declined to do. Some male slaves refused to do washing for this reason. Cooking was usually the task of women, as was sewing and some forms of child care. Sometimes masters punished males by forcing them to work with women labor gangs in the fields or compelling them to wash the family's clothes and attend to house-cleaning. So great was their shame before their fellows that many ran off and suffered the lash on their backs rather than submit to the discipline.[40]

Another area where black women became special captives was in their role as breeders of children and sex objects. Many black women were forced to breed like animals to ensure the master a steady supply of workers. Black women were often impregnated as they served as receptacles to satisfy the sexual desires of men, black and white.

Proponents of the pathology-disorganization perspective suggest that it was the sexual relations which black women had with white men that gave the former power which black men did not have. Jessie Bernard holds that "because they were useful in the role of breeders as well as that of workers, female slaves were strategically better off than male slaves."[41] And E. Franklin Frazier goes so far as to see the positive transmission of white culture to blacks through the intimate relations of slave women and white men.[42] Social scientists, looking at black life in the South long after slavery, continued to maintain the thesis that the rape of black women by white men somehow gave black women an advantage and served to emasculate the black man. John Dollard's *Caste and Class in a Southern Town* is a case in point.[43] Stanford Lyman has summarized this convoluted kind of thinking:

> The sexual gain provides white men, by virtue of their superior caste position, with two classes of women—white women, from whom they draw their sweethearts and wives, and black women, of whom they take sexual advantage. . . But black women too may find a gain in this situation, because they are freer to express otherwise inhibited sexual impulses and are protected from reproach because they dare not refuse a white man's bidding. Moreover, by having sexual relations with white men, black women may achieve an otherwise forbidden sense of equality with whites or a sense of degrading these same white men who hold them in disrepute. It is black men who suffer a sense of real deprivation and demoralization. They cannot protect their own women, and this indignity compromises their manhood.[44]

In addition to undergoing the helplessness and psychological pain of being constantly raped, the black woman, instead of getting power, generally got more babies. Unlike traditional Africa, where having babies gave the black woman a great deal of esteem and status, in slavery continual childbearing generally impaired the black woman's health, increased her suffering and grief, and shortened her life. The white wife of a slave owner recorded this account in her diary:

> In considering the whole condition of the people on this plantation, it appears to me that the principal hardships fall to the lot of the women. . . Fanny has had six children; all dead but one. She

came to beg to have her work in the field lightened. Nanny has had three children; two of them dead. . . Leah has had six children; three are dead. Sophy . . . is suffering fearfully; she had had ten children born; five of them are dead. Sally had had two miscarriages and three children born, one of whom is dead. She came complaining of incessant pain and weakness in her back. Sarah . . . She has had four miscarriages, had brought seven children into the world, five of whom were dead, and was again with child. She complained of dreadful pains in the back, an internal tumor which swells with the exertion of working in the fields; probably, I think, she is ruptured. . . Molly . . . Hers was the best account I have yet received; she had had nine children, and six of them were still alive. . . There was hardly one of these women . . . who might not have been a candidate for a bed in a hospital, and they had come to see me after working all day in the fields.[45]

When social scientists are not claiming that sex gave black women matriarchal power in slavery, they look at the black mammy type as the ultimate matriarch, claiming that black women have "more often been loved . . . not only as sex partners but also as nurses or 'mammies.' "[46] The fact is that "like the majority of slave men, slave women, for the most part, were field workers."[47] The "Black mammy stereotypes which presume to capture the essence of the Black woman's role in slavery"[48] obscure the reality that even the so-called black mammy was no more than a powerless beast of burden, like any other slave, despite her alleged propensity to be "sassy" to white folks. Blassingame documented that life for house servants, including black mammies, was no sinecure.[49] House servants not only had numerous chores, but also had to sometimes "do double duty as field hands."[50] James Curry, a former slave, gave this account of the day-to-day life of a black mammy:

My mother's labor was very hard. She would go to the house in the morning, take her pail upon her head, and go away to the cow-pen, and milk fourteen cows. She then put on the bread for the family breakfast, and got the cream ready for churning, and set a little child to churn it, she having the care of from ten to fifteen children, whose mothers worked in the field. After clearing away the family breakfast, she got breakfast for the slaves; which consisted of warm corn bread and buttermilk, and was taken at twelve o'clock. In the meantime, she had beds to make, rooms to sweep, etc. Then she cooked the family dinner, which was simply plain meat, vegetables, and bread. Then the slaves' dinner was to be ready at from eight to nine o'clock in the evening. . . (She cooked for from twenty-five to thirty-five, taking the family and the slaves together . . .). At night she had the cows to milk again. . . This was her work day by day. Then in the course of the week, she had the washing and ironing to do for her master's family . . . and for her husband, seven children and herself.[51]

One would think that a house servant and mammy so faithful and hardworking would be practically exempt from punishment and indeed have a high status in her master's house, but Curry goes on to say:

> One of the most trying scenes I ever passed through, when I would have laid my life to protect her if I had dared, was this: After she had raised my master's children, one of his daughters, a young girl, came into the kitchen one day, and for some trifle about the dinner, she struck my mother, who pushed her away, and she fell on the floor. Her father was not at home. When he came, which was while the slaves were eating in the kitchen, she told him about it. He came down, called my mother out, and, with a hickory rod, he beat her fifteen or twenty strokes, then called his daughter and told her to take her satisfaction on her, and she did beat her until she was satisfied. Oh! it was dreadful, to see this girl whom my poor mother had taken care of from her childhood, thus beating her, and I must stand there, and did not dare to crook my finger in her defense.[52]

Blassingame maintains that most slaves preferred to be field slaves for the house slave had to be "at the beck and call of the master day and night" and be subjected to his "every capricious, vengeful, or sadistic whim."[53] Another former slave verifies this statement by reporting:

> One day my master was dining with a gentleman who had a wife as black as dat hat. A young colored woman, as likely for her color as any lady in dis assembly (a laugh), waited on table. She happened to spill a little gravy on the gown of the mistress. The gentleman took his carving knife, dragged her out to wood pile, and cut her head off; den wash his hands, come in and finish his dinner like nothing had happened![54]

Slavery finally ended; but the Civil War quite clearly gave indications to black women that they were not going to develop matriarchal power or escape being special captives. Leon F. Litwack gives this account:

> Not only did some Union soldiers sexually assault any women they found in a slave cabin but they had no compunctions about committing the act in the presence of her family. . . In some such instances, the husband or children of the intended victim had to be forcibly restrained from coming to her assistance. Beyond the exploitation of sexual assault, black women could be subjected to further brutality and sadism, as was most graphically illustrated in an incident involving some Connecticut soldiers stationed in Virginia. After seizing two "niger wenches," they "turned them upon their heads, & put tobacco, chips, stocks, lighted cigars & sand into their behinds." Without explanation, some Union soldiers in Hanover County, Virginia, stopped five young black women and cut their arms, legs, and backs with razors.[55]

It must be kept in mind that this type of treatment was meted out to black women by white men who supposedly had come to free them, and that many black women were faced with prejudice and barbarism as bitter as that which they had left behind.

The Free Black During and After Slavery

Leon Litwack shows that free blacks were hardly any better off than slaves.[56] Though free blacks had greater freedom of choice and mobility and a few more rights than slaves, they were still the victims of vicious racial prejudice and discrimination, still relegated to a low, inferior position of economic powerlessness, and still vigorously denied even elementary citizenship rights.

Patriarchy in the free black community was virtually nonexistent, since it depended on the ability of black men to provide for their families without their women having to work outside the home. Free black men seemed to have a full grasp of the reality that the survival of the black family depended largely on black women as workers, and that black men were hardly in a position economically or politically to start acting like they could carry black burdens alone.

In fact, Rosalyn Terborg-Penn holds that a prevalent attitude among prominent nineteenth-century black men both during and after slavery was that black women were the key to black survival and advancement.[57] Martin Delaney, a major black leader of his day, wrote that "no people are ever elevated above the condition of their females."[58] Just as did many other black male reformers and leaders, he called for the education of black women so they could rise above being "washerwomen, chamber-maids, children's traveling nurses, common house servants, and menials,"[59] and take their places beside black men in working for the total liberation of black people.

With this type of attitude toward women, free black men were often strong advocates of female equality. Terborg-Penn writes that: "On the whole during the antebellum period, Black male leaders were more sympathetic to women's rights than white male leaders."[60] Benjamin Quarles has pointed out that: "In the viewpoint of the Negro abolitionist the whole struggle for human freedom embraced the rights of women."[61] A number of nineteenth-century black men pleaded the cause of black women, men such as Frederick Douglass, a staunch supporter of women's rights, and Alexander Crummell, a leading black scholar who wrote a scathing attack on the plight of black women. But black women were highly capable of pleading their own cause. In slavery, the slave woman emerged as a powerful survivalist worker in her role as special captive. They would not only emerge as survivalist workers, but also as workers for achievement and social change. "O, ye daughters of Africa, awake! awake! arise!" was the call of Maria Stewart, the first black woman to make a public address on behalf of blacks in America.[62] Many black women responded.

Nineteenth-century black women combined their roles as survivalists, achievers and agents of social change. They participated in the abolitionist movement from its inception, the greatest example being Harriet Tubman who clearly showed that black women were not lacking in the daring, courage and toughness generally associated with males. They participated in the struggle for women's rights amidst widespread, palpable racial prejudice on the part of white women. Sojourner Truth, the greatest example of this participation, said:

> I feel that if I have to answer for the deeds done in my body just as much as man, I have a right to have just as much as a man.... Then that little man in black there, he says women can't have as much rights as men, because Christ wasn't a woman! Where did your Christ come from? Where did your Christ come from? From God and a woman! Man had nothing to do with him... If the first woman God ever made was strong enough to turn the world upside down all alone, these women together ought to be able to turn it back, and get it right side up again! And now that they are asking to do it, the men better let them.[63]

Nineteenth-century black women allied themselves with white women in an effort to "wipe out illiteracy among the millions of former slaves."[64] If the black church was male-dominated, black schools were dominated by black women. They formed women's clubs designed to educate, refine and uplift black women so that they could become more active in the liberation and reconstruction of black life. Thousands of these clubs were formed nationwide in the late nineteenth century, and were second only to the black church in providing social welfare services to the black community. These women were not lazy, dependent, social butterflies placed on a pedestal. They were wives, cooks, mothers and lovers; yet they were self-sacrificing, committed women ever seeking to relieve the suffering of their black brothers and sisters and of humanity.

There were, of course, a great number of black women during the nineteenth century, both slave and free, who were so caught up in survival that they led harsh, stunted, dead-end lives. There were also some who were so caught up in their own individual success and achievements that they had little concern for other blacks. But the highest model of black womanhood was when black women were able to combine the three roles. This model was prevalent among nineteenth-century black women and was carried over into the early parts of the twentieth century. When a woman was able to combine these three roles, they were often referred to as "race women." The nineteenth and twentieth centuries produced a number of such women. Already mentioned have been Harriet Tubman and Sojourner Truth. There were also Fannie M. Barrier, an ardent abolitionist; Ida B. Wells, a crusader in the fight against lynching; Nannie Helen Burroughs, a teacher of race pride and founder of a school for black girls; Fannie Coppin, a founder of a school as well; Anna J. Cooper, who wrote a book about the conditions of the black woman in the South; Mary Church Terrell, one of the most intelligent and committed fighters for black rights, women's rights and human rights that the United States has ever produced; and Mary McCleod Bethune, the great educator and advisor to President Franklin D. Roosevelt.

As race women, these black women put racism before sexism or made attacks against sexism mainly as a by-product of attacks against racism. These women became role models to which millions of other black women aspired. They, and thousands of others like them, pleaded with black women to maintain their position as equals. Their chief interest seemed to be to work with black men, not to dominate them. "For woman's cause is man's," wrote Anna J. Cooper. "They rise or sink together, dwarfed or godlike, bond or free."[65]

Black Women and Public Policy

It is consistent and proper that despite black women's survival of chattel slavery, where they served as special captives, achieving amidst the most oppressive odds and working to make the United States truly a democracy, the image that predominates is one of them as sexually promiscuous welfare recipients and matriarchs. This prevailing image is quite consistent with the norms of a sexist and racist society.

For black women, racism takes precedence over sexism. For even when white women show strengths similar to black women in the survival of the family, they are not viewed as negatively as black women are. Cynthia Epstein writes that: "There have been instances of strong mother figures in American history (immigrant mothers and pioneer mothers) who have been idealized as women who made it possible for their families to endure in punishing situations." But, she added, "Somehow these other women were subjected to a different set of norms," and were not viewed as exhibiting "masculine or, worse, 'castrating' behavior."[66]

Jessie Bernard also suggests how differently black women are viewed when they are, in essence, playing a role similar to that of women in other ethnic groups. She observes:

> The fact that women contribute to the support of the family need not, in and of itself, lower the strategic position of their husbands. In the little ghetto communities of Eastern Europe, the woman who married a scholar and supported him in his studies was honored: it was a genuine privilege to support a learned man— nor was his masculinity diminished because he was supported by his wife. And many immigrants' wives in the United States found it necessary to step in to earn money during their husbands' periods of unemployment. Although there was no special honor in the "matriarchal" position, neither was there any disgrace. A husband may have felt chagrin or humiliation, but his wife knew he was a man, the world knew he was a man, so he knew it too.[67]

But somehow Bernard feels this does not apply to the black man for, in her words, "The Negro husband is not in the scholar's position nor has the outside world allowed him to cultivate his masculine honor."[68] The implication is that when white women help to support their men it is an acceptable necessity, but when black women do so, it is castrating because the black man has not been allowed "to cultivate his masculine honor." This, of course, is merely another call for black patriarchy.

The three major roles black women have played historically in the black family and community represent a culture counter to a sexist society and to male chauvinistic deviations in the black community. It has already been shown that patriarchy is not in the interest of the black family and the community. Also, the rise of feminism in the white community shows that it is an undesirable feature of life for many white people as well. What must be highlighted is that the call for patriarchy on the public policy level is a cruel hoax played on black men.

It is highly questionable whether public policymakers are sincerely interested in establishing a black patriarchy. For patriarchy extends farther than male rule of the family. It extends to male rule of society. As Kate Millet maintains, the family becomes "both mirror of and a connection with the larger society; a patriarchal unit within a patriarchal whole."[69] To establish a black patriarchy would mean, in essence, white men sharing real power and not just symbolic power with black men. There has been little or no indication that white men are willing to do that; and there has been ample evidence that they are not willing to do so without a struggle.

It is a cruel hoax to demand that black men live up to the patriarchal model and then do practically everything conceivable to make sure that the great majority of them will never be able do so. It is even a crueler hoax to hold that the black man is ruled by a matriarchy, the very opposite of the patriarchal ideal. In essence, this is saying that the black man is not a man. So long as the black man incorporates the patriarchal ideal as a part of his personality and manhood, he will continue to experience inner frustration, tension and rage.

Public policies and programs centering basically around black women give strong evidence that racism is still too prevalent to give black men real power. At present, most public policies and programs are geared mainly toward keeping black women at a subsistence, poverty level. Very little is done on the public policy level to take advantage of the black woman's tradition as an achiever. As a result, thousands of black women have had their promise and potential stifled generation after generation, regardless of who was in political office. The great voices of black women calling for much needed social change have all but been ignored.

Public policy has aligned itself with the media, public opinion and the social sciences in presenting a negative image of the black woman. It is precisely the stereotypic, racist image of black women as mammies, matriarchs, permissive sex objects, welfare bums and emasculators that must be totally destroyed so that a more realistic assessment of black women as hard-working, striving, achieving people seeking to improve the quality of their lives can emerge. It is precisely this type of divide-and-conquer tradition of racism that makes it paramount for black women to keep being strong, keep surviving, keep seeking to rise above poverty and degradation and, more importantly, keep on fighting for the massive changes necessary for the full liberation and self-determination of black women, black men and their children.

NOTES

[1]See John H. Bracey, Jr., August Meier and Elliott Rudwick, eds., *Black Matriarchy: Myth or Reality* (Belmont, Cal.: Wadsworth Publishing, 1971).

[2]Erlene Stetson, "Studying Slavery: Some Literary and Pedagogical Considerations on the Black Female Slave," in Gloria T. Hull, Patricia Bell Scott and Barbara Smith, eds., *All the Women Are White, All the Blacks Are Men, But Some of Us Are Brave: Black Women's Studies* (Old Westbury, N. Y.: The Feminist Press, 1982), pp. 61-85.

[3]Horace Cayton and St. Clair Drake, *Black Metropolis: A Study of Negro Life in A Northern City* (New York: Harcourt Brace & Co., 1945), p. 385.

[4]Daniel Patrick Moynihan, *The Negro Family: The Case for National Action* (Washington, D.C.: U.S. Department of Labor, Office of Policy Planning and Research, 1965), p. 39.

[5]E. Franklin Frazier, *The Negro Family in the United States* (Chicago: University of Chicago Press, 1939).

[6]Gunnar Myrdal, *An American Dilemma: The Negro Problem and Modern Democracy* (New York: Harpers & Bros., 1944), pp. 930-931.

[7]Mozell Hill, "The All-Negro Society in Oklahoma" (Unpublished Ph.D. Dissertation, University of Chicago, 1946), p. 94.

[8]Charles S. Johnson, *Growing Up in the Black Belt: Negro Youth in the Rural South* (1941; reprint, New York: Schocken Books, 1967), p. 78.

[9]Kate Millett, *Sexual Politics* (Garden City, N. Y.: Doubleday, 1970), p. 39.

[10]W.E.B. Du Bois, *The Negro American Family* (Atlanta: Atlanta University Press, 1908; New York: Negro Universities Press, Greenwood Publishing, 1969).

[11]Andrew Billingsley, *Black Families in White America* (Englewood Cliffs, N. J.: Prentice-Hall, 1968), pp. 4-6, 22.

[12]Ibid., pp. 15-21.

[13]Ibid., p. 143.

[14]Ibid., pp. 97-122.

[15]See Robert B. Hill, *The Strengths of Black Families* (New York: Emerson Hall Publishers, Inc., distributed by Independent Publishers Group, 1972).

[16]Joyce Ladner, *Tomorrow's Tomorrow: The Black Woman* (Garden City, N. Y.: Doubleday, 1971), p. xxi.

[17]See Robert Staples, *The Black Woman in America: Sex, Marriage and the Family* (Chicago: Nelson-Hall Publishers, 1973).

[18]Ladner, op. cit., p. 35.

[19]Staples, op. cit., p. 33.

[20]Ibid.

[21]Wade Nobles, "Africanity: Its Role in Black Families," *The Black Scholar* 5:9 (June 1974): 10-17.

[22]Niara Sudarkasa, "African and Afro-American Family Structure: A Comparison," *The Black Scholar* 11:8 (November/December 1980): 37-60.

[23]Ibid., p. 48.

[24]Niara Sudarkasa, "An Exposition on the Value Premises Underlying Black Families Studies," *Journal of the National Medical Association* 67: 3 (May 1975): 238.

[25]Elmer P. and Joanne Mitchell Martin, *The Black Extended Family* (Chicago: University of Chicago Press, 1978).

[26]See Joyce Aschenbrenner, *Lifelines: Black Families in Chicago* (New York: Holt, Rinehart & Winston, 1975); Demitri B. Shimkin, Edith M.

Shimkin and Dennis Frate, eds., *The Extended Family in Black Societies* (The Hague: Mouton Publishers, 1978); and Carol B. Stack, *All Our Kin: Strategies for Survival in a Black Community* (New York: Harper & Row, 1974).

[27]Jomo Kenyatta, *Facing Mount Kenya: The Traditional Life of the Kikuyu* (New York: Vintage Books, 1965), p. 158.

[28]John W. Blassingame, *The Slave Community: Plantation Life in the Antebellum South,* revised and enlarged ed. (New York and Oxford: Oxford University Press, 1979), p. 178.

[29]Ibid., p. 172.

[30]Eugene Genovese, *Roll, Jordan, Roll: The World the Slaves Made* (New York: Pantheon Books, 1974), p. 501.

[31]Blassingame, op. cit., p. 178.

[32]Merle Hodge, "The Shadow of the Whip: A Comment on Male-Female Relations in the Caribbean," in Orde Coombs, comp., *Is Massa Day Dead? Black Moods in the Caribbean* (Garden City, N. Y.: Anchor Books, 1974), pp. 111-118.

[33]Angela Y. Davis, *Women, Race, and Class* (New York: Random House, 1981), p. 18.

[34]Leslie H. Owens, *This Species of Property: Slave Life and Culture in the Old South* (New York: Oxford University Press, 1976), p. 39.

[35]W.E.B. Du Bois, *The Gift of Black Folk: The Negroes in the Making of America* (Boston: The Stratford Co., 1924), p. 262.

[36]Quoted in Bert J. Loewenberg and Ruth Bogin, eds., *Black Women in Nineteenth-Century American Life: Their Words, Their Thoughts, Their Feelings* (University Park, Pa.: Pennsylvania State University Press, 1976), p. 235.

[37]Ibid.

[38]Elmer P. and Joanne Mitchell Martin, "The Black Woman: Cultural and Economic Captive," in Pauline Kolenda, ed., *Contemporary Cultures For and Against Women* (Houston, Tex.: Department of Anthropology, University of Houston Central Campus, 1981): 235-253.

[39]Owens, op. cit., p. 195.

[40]Ibid.

[41]Jessie Bernard, *Marriage and Family Among Negroes* (Englewood Cliffs, N. J.: Prentice-Hall, 1966), p. 68.

[42]Frazier, op. cit., p. 69.

[43]John Dollard, *Caste and Class in a Southern Town* (New York: Doubleday and Co., 1937).

[44]Stanford M. Lyman, *The Black American in Sociological Thought* (New York: Putnam, 1972), pp. 79-80.

[45]Frances A. Kemble, quoted in John Anthony Scott, ed., *Frances Ann Kemble's Journal of a Resistance on a Georgia Plantation in 1838-1839* (New York: Alfred A. Knopf, 1961), pp. 224-241.

[46]Bernard, op. cit., p. 69.

[47]Davis, op. cit., p. 5.

[48]Ibid.

[49]Blassingame, op. cit., p. 155.

[50]Genovese, op. cit., p. 339.

[51]Quoted in John W. Blassingame, ed., *Slave Testimony: Two Centuries of Letters, Speeches, Interviews and Autobiographies* (Baton Rouge, La.: Louisiana State University Press, 1977), pp. 128-129.

[52]Ibid., pp. 132-133.

[53]Blassingame, *The Slave Community*, op. cit., p. 158.

[54]Blassingame, *Slave Testimony*, op. cit., pp. 125-126.

[55]Leon F. Litwack, *Been in the Storm So Long: The Aftermath of Slavery* (New York: Alfred A. Knopf, 1979), p. 130.

[56]See Leon F. Litwack, *North of Slavery: The Negro in the Free States, 1790-1860* (Chicago: University of Chicago Press, 1961).

[57]Rosalyn Terborg-Penn, "Black Male Perspectives on the Nineteenth-Century Woman," in Sharon Harley and Rosalyn Terborg-Penn, eds., *The Afro-American Woman: Struggles and Images* (Port Washington, N. Y.: Kennikat Press, National University Publications, 1978), pp. 28-42.

[58]Martin Delaney, *The Condition, Elevation, Images, and Destiny of the Colored People of the United States of America Politically Considered* (1852; reprint with a new introduction, New York: Arno Press, 1968), p. 199.

[59]Ibid.

[60]Terborg-Penn, op. cit., p. 28.

[61]Benjamin Quarles, *Black Abolitionists* (New York: Oxford University Press, 1969), p. 177.

[62]Quoted in Loewenberg and Bogin, op. cit., p. 187.

[63]Ibid., p. 236.

[64]Davis, op. cit., p. 107.

[65]Anna J. Cooper, *A Voice From the South By a Black Woman of the South* (Xenia, Ohio: The Aldine Printing House, 1892), p. 192.

[66]Cynthia Fuchs Epstein, "Persistent Effects of the Multiple Negative: Explaining the Success of Black Professional Women," in Mark Abrahamson, Ephraim Mizruchi and Carlton Hornung, *Stratification and Mobility* (New York: Macmillan Publishing, 1976), pp. 306, 311.

[67]Bernard, op. cit., p. 95.

[68]Ibid.

[69]Millett, op. cit., p. 35.

WOMEN, ETHNICITY, AND FAMILY VIOLENCE: IMPLICATIONS FOR SOCIAL POLICY

Suzanne K. Steinmetz and Joy Pellicciaro

University of Delaware

Introduction

When examining the impact of gender and ethnicity on interpersonal violence, a clear understanding of these terms is important. Three major problems that make difficult the use of "ethnic" as an identifying variable need to be addressed: the definitional problem; the confounding of social class and ethnicity; and the culture-bound definition of behavior.

Defining Ethnicity

What exactly is an ethnic group? Webster's defines "ethnic" as "of or relating to races or large groups of people classified according to common traits and customs."[1] In the social sciences, ethnic may refer to the common cultural heritage shared by a group of people from a specific country, e.g., the Polish and their homeland, Poland. Ethnic can also refer to people who share a common religious background such as the Jewish. Finally, ethnic is used to characterize racial groups, e.g., blacks.

Categorizing people by these broad definitions, however, presents problems when conducting research or developing social policy. For example, under a recently repealed 1970 state of Louisiana "Black Blood" law, a citizen was considered to be black if more than one-thirty-second of his of her ancestry was of Negro blood.[2] Yet eligibility for the Employment Assistance Program for adult Indians requires an applicant, if not an enrolled member of an eligible tribe, to possess "at least one-half degree of Indian blood which is not derived from a tribe whose relationship is terminated by an Act of Congress."[3]

To qualify as "Hispanic" for eligibility in minority programs, a Spanish surname is the only attribute needed. However, some Hispanics do not have "Spanish" surnames and using "Spanish-speaking" as a mechanism for identifying Hispanics fails to recognize that Brazilians speak Portuguese.

The 1980 census definition for Hispanics attempted to remedy these problems:

> Persons of Spanish origin or descent are those who classify themselves in one of the specific Spanish origin categories listed on the questionnaire—Mexican, Puerto Rican, or Cuban—as well as those who indicated that they were of other Spanish/Hispanic origin . . . "[O]ther Spanish/Hispanic origin" are those whose origins are from Spain or Central or South America or they are Spanish origin persons identifying themselves generally as Spanish, Spanish American, Hispano, Latino, etc. Persons of Spanish origins can be of any race.[4]

Unfortunately, as a way of classifying people into meaningful categories, this definition is virtually useless. As Carmela Lacayo notes, "While Hispanics share a language and a certain cultural heritage that is common to all, heterogeneity is more nearly the hallmark than homogeneity."[5] The research on Mexican Americans provides an excellent illustration of this problem. Since this research is frequently based on Spanish surnames in census data, and 40 percent of this group represents non-Mexican groups (Puerto Ricans, Cubans, etc.), the significant variations in age, income, family size and occupational attainment between Mexican Americans and other Hispanic groups are distorted.[6]

Black scholars also decry the methodological practice of considering blacks as a single unit. They suggest that there is no monolithic black group, because among black Americans there are as many differences as between black Americans and white Americans.[7] It is clear that the use of ethnicity as a classifying variable is problematic.

Confounding Social Class and Ethnicity

A second problem to be addressed is the confounding of social class and ethnicity when using these variables to attribute specific characteristics or behaviors to particular populations. Social class—specifically the conditions of occupational life—is the primary influence on parental values.[8] Numerous studies have documented the relationship between social class and the use of physical violence to resolve conflicts.[9] Because of their lower income levels and higher unemployment rates, minority groups in the United States appear to have correspondingly higher rates of family violence than do white Americans. However, when the data are controlled for social class, these differences disappear.[10]

Since many of the statistics on abuse are collected from public service agencies that serve lower-class clients, their abuse becomes a public record and is thus more visible. Middle- and upper-class citizens have resources that enable them to rely on private agencies, private physicians, private counselors, etc., and therefore their abuse escapes public notice. Inasmuch as minority groups are the most easily identified, the statistics are often compiled on the basis of "white" and "nonwhite" or "white, black, Hispanic and other." Because a greater percentage of the black population is classified as lower class (based on occupation and income), they tend to be overrepresented in these studies.

Culturally Bound Definitions of Abuse

Finally, in analyzing data on violence, the most complex factor of all is the need to separate culturally bound definitions of abuse. As James Garbarino and Aaron Ebata note in their discussion of child abuse, this perspective is:

> A necessary pre-condition for dealing with cultural and ethnic factors in child maltreatment because any conclusion about who abuses and how much they abuse depends upon a culturally validated definition of what abuse is.[11]

A poignant example of this culturally bound definition was reported by a social worker attending the 1977 conference on family law and family violence held in Montreal. A colleague received a complaint of child abuse involving a Puerto Rican mother who forced her child to kneel for extended periods of time in the alley beside their apartment building. Another social worker, herself Puerto Rican, explained that in Puerto Rico, children are often sent into the yard or garden to kneel, pray, and meditate on their wrongdoings. When transposed to the alley of New York, such behavior may seem abusive, but it is compatible with Puerto Rican child-rearing practices and much preferred to spanking or hitting a child.

One observes similar variations in the ways women perceive what it is to be battered. For example, some women who have sought shelter against spousal abuse report that they have been "beaten up," which they describe as frightening verbal abuse, the threat of physical abuse and, perhaps, some slaps. Other women, who have experienced physical injury at the hands of their husbands, did not consider themselves to be battered when interviewed.

Insight into how abuse can take different forms and different meanings in families from two very different ethnic groups is offered from an ethnopsychiatric perspective by John Spiegel. By contrasting the highly interactive Italian-American family, which has a greater tolerance for aggressive behavior between family members, with the moralistic Irish-American family, which uses guilt to control transgressions, he shows that acceptable levels of physical violence vary from culture to culture.[12]

Leanor Johnson has analyzed the effect of writers' different perspectives on the interpretation of data on black families.[13] She tabulated 7017 articles which had appeared in sociology and social work journals over a thirteen-year period (1965-1978), categorizing them according to Walter Allen's[14] three theoretical perspectives or value orientations: cultural equivalence, in which black families are compared to and found to share white middle-class family norms; cultural deviance, in which black families are compared to white middle-class norms and found to deviate (explicitly or implicitly interpreted as pathological); and cultural variance, in which black cultural patterns are explained primarily by use of black values and experiences. The analysis revealed that 44 percent of the data pertaining to black family roles, structures and functions were interpreted through the cultural equivalence perspective, 29 percent from the cultural deviance view, and 27 percent from the cultural variance perspective.

These examples demonstrate the effects of different cultural expectations on the interpretations of data from different ethnic groups.

The Culture of Violence Theory

The most commonly used theory for examining the influence of culture on violence is the "culture of violence" theory, which suggests that the differential distribution of violence is a function of the cultural norms and values concerning violence.[15] This theory predicts that a greater degree of violence will occur in those families belonging to a culture or subculture in which socialization practices are deeply embedded in violence, rather than predicting violence from an excess of deprivation and stress or the lack of alternative resources for resolving conflicts.

There is considerable support for this position. The image of machismo among Latino males has often been utilized as an example of cultural expectation towards the appropriateness of violence.[16] Marvin Wolfgang and Franco Ferracuti found that groups with high rates of homicide also were characterized by extremely high rates of rape and aggravated assault, a characteristic which provides support for a sub-culture of violence.[17]

Lynn Curtis[18] cautions that values should not be considered as in-tervening variables in violent behavior. Rather, he posits that values and behavior are but two of the many factors affecting violence, with neither having a causal relationship with the outcome. He defines a black poverty subculture in which economic marginality and institu-tional racism are determinants of the behavior of poor, young black males, and in which contracultural values and behaviors lead to con-flict and violence.

Noel Cazenave and Murray Straus,[19] in interpreting black spousal violence, also question the rationale for a culture of violence theory. As alternative explanations of such behavior, they suggest that social structural (such as discrimination and unemployment) or situational conditions may lead to family violence, which then develops into vio-lent attitudes, rather than violent cultural attitudes causing violent behavior. From the same data, which show lower rates of corporal pun-ishment, sibling violence and parent abuse for blacks than for whites, the researchers find an equally salient "culture of nonviolence."

In his analysis of black male familial roles in American society, Cazenave[20] finds support for Jackson Toby's[21] concept of the mascu-line ideal. Cazenave postulates that the socialization of males in Ameri-can society leads to certain expectations which determine their behav-ior and their perceptions of themselves. The black man's quest for gender identity places him in the predicament of proving his manhood without having access to the means of achieving it. As an alternative, he may turn to violence to attain his masculinity. Lacking the visible attributes of a higher social class, the lower-class black male may use physical violence as a compensatory resource.

Ethnic Comparisons of Family Violence

In a study of family violence using 2,143 intact families,[22] the methods for resolving family conflicts were compared for blacks, whites, Jewish and others (American Indian, Asian, etc.). The data presented in Table 1 suggest that while a greater percentage of blacks engage in wife abuse than do other groups, they have the lowest percentage of siblings en-gaging in violence and essentially identical percentages of child abusers as do white parents. In contrast, a considerably smaller percentage of Jewish husbands use violence on their wives than do black husbands, yet a comparison of black and Jewish wives reveals that a similar percentage of both groups use violence against their husbands. Overall, a smaller percentage of white families engage in each act except for sibling abuse. Unfortunately, the composition of "others" is so diverse that meaningful comparisons are not possible.

TABLE 1
COMPARISON OF THE PERCENTAGE OF FAMILIES
ENGAGING IN VIOLENCE BY ETHNICITY

Ethnicity	Sibling	Parent/Child	Husband/Wife	Wife/Husband
White	50	14	3	4
Black	51	15	11	8
Jewish	45	7	2	7
Other	56	18	5	10

Source: Adapted from Murray A. Straus, Richard J. Gelles and Suzanne K. Steinmetz, *Behind Closed Doors: Violence in American Families* (New York: Doubleday, 1980), pp. 128-129.

Cazenave and Straus, in a secondary analysis of the national data cited above, found that blacks and whites had similar rates of child abuse, but that blacks were less likely to report sibling abuse or parent abuse than whites.[23] Furthermore, over twice as many black husbands as white husbands slapped their wives during the previous year (11 percent versus 5 percent), and black wives and white wives showed a similar pattern of slapping (6 percent versus 3 percent). For the variable "beat-up," 8 percent of the black husbands and 4 percent of the white husbands had engaged in this behavior.

When income was controlled, however, racial variations disappeared, and in some instances the relationships were reversed. For example, at the highest income levels ($12,000 to $19,000 and over $20,000 per year), blacks were less likely than whites to report sibling, marital or parent abuse. Blacks at the very lowest level, with incomes below $6,000 per year, were also less likely than whites to report marital abuse. Only in the group with incomes of $6,000 to $11,999 (which constituted the largest group for blacks) were blacks more likely than whites to engage in spousal violence.

Lauderdale, Valiunas and Anderson,[24] in a study of validated cases of child abuse and neglect in Texas in the period from 1975 to 1977, found that the rates for all types of abuse were highest among blacks, followed by Mexican Americans, with Anglos having the lowest rates. However, when the analysis was limited to physical abuse (i.e., neglect omitted), Anglos had the highest proportion of abuse followed by blacks and Mexican Americans. These data also support the importance of income as a confounding variable.

William Stacy and Anson Shupe,[25] in their study of 542 Dallas-Ft. Worth women using shelters for physically abused women, developed a severity index to compare the relative violence of women batterers in four racial/ethnic groups. They found that black men were the most likely to use severe violence against women, followed by Hispanics, white-Anglos and "others" (Native Americans and Asians). Again, a confounding variable may be social class, inasmuch as the researchers found mostly lower-middle and lower-class women at the shelters.

Using a series of vignettes in a survey of three hundred professionals (lawyers, pediatricians, social workers, police) and 1100 lay persons, Giovannoni and Becerra[26] attempted to ascertain ethnic differences in the attribution of seriousness to acts of mistreatment. The study found that 94 percent of the time, blacks and Hispanics gave a more serious rating to the vignette than did Anglos. Furthermore, education and income were inversely related to the ratings of seriousness: the lower their incomes and the lower their education, the more likely were blacks and Hispanics to see certain behaviors as abusive.

Differences between blacks and whites in their perceptions of the seriousness of the problem of abuse were noted in a 1981 poll conducted by Louis Harris and Associates.[27] The data in Table 2 indicate that in all three categories of victims rated, similar percentages of black and white respondents knew a victim of "wife abuse" (25 percent versus 27 percent); "child abuse" (25 percent versus percent 23 percent); and "abuse of the elderly" (19 percent versus 15 percent). To the question, "How serious a problem do you think these categories of abuse are in the U.S.?," the percentage of both blacks and whites who rated the problem of abuse as "very serious" was two to three times as high as the percentage who knew a victim of abuse. However, differences between blacks and whites were marked. A much greater number of blacks were likely to rate each category of family abuse as a very serious problem than were whites.

TABLE 2
COMPARISONS OF KNOWN VICTIMS AND SERIOUSNESS
OF FAMILY VIOLENCE BY RACE

Race	Known Victim of Abuse (Percent)			Seriousness of Abuse (Percent)		
	Wife	Child	Elderly	Wife	Child	Elderly
Black	25	25	19	72	59	58
White	27	23	15	61	40	36

Source: Adapted from U.S. Department of Justice, *Sourcebook of Criminal Justice Statistics* (Washington, D.C.: Government Printing Office, 1982), p. 278.

A study of abuse and neglect conducted in Hawaii during 1976 and 1977 revealed that Japanese Americans had significantly lower rates of abuse (3.5 percent versus 6.5 percent) than Samoan Americans.[28] Japanese Americans represent 27 percent of the population, while Samoan Americans constitute less than 1 percent of the population. Although Samoan Americans had fewer cases of abuse, they had an inordinate number of abuse cases for such a small percentage of the population. The impact of social class is evident in these findings: Samoan Americans constitute the lowest social group in Hawaii. It is possible that if income/social class were controlled, the differences in rates between Samoan Americans and the more affluent Japanese Americans might disappear.

One of the few studies to systematically assess the ethnic differences in family violence in the United States was undertaken by Robert and Caroline Blanchard.[29] They administered a modification of the conflict tactic scales used by Straus, Gelles and Steinmetz[30] to 465 college students in Hawaii. The sample was divided into European, Japanese, Chinese, Filipino and Hawaiian/part Hawaiian. Subjects were asked about violence towards any family member rather than a specific family member, i.e., parent, sibling, spouse. The researchers found that Hawaiian students had the highest violence scores, with a mean score of 7.8, followed by Caucasians with 4.2, Filipinos, 3.75, and Chinese, 3.20. As in the earlier study by Dubanski and Snyder, the lowest scores were obtained by the Japanese with a mean score of 3.05. These scores, however, did not include the categories of slap, push, grab or shove, because they were not considered violent enough acts to qualify "as a violent crime charge or . . . inspire a reputation as a bully."[31]

Given the importance of financial resources in lowering the potential for domestic violence, or in enabling an abused woman to leave a violent partner, it is clear that minority women are at increased risks of being abused. Not only are their partners less likely to possess the higher levels of education, occupational prestige or incomes which are related to lower levels of violence, but these women have to contend with the macho ideology and the likelihood that they may be employed (while their husbands are unemployed) and/or receiving a higher income. These factors—the women's greater likelihood of being abused and, concomitantly, their greater likelihood of finding employment (or being eligible for welfare)—may be contributing factors behind the exceedingly high rate of female-headed Puerto Rican families and black families. On the other hand, their own limited resources, relative to non-minority families, may act to keep these women in abusing relationships.

Women as Victims and Perpetrators

As Margaret Mead showed in her classic study entitled *Sex and Temperament*,[32] aggressive interaction is primarily a learned behavior which, depending on the society, may be either a masculine or feminine characteristic. Thus to explain the phenomenon, it is necessary to consider the socialization practices and the economic and social structures of American society, as well as differences between individuals.[33]

Spousal Violence

American women have been socialized to be feminine, which implies non-aggressive behavior. They also have been trained to believe that their primary role is caring for others: husband, children, parents and other kin. Yet, women are not only victims but also perpetrators of domestic violence. They predominate as child abusers, which is not surprising since they have the prime responsibility for child care. They are also, however, active participants in spousal violence. The percentage of wives who use physical violence on their husbands, as well as the frequency with which they engage in spousal abuse, is equal to or in some cases slightly exceeds that used by husbands against their wives, a finding that is supported cross-culturally.[34]

Roughly one-half to three-fourths of all couples have experienced at least one incident of spousal violence. In about 20 percent of these families the violence is frequent; and about 5 to 7 percent endure severe beatings.[35] However, the male's greater size, strength and experience in contact sports and fights predispose him to produce considerably more injury when he does use violence, as compared to what he experiences as a victim. In two separate incidence studies, Steinmetz[36] found a 13:1 ratio of husband to wife battering. Only in spousal homicide are the outcomes essentially equal. About 19 percent of all homicides involve family relationships, one-half of which are spouse killing spouse, and 43 percent of these victims are husbands.[37]

Kersti Yllo,[38] using American states as units of analysis for assessing women's status, has found a curvilinear pattern between rates of violence and women's status. The highest levels of violence are in those states where women's overall status is lowest. The rate drops as status improves.

In another study focusing on the impact of husbands' and wives' status on violence,[39] individual educational and occupational attainments were found to be related to physically and psychologically abusive behaviors. Status inconsistency, especially the husband's underachievement in occupation, and status incompatibility, i.e., the wife's occupation is high relative to her husband's, are likely to result in life-threatening abuse—beating or use of a weapon. Couples with an over-achieving husband experienced considerably lower levels of spousal violence. As women continue to strive for equality, a readjustment in the male/female power structure can be expected to produce a short-term increase in violence. Only when egalitarian rather than male-superiority norms prevail can we expect to see a reduction in spousal violence.[40]

Such acceptance may be delayed among certain minority groups. Many Puerto Rican men have not been able to accept their wives' higher income. Since 56 percent of Puerto Rican families are currently headed by women,[41] one can speculate about the causal sequence of this finding. Does this represent the inability of males to adjust to their wives' employment (and possibly higher income levels) while their likelihood of unemployment is great; or have these families become "female-headed," with the wife now seeking employment because their husbands were unable to find employment and deserted them out of guilt, shame or the inability to resolve the differences between their macho image and reality?

Child Abuse

Spousal abuse is not the only form of violence in which women are involved. Straus, et al.,[42] found that 68 percent of mothers were the perpetrators of violence against children, compared to 58 percent of the fathers. Also, when acts of violence carrying a high risk for serious injury (kicking, biting, punching, threatening to use or using a gun or knife) were compared for mothers and fathers, 4.4 percent of the mothers and 2.7 percent of the fathers committed these extremely violent acts. This represents a 62 percent greater rate of this type of child abuse by mothers than by fathers.

Comparisons of black parents and white parents in their approval of and use of slapping and spanking are of interest. Cazenave and Straus[43] found that black parents had slightly higher rates of approval of slapping and spanking a twelve-year old than did white parents (83 percent versus 81 percent). Black parents, however, were less likely than white parents (51 percent versus 59 percent) to report having actually spanked during the previous year. The use of the more severe acts of child abuse (biting, punching, beating up, threatening or using a weapon) were quite similar for the two groups (15 percent versus 14 percent respectively).

When income was controlled, blacks in the higher income groups ($12,000 and above) were less likely than whites to have engaged in child abuse during the previous year. Similarly, when the sample considered white-collar groups, blacks had consistently lower child abuse scores (7 percent for blacks versus 12 percent for whites). However, when parents who held blue-collar jobs were compared, black parents were slightly more likely to be abusive than white parents (18 percent versus 15 percent).

The impact of teen pregnancy is especially acute among minority families. In her study of low-income, black teenage girls, Joyce Ladner[44] found a lack of stigma attached to premarital sex and motherhood, with sexual activity viewed as a human function rather than a moral issue. Most girls in the study strongly opposed both abortion and contraception due to a lack of information, misinformation, and/or moral reasons, with marriage also viewed negatively. As Eleanor Engram[45] asserts, black unwed motherhood is not understood because of a lack of awareness of the underlying values of black procreation, fecundity and fertility.

Unfortunately, early pregnancy, regardless of the value system that positively views this choice, does set the stage for child abuse by the young mother. These mothers, because of poor nutrition and prenatal care, have a disproportionately large number of low birth weight and premature babies who suffer from hyperactivity and/or minimal brain damage. The mother-child bond is difficult to establish because these children are often difficult to care for. They require extra attention, and the mother's lack of experience results in these babies being at high risk for abuse. Leo Stern[46] found that the incidence of physical abuse of low birth weight infants is approximately triple that of normal infants. Further complicating this situation is the poor postpartum nutrition of the mother—the typical teen diet characterized by "grazing" on "junk" food, which along with the problems of caring for the infants are likely to increase stress and hypertension.

In the cycles of poverty and early pregnancy, disproportionately minority conditions, both the mother and her baby are victims. Richard Gelles found that 23 percent, Mildred Pagelow found that 60 percent, and William Stacy and Anson Shuple found that 42 percent of the women in their studies had experienced battering during pregnancy.[47]

Elder Abuse

As a result of increased longevity a large number of families are now characterized by three, and some even by four, generations. One of the unforeseen consequences of this change in the United States demographic profile is that at the point in our parents' lives when they need help and become dependent on their children, usually in their late seventies, their children are also likely to be facing the consequences of old age—impending retirement, loss of a spouse and diminishing physical abilities. Not only are the elderly likely to face a loss of resources such as income, power and money which earlier had "protected" them from abuse, but as their needs increase, the stress experienced by the caregivers in fulfilling these needs increases significantly their likelihood of abusing the elders.

One study found that elders who were extremely dependent on their caregivers for providing tasks of daily living (help with household tasks, personal grooming, finances, mobility, social/emotional needs and mental health needs) were much more likely to be abused than elders who were less dependent. Furthermore, caregivers experiencing high levels of stress resulting from these tasks had elder abuse scores that were seventeen times higher than families with low levels of dependency-related stress.[48]

Since women constitute the majority not only of elderly needing care (80 percent in Helen O'Malley's 1979 study; 84.5 percent in Steinmetz[49]), but also of the caregivers (90 percent in O'Malley; 93 percent in Steinmetz[50]), this problem of elder abuse is almost entirely a "woman's" problem. Women are in double jeopardy as abusers of the elderly and as abused elderly. However, minority women are considerably more likely to face elder abuse than their white counterparts.

Black elderly women are more likely to live in multigenerational households; a greater percentage live in poverty (42 percent of black women versus 16 percent of white women over sixty-five years of age); and older blacks are in signficantly poorer health even when income, gender and social class are controlled.[51] Based on our knowledge of the factors characteristic of abusive families and the conditions noted above, black women are at an increased risk of being abused.

Public Policy, Ethnicity, and Family Violence

Historically, the right of American families to monitor their own personal affairs, including physical violence between family members, has been implicitly sanctioned through limited legislation or the lack of legislation. Although women in colonial America appear to have been offered some protection by laws such as the Massachusetts statute which decreed peaceful cohabitation between men and women, attitudes towards the husband's use of violence to "discipline" his wife had changed by the nineteenth century.[52]

In 1824 a Mississippi court ruled that a husband could chastise his wife "in case of great emergency" and with "salutory restraints."[53] This law was based on the ancient law which gave the right to a husband to chastise his wife with a whip or rattan no bigger than his thumb. Until recently the prevailing viewpoint has echoed a ruling of over one hundred years ago, when a North Carolina court found that a husband had no right to chastise his wife under any circumstance, but that "[i]f no permanent injury has been inflicted nor malice, cruelty nor dangerous violence shown by the husband, it is better to draw the curtain, shut out the public gaze, and leave the parties to forget and forgive."[54]

Currently, American society is recognizing that individual rights can be protected only when violence in personal relations becomes public business. Contemporary research has not, however, examined the relationship between the incidence of domestic violence and the cultural expectations of various ethnic groups. Using the cultural variance perspective, Leanor Johnson[55] makes a plea for more black researchers to identify that which is unique and functional in black families, while Eleanor Engram[56] calls for public policy that recognizes the strengths as well as the weaknesses of black American families.

Discriminatory practices against minorities and women, both in job availability and wage compensation, must be eliminated. Until economic and sexual equality are achieved by all individuals, one can expect unequal treatment of those with the fewest resources who are also those most at risk of family violence. A condition of "triple jeopardy" has been ascribed to the "young, black female . . . and subsequently her children,"[57] and also the Hispanic woman who is "old, poor, and minority."[58] The unifying factors for these two diverse groups are their explicitly female minority status, but the equally significant variable implicit in both descriptions is that these populations represent those most susceptible to poverty and its negative social and economic derivations.

One cannot overlook the realities of educational and employment opportunities under varying economic conditions and the impact of public services and assistance programs on family violence. However, the attitudes and values imparted to all Americans through the media, school systems, corporate entities and families must also be considered. The society cannot praise aggression and violence under the "right" conditions—Rocky/Rambo heroes of the 1980s, Bruce Lee of the 1970s or John Wayne of earlier generations; the "shoot first, ask-questions-later mentality" of many police training academies; the use of bombs to control our enemies—without expecting cultural spillover into other areas of the social order. On the same note, one cannot expect parents to simultaneously abhor child abuse yet consider a good spanking as a necessary requisite in order to be a good parent, without expecting the spanking to turn into abuse when a parent is under stress.

Bernard and Bernard, in their study on the impact of modeling abusive behavior, found that the "most striking aspect of modeling is the extent to which students indulge in the same forms of abuse as they experienced or observed in their families of origin." They concluded that children in American homes are "not only educated to be violent, but are even taught how to be violent."[59]

Patricia Ulbrich and John Huber[60] reported that although parents hitting one another did not affect students' attitudes about women's roles, it did affect attitudes about the use of violence against women. Men who had observed their fathers hitting their mothers were more likely to approve of violence against women. This study was further supported by Stacy and Shupe, who found that 60 percent of women-batterers had witnessed physical violence between their parents, and 40 percent had been neglected and 40 percent abused as children.[61]

The cyclical relationship between all forms of family violence has been well documented. Abused children become violent siblings, abusive spouses, and abusive caregivers to elderly parents. The cycle continues from generation to generation, fueled by a lack of education, inadequate financial means, unstable or overstressed kinship networks, insufficient and inappropriate social services, and a value system that rewards male machismo and aggression/violence in general.

It is difficult to believe that as a society we want to eliminate family violence when so little is done to change the structural conditions which virtually assure its continuity, and so much is done to reinforce the importance of having money, power, prestige and control over others and utilize whatever means are necessary to accomplish these ends. Inasmuch as economic reforms are more efficacious to legislate than cultural norms, and can elicit the primary goal of increasing the quality of life for families as well as the secondary function of reducing violence, public policy must concentrate on extensive structural improvements.

NOTES

[1] *Webster's New Collegiate Dictionary*, s.v., "ethnic."

[2] Frances Frank Marcus, "Louisiana Repeals Black Blood Law," *The New York Times* (July 6, 1983), p. A10.

[3]U.S. Code of Federal Regulations, Title 25, Ch. 1, Part 26.1(g) (4-1-85).

[4]U.S. Bureau of the Census, *1980 Census Supplementary Report*, PC 80-51-6, "Age, Sex, Race and Spanish Origin of the Population by Regions—Divisions and State" (Washington, D.C.: Government Printing Office, 1980).

[5]Carmela G. Lacayo, "Triple Jeopardy: The Hispanic Elderly in the United States," *State of Hispanic America* 2 (1982): 57-58.

[6]See Lionel A. Maldonado, "Altered States: Chicanos in the Labor Force," in Winston Van Horne, ed., *Ethnicity and the Work Force* (Milwaukee, Wis.: University of Wisconsin System American Ethnic Studies Coordinating Committee, 1985); and Philip Garcia and Lionel Maldonado, "America's Mexicans: A Plea for Specificity," *Social Science Journal* 19:1 (April 1982): 9-24.

[7]See James E. Blackwell, *The Black Community: Diversity and Unity* (New York: Harper and Row, 1975).

[8]See Melvin L. Kohn, *Class and Conformity—A Study in Values* (Homewood, Ill.: Dorsey Press, 1977).

[9]See Howard R. Erlanger, "Social Class and Corporal Punishment: A Reassessment," *American Sociological Review* 39:1 (February 1974): 68-85; Suzanne K. Steinmetz, "The Battered Husband Syndrome," *Victimology* 2:3-4 (1977-78): 499-509; and Murray A. Straus, Richard J. Gelles and Suzanne K. Steinmetz, *Behind Closed Doors: Violence in American Families* (New York: Doubleday, 1980).

[10]See Suzanne K. Steinmetz and Murray A. Straus, eds., *Violence in the Family* (New York: Harper and Row, 1974).

[11]James Garbarino and Aaron Ebata, "The Significance of Ethnic and Cultural Differences in Child Maltreatment," *Journal of Marriage and the Family* 45:4 (November 1983): 773.

[12]John P. Spiegel, "Ethnopsychiatric Dimensions in Family Violence," in Maurice R. Green, ed., *Violence and the Family* (Houston: Selected Symposium 47, Annals of the American Academy of Political and Social Sciences, 1979), pp. 79-89.

[13]See Leanor B. Johnson, "Perspectives on Black Family Empirical Research: 1965-1978," in Henriette Pipes McAdoo, ed., *Black Families* (Beverly Hills, Cal.: Sage Publications, 1981), pp. 87-102.

[14]See Walter R. Allen, "The Search for Applicable Theories of Black Family Life," *Journal of Marriage and the Family* 40:1 (Fall 1978): 111-129.

[15]See Marvin E. Wolfgang and Franco Ferracuti, *The Subculture of Violence* (London: Social Science Paperbacks, 1967).

[16]Evelyn P. Stevens, "Machismo and Marianismo," *Society* 10:6 (Sept./Oct. 1973): 57-63.

[17]Wolfgang and Ferracuti, op. cit.

[18]Lynn A. Curtis, *Violence, Race, and Culture* (Lexington, Mass.: Lexington Books, 1975).

[19]Noel A. Cazenave and Murray A. Straus, "Race, Class, Network Embeddedness and Family Violence: A Search for Potent Support Systems," *Journal of Comparative Family Studies* X:3 (Autumn 1979): 281-300.

[20]Noel A. Cazenave, "Black Men in America: The Quest for 'Manhood,' " in Henriette Pipes McAdoo, ed., *Black Families* (Beverly Hills, Cal.: Sage Publications, 1981), pp. 176-185.

[21]See Jackson Toby, "Violence and the Masculine Ideal: Some Quantitative Data," in Marvin E. Wolfgang, ed., *Patterns of Violence* (Philadelphia: Vol. 34, Annals of the American Academy of Political and Social Sciences, 1966), pp. 20-27.

[22]Straus, Gelles and Steinmetz, op. cit.

[23]Cazenave and Straus, op. cit.

[24]M. Lauderdale, A. Valiunas and M. Anderson, "Race, Ethnicity, and Child Maltreatment: An Empirical Analysis," *Child Abuse and Neglect* 4:3 (1980): 163-169.

[25]William Stacy and Anson Shupe, *The Family Secret: Domestic Violence in America* (Boston: Beacon Press, 1983).

[26]J. M. Giovannoni and R. M. Becerra, *Defining Child Abuse* (New York: The Free Press, 1979).

[27]U.S. Department of Justice, *Sourcebook of Criminal Justice Statistics* (Washington, D.C.: Government Printing Office, 1982).

[28]R. A. Dubanski and K. Snyder, "Patterns of Child Abuse and Neglect in Japanese- and Samoan-Americans," *Child Abuse and Neglect* 4:4 (1980): 217-225.

[29]Robert H. and D. Caroline Blanchard, "Hawaii: Violence, A Preliminary Analysis," in Arnold P. Goldstein and Marshall H. Segall, eds., *Aggression in Global Perspective* (New York: Pergamon Press, 1983).

[30]See Straus, Gelles and Steinmetz, op. cit.

[31]Blanchard and Blanchard, op. cit., p. 182.

[32]Margaret Mead, *Sex and Temperament in Three Primitive Societies* (New York: Morrow Publishing, 1935).

[33]Suzanne K. Steinmetz, "Women and Violence: Victims and Perpetrators," *American Journal of Psychotherapy* 34:3 (July 1980): 334-350.

[34]See Steinmetz, "The Battered Husband Syndrome," op. cit.; Straus, Gelles and Steinmetz, op. cit.; and Steinmetz, "A Cross-Cultural Comparison," op. cit.

[35]See Richard J. Gelles, *The Violent Home* (Beverly Hills, Cal.: Sage Publications, 1974); Suzanne K. Steinmetz, *The Cycle of Violence: Assertive, Aggressive, and Abusive Family Interaction* (New York: Praeger Publishers, 1977); and Straus, Gelles and Steinmetz, op. cit.

[36]See Steinmetz, "The Battered Husband Syndrome," op. cit.; and Suzanne K. Steinmetz, "Family Violence: Past, Present and Future," in Marvin Sussman and Suzanne K. Steinmetz, eds., *Handbook of Marriage and the Family* (New York: Plenum Publishers, 1986).

[37]U.S. Department of Justice, *FBI Uniform Crime Reports*, op. cit.

[38]Kersti Yllo, "Sexual Equality and Violence Against Wives in American States," *Journal of Comparative Family Studies* XIV:1 (Spring 1983): 67-86.

[39]Carlton A. Hornung, B. Claire McCullough and Taichi Sugimoto, "Status Relationships in Marriage: Risk Factors in Spouse Abuse," *Journal of Marriage and the Family* 43:3 (August 1981): 675-692.

[40]See Steinmetz and Straus, op. cit.

[41]Maria Elena Torano and Lourdes Alvarez, "Hispanas: Success in America," *State of Hispanic America* 2 (1982): 149-167.

[42]Straus, Gelles and Steinmetz, op. cit.

[43]Cazenave and Straus, op. cit.

[44]Joyce A. Ladner, *Tomorrow's Tomorrow* (New York: Doubleday, 1971).

[45]Eleanor Engram, *Science, Myth, Reality: The Black Family in One-Half Century of Research* (Westport, Conn.: Greenwood Press, 1982).

[46]Leo Stern, "The High Risk Infant and Battering," in U.S. Department of Health, Education and Welfare, *Child Abuse and Developmental Disabilities: Essays* (Washington, D.C.: Government Printing Office, 1979), pp. 20-24.

[47]See Richard J. Gelles, "Violence and Pregnancy: A Note on the Extent of the Problem and Needed Services," *Family Coordinator* 24:1 (January 1975): 81-86; Mildred Daley Pagelow, *Woman-Battering: Victims and Their Experiences* (Beverly Hills, Cal.: Sage Publications, 1981); and Stacy and Shupe, op. cit.

[48]Suzanne K. Steinmetz, "Elder Abuse: One-Fifth of Our Population At Risk?" Testimony delivered before the House of Representatives, Committee on Aging, Subcommittee on Health and Long-Term Care (May 10, 1985).

[49]See Helen O'Malley, Howard Segars, Rubin Perez, Victoria Mitchell and George M. Knuepfel, *Elder Abuse in Massachusetts: A Survey of Professionals and Paraprofessionals* (Boston: Legal Research and Sources for the Elderly, 1979); Steinmetz, "A Cross-Cultural Comparison," op. cit.; and Steinmetz, "Elder Abuse," op. cit.

[50]Ibid.

[51]James J. Dowd and Vern L. Bengston, "Aging in Minority Populations: An Examination of the Double Jeopardy Hypothesis," *Journal of Gerontology* 33:3 (May 1978): 427-436.

[52]See Steinmetz, "A Cross-Cultural Comparison," op. cit.

[53]*Bradley* v. *State*, 1 Miss. Rep (Walker) 156, 158 (1824).

[54]*State* v. *Oliver*, 70 N. Car. 60, 61-62 (1874).

[55]Johnson, op. cit.

[56]Engram, op. cit.

[57]Mildred Daley Pagelow, *Family Violence* (New York: Praeger Publishers, 1984), p. 52.

[58]Lacayo, op. cit., p. 52.

[59]Bernard and Bernard, op. cit., p. 286.

[60]Patricia Ulbrich and John Huber, "Observing Parental Violence: Distribution and Effects," *Journal of Marriage and the Family* 43:3 (August 1981): 623-631.

[61]Stacy and Shupe, op. cit.